The Lesser Key of Solomon

THE LESSER KEY OF SOLOMON

LEMEGETON CLAVICULA SALOMONIS

Detailing the Ceremonial Art of
Commanding Spirits Both Good and Evil

Joseph H. Peterson, Editor

WEISERBOOKS
York Beach, Maine, USA

First published in 2001 by
Weiser Books
P.O. Box 612
York Beach, ME 03910-0612
www.weiserbooks.com

Library of Congress Cataloging-in-Publication Data

   Clavicula Salomonis. English
     The lesser key of Solomon : lemegeton clavicula Salomonis / Joseph
  H. Peterson, editor
      p. cm.
     Includes bibliographical references and index.
     ISBN 1–57863–220–X (alk. paper); ISBN 1-57863-256-0 (pbk. : alk. paper)
     1. Magic—Early works to 1800. 2. Magic, Jewish—Early works to
  1800. I. Peterson, Joseph H. II. Title.

   BF1601.C4313 2001
   133.4'3—dc21   00–068529

MV

Typeset in 12 pt. Adobe Caslon
Cover design by Ed Stevens

Printed in the United States of America

08 07 06 05 04 03 02 01
8 7 6 5 4 3 2 1

The paper used in this publication meets all the minimum requirements of
the American National Standard for Information Sciences–Permanence of
Paper for Printed Library Materials Z39.48–1992 (R1997).

CONTENTS

Emendments, *Lesser Key of Solomon*, edited by Joseph H. Peterson (2001)

Since Publication the following emendments are to be noted:

Page	Error	Correction
xii, l. 3	The name Lemegeton was probably naively invented because of the compiler's ignorance of Latin.	Replace with: The title Lemegeton was no doubt adopted from a reference cited in Ars Notoria, which describes it as Solomon's "treatise of spiritual and secret experiments" (tractu spiritualium & secretorum experimentorum). See page 170 below. Ars Notoria mentions another Solomonic title, Helisoe, which is likewise noticed by the compiler of the Lesser Key; see pages 6 and 166 below.
xiii, l. 13		Add: Other manuscripts not utilized include Sloane 3824, titled "Longobardus", a precursor to the Lesser Key; Wellcome MS 4665, a copy by Hockley; and Wellcome 3203, Lea's copy of Hockley's.
16, footnote 37.	H and S2 reads	should read: H and S2 read
22, l. 7, and p. 243, l. 18	"He appeareth when the Sun is in some of the Southern signs, in a human shape."	Add footnote: Clm 849 reads "Apparet in signo medici cum suscipit figuram humanam; [est] doctor opti[m]us mulierum, et facit ardere in amorem virorum" (He appears in the form of a doctor (medici, not meridii=southern as in Weyer) when he takes on a human form. He is a most excellent doctor of women, and he makes them burn with love for men.) For text see Kieckhefer, Forbidden Rites (University Park Pennsylvania: Pennsylvania State University Press, 1998, pp. 291-293.)
39, l. 13	... in time of acction &c.	Add footnote: This spirit occurs as one invoked into a crystal in order to discover a thief, treasure, etc. variously given as Andromalcum, Andromalce, and Andrewemalcus. See Sloane 3847 fol. 17r-18r for an example.
47, footnote 133	"(in Hebrew letters"	should read: "(in Hebrew letters)"
53, l. 11	thou aft	should read: thou art
59, l. 1	PART I: OF THE ARTE GOETIA	should read: PART II: THE ART THEURGIA GOETIA
114, l. 15		Add the following drawing:
130, l. 17	signals	should read: signall [i.e. extraordinary]
134, l. 6	Panae1	should read: Panael
134, l. 9	Mechie1	should read: Mechiel
137, footnote 116		Add: The formulas below differ somewhat from Paracelsus' original, Sudhoff, Paracelsus: Sämtliche Werke. Abt. 1, Bd. 14: Das Volumen primum der Philosophia magna, Oldenbourg: München [u.a.] 1933: Aries: Iron 1 Lot, Gold half Lot, Silver 1 Dr., Copper half Dr.; Taurus: Copper 1 Oz., Iron half Oz., Tin 1 Dr., Gold 2 Oz.; Virgo: Copper 1 Dr., Gold half Oz., Silver 2 Dr., Tin half Dr.; Aquarius: Gold 1 Lot, Silver 1 Oz., Lead 2 Dr., Iron 1 Dr.; Pisces: Gold 1 Dr., Silver 2 Dr., Tin 4 Dr., Iron 1 Dr., Copper 1 Dr. Paulina basically follows Turner's translation, except for mistakenly omitting Silver in the seal of Aries.
240, l. 26	exocista	should read: exorcista
245, l. 9	Procell	should read: Procell [Pucel]
[20. Byleth]	jufferit	should read: jusserit
[22. Paymon]	fustineat	should read: sustineat
[23. Belial]	circirer	should read: circirer [*circiter]
[23. Belial]	didiciste	should read: didicisse
[29. Forras]	corundem	should read: eorundem
[43. Focalor]	three legions	should read: <three> [thirty] legions
[52. Amduscias]	fistit	should read: sistit
[57. Orobas]	idoltum	should read: idolum
[62. Balam]	responet	should read: respondet

ACKNOWLEDGMENTS

I would like to thank the British Museum for allowing me to study the manuscripts firsthand, and for their help in preparing microfilm copies. I am particularly grateful for the high quality negative of Sloane 3825, which they prepared specially.

Abbreviations

C   A. Crowley [and S.L. Mathers], *The Goetia* (York Beach, ME: Samuel Weiser, 1995).

H   Harley MS 6483, British Library.

MS(S)   Manuscript(s).

P   Paracelsus, *Archidoxes of Magic*, translated by Robert Turner (1656, reprint New York: Samuel Weiser, 1975).

r   Recto.

sec. man.   *secunda manu*, i.e., written in a different handwriting.

S1   Sloane MS 2731, British Library.

S2   Sloane MS 3648, British Library.

S3   Sloane MS 3825, British Library.

T   Johannes Trithemius, *Steganographia* (Darmbstadii, 1621).

v   Verso.

W   Johann Weyer, *Pseudomonarchia daemonum*, in *Opera Omnia* (Amstelodami, 1660, pp. 649–666). English translation in R. Scot, *The Discoverie of Witchcraft* (1584, reprint New York: Dover Publications, 1972, pp. 217-227).

[ ]   Alternate wording or explanation

< >   Makes an error or accretion in the text that should be disregarded.

INTRODUCTION

The *Lemegeton* is a popular handbook of sorcery known from the 17th century[1] in more or less the same form as I will present it. Most of the material, however, is found in varying forms in earlier manuscripts, and some of the material dates back as early as the 14th century or earlier.[2] In a 1531 list of magical texts, Heinrich Cornelius Agrippa mentioned three of the books of the *Lemegeton* in the same breath, *Ars Almadel, Ars Notoria,* and *Ars Paulina*.[3] The relevant passage is found in a chapter titled "Theurgia,"[4] and the chapter which precedes it is titled "Goetia."[5] *Goetia* and *Theurgia Goetia* are the names of the remaining books of the *Lemegeton*. This list was repeated by Agrippa's student, Johann Weyer (a.k.a. Wier, or Wierus), in 1531. Reginald Scot, who relied to some extent on Weyer, does likewise.[6]

---

1   The date 1641 occurs in the text and may indicate that its present form dates from then.

2   To this period has been dated an important text of the Solomonic literature, *Liber Juratus*, or *The Sworn Book of Honorius*, which has important connections with our present work.

3   *De incertitudine et vanitate omnium scientarum et artium* (Paris, 1531, folios 54v-56v): "Eius itaque scholae sunt, ars Almadel, ars Notoria, ars Paulina, ars Reuelationum, & eius modi superstitionum plura, quae eo ipso sunt pernicisiorum, quo apparent imperitis diuiniora." (Of this school therefore is the Art Almadel, the Notory Art, the Pauline Art, the Art of Revelations, and many similar superstitions, which are so much the more pernicious, by how much they seem the more divine to the ignorant.)

4   Agrippa classified these three magical books as belonging to "theurgia," that category of magic which works through the agency of the good angels and God.

5   According to Agrippa, Goetia is the other major category of ceremonial magic. He believed that goetia works through the agency of "unclean spirits."

6   Reginald Scot, *Discoverie of Witchcraft* (1584, reprint New York: Dover Publications, 1972), Book 16, chapters 31 and 42.

Weyer included a text closely related to the *Goetia*.[7] Thus the bulk of the materials were possibly collected together before 1531.

The name *Lemegeton* was probably naively invented because of the compiler's ignorance of Latin. He or she was no doubt familiar with the *Clavicula Salomonis (Key of Solomon)*[8] and wanted to title this work the *Little Key of Solomon*; this became *Lemegeton Clavicula Salomonis*.

The major texts used for this edition have all been from the British Library Manuscript collection. They include Harley MS 6483, and Sloane MSS 2731, 3825, and 3648.

Harley 6483 is cataloged as *Liber Malorum Spirituum*. Its description reads as follows:

> A Quarto, containing all the Names, Orders, & Offices of all the spirits Salomon ever conversed with: the Seals & Characters belonging to each Spirit; & the manner of calling them forth to visible appearance. - Some of these spirits are in Enoch's Tables described in the former volume, but their seals & characters how they may be known are omitted, which are therefore in this book at large set forth.[9]

Harley 6483 is probably the latest manuscript and contains much additional material, with extracts from de Abano's *Heptameron* replacing much of the instructions included in Book 1 of the other manuscripts. It is handsomely written, with circles drawn around the sigils, and Hebrew lettering supplied in many places.[10] It is dated 1712–1713. Note that Harley shares many readings with Sloane 3648. In fact, a dependence of both on a common ancestor can reasonably be established. Given the number of deviations from the majority, Harley 6483 is among the least reliable of the manuscripts.

Sloane 2731 is cataloged as *Clavicula Salomonis*. It is important because it has been compiled from multiple versions, including Sloane 3648. This text is,

---

7   Weyer, *De Praestigiis Daemonum*. Scot, *Discoverie of Witchcraft*, includes an English translation in Book 16, chapter 2. See below and Appendix 2 of the present volume.

8   For Latin examples of the *Key of Solomon*, see British Library Additional MS 10862 (17th century) and Sloane 2383. For an English translation, see *The Key of Solomon the King (Clavicula Salomonis)*, first translated and edited from ancient manuscripts in the British Museum by S. Liddell MacGregor Mathers (London: George Redway, 1889. Reissued, York Beach, ME: Samuel Weiser, 2000).

9   British Museum. Dept. of Manuscripts, *A Catalogue of the Harleian Manuscripts in the British Museum*, vol. III (London: G. Eyre and A. Strahan, 1808–12), p. 369.

10 For examples, see Appendix 3. Mathers judged these to be "manifestly incorrect in orthography," but includes them anyway, "such as they are."

unfortunately, incomplete, makes arbitrary rearrangements in the text, has many careless mistakes, and omits all of Book 5. It is dated January 18, 1686.

Sloane 3825 is cataloged as *Treatise on Magic* and includes two articles, *Janua Magica reserata* (fol. 1 ff.) and *Clavicula Solomonis, The Little Key of Solomon* (fol. 100r ff.). Carefully written and legible, it is also a more complete and internally consistent text. It has the most consistently reliable readings of the available manuscripts as well and is interesting in that it contains a shorter version of *The Notary Art*, to which has been added the remaining portions as found in Robert Turner's translation.[11]

Sloane 3648, a collective codex, also contains pieces of Agrippa and Paracelsus. This manuscript also dates from the 17th century and was apparently used by the writer of Sloane 2731. It is carelessly written, with poorly executed drawings.

I have followed Sloane 3825 for this edition, except for the *Ars Notoria*. For the latter, the manuscripts are clearly dependent on Robert Turner's translation. I have therefore used his 1657 printed edition as my primary source. Variants from other manuscripts are noted in square brackets [ ]. Also in square brackets are the folio numbers from Sloane 3825. I have resisted the temptation to modernize the language.

PARTS OF THE *LEMEGETON*

Goetia

Goetia is a Greek term more or less synonymous with magic, but with negative connotations, as distinguished from the more elevated *Theurgia* ("working of a god"). The compiler of the *Lemegeton* certainly recognized this distinction. The first book, *Goetia*, corresponds closely with the catalog of demons published by Johann Weyer as *Pseudomonarchia daemonum*, included as an appendix to his *De Praestigiis Daemonum* (1563).[12] Weyer referred to his source manuscript as *Liber officiorum spirituum, seu Liber dictus Empto.*

---

11   Robert Turner of Holshot, *Ars Notoria: the Notory Art of Solomon, shewing the cabalistical key of magical operations, the liberal sciences, divine revelation, and the art of memory. Whereunto is added an Astrological Catechism, fully demonstrating the art of Judicial Astrology ... Written originally in Latine [by Apollonius, Leovitius, and others. Collected] and now Englished by R. Turner, Filomathes.* (London: 1657)

12   For example, the edition published at Basileae: Ex Officina Oporiniana, 1583. Unfortunately, *Pseudomonarchia daemonum* was not included in the recent edition published as *Witches, Devils, and Doctors in the Renaissance* by George Mora et al. (Tempe, Arizona: Medieval & Renaissance texts and studies 1998). Note that Weyer discusses Goetia and Theurgia in Book II, chapter ii.

Salomonis, de principibus & regibus dæmoniorum ("Book of the offices of spirits, or the Book of sayings of Empto. Solomon concerning the princes and kings of the demons"). It includes variations in many of the names, showing that it had been redacted by the time Weyer obtained it, so it evidently dates from long before 1563. In Weyer's text, there are no demonic seals, and the demons are invoked by a simple conjuration, not the elaborate ritual found in the *Lemegeton*.

The most striking difference between Weyer's text and the *Goetia* is the order of spirits. I see no explanation for the difference; it's almost as if a stack of cards got scrambled. There are also four additional spirits found in the *Goetia* that aren't in Weyer (number 3, Vassago, and the last three, Seere, Dantalion, and Andromalius).

Other anomalies may be of more significance. One is that the fourth spirit in Weyer's text, Pruflas (alias Bufas), was accidently left out of Reginald Scot's English translation, or was already missing from the edition used by Scot (a manuscript dated 1570). It is also the only spirit from Weyer's list that is not found in the *Lemegeton*. If a specific edition can be found that introduced this defect, it might allow us to fix the date of the composition of the *Goetia* in its present form.

The *Goetia* does, in fact, seem dependant on Scot, faithfully copying his frequent mistranslations, elaborations, and omissions. A possible exception is a passage in the description of Valefar (spirit 6) that, in Weyer's Latin, reads "& capite latronis." The *Goetia* renders this "a man's head lowring," while Scot reads "the head of a thief." See Appendix 2 for the full text of the *Pseudomonarchia daemonum*.

We can identify two other sources utilized by the compiler of the *Goetia*. One is Agrippa's *Three Books of Occult Philosophy*.[13] The Hebrew lettering which appears on the brass vessel (figure 7) is clearly based on Agrippa's "Scale of the Number Seven." Likewise, the magical circle is based on Agrippa's "Scale of the Number Ten."[14] The other source utilized is a small book titled *Heptameron, or Elements of Magic* by Peter de Abano.[15] This appears to have been the basis for the goetic rituals.

---

[13] Heinrich Cornelius Agrippa, *Three Books of Occult Philosophy* (London: Gregory Moule, 1651).

[14] Agrippa, *Three Books of Occult Philosophy*, Book II, chapters 10 and 13 respectively, pp. 202 and 212.

[15] Published with *Henry Cornelius Agrippa his fourth book of occult philosophy. Of geomancie. Magical elements of Peter de Abano. Astronomical geomancie. The nature of spirits. Arbatel of magick. The species or several kindes of magick.* Translated into English by Robert Turner (London: Printed by J.C. for John Harrison, 1655).

Theurgia Goetia

Slightly less diabolical is the second book, *Theurgia Goetia*. This text has close parallels with Book One of Trithemius' *Steganographia*.[16] Although the abundant spirit seals are not found in Trithemius, those few that can be found match exactly. For example, these four seals are found in *Steganographia* I, chapter xi, dealing with Usiel and his subordinates:

Compare these with the following seals found in the *Lemegeton* in the section dealing with the eleventh spirit, Usiel, and his subordinates Adan, Ansoel, Magni, and Abariel:

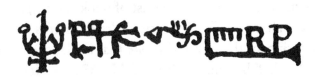

It should be noted that Trithemius' conjurations are actually his examples of hidden writing ("steganography") and do not correspond with the conjurations found in *Theugia Goetia*. Written in 1500, *Steganographia* was not published until 1608. It was, however, widely circulated in manuscript form. Where the majority of manuscripts agree, they also agree with the *Steganographia*. This is highly significant, in that it allows us to gauge the degree of degradation of the various *Lemegeton* manuscripts by the number of times they deviate from the *Steganographia*.

Ars Paulina

The spirits in Part 1 of *Ars Paulina* coincide exactly with those found in Book 2 of Trithemius' *Steganographia*. Trithemius cites Raziel several times as an authority for these angels,[17] but I have been unable to match up any of the lists of

---

16   Johann Trithemius, *Steganographia* (Frankfurt, 1606; the edition I have used is Darmbstadii, 1621).

17   e.g., T2.12 "Omnes autem huius horæ principes, duces & comites (secundum sententiam Razielis) formas assumunt ad placitum operantis." He also mentions "secundum Salomonem & Razielem" (T2.14.).

spirits with those found in *Sepher Ha-Razim*.[18] According to Thorndike,[19] the "The Pauline art," was purported to have been discovered by the Apostle Paul after he had been snatched up to the third heaven, and delivered by him at Corinth. Robert Turner mentions a 16th-century manuscript in the Bibliothèque Nationale.[20] Although this text is based on earlier versions, repeated mention of the year 1641 and guns, shows a late redaction. The "table of practice" has similarities with Dee's "holy table." In the former, the seven seals have the characters of the seven planets, which also occur in the *Magical Calendar* (published in 1620, but with possible connections with Trithemius).[21]

The descriptions of the seals for each sign of the Zodiac are evidently abstracted from Paracelsus, *The Second Treatise of Celestial Medicines*, (*Archidoxes of Magic*) translated by Robert Turner in 1656 (pp. 136 ff.)

Ars Almadel

In 1608, Trithemius mentioned a long list of books on magic, including the book *Almadel attributed to King Solomon*.[22] *Ars Almadel* is also found in the Hebrew manuscripts of the *Key of Solomon* (ed. Gollancz), *Sepher Maphteah Shelomoh* (1914, fol. 20b), and in Oriental MS 6360, a Hebrew manuscript recently acquired by the British Library.[23] Johann Weyer seems to associate the art with an Arab magician of the same name.[24] Robert Turner mentions a 15th-century manuscript in Florence.[25]

---

18 See *Sepher Ha-Razim*, translated by Michael A. Morgan (Chico, California: Scholars Press, 1983). I have also compared the lists of names with those found in the *Book of the Angel Raziel*, from Sloane MS 3846.

19 Lynn Thorndike, *Magic and Experimental Science* (New York: Columbia University Press, 1923), chapter xlix, pp. 279 ff.

20 Bibliothèque Nationale MS 7170A. See Robert Turner, *Elizabethan Magic* (Shaftesbury: Element, 1989), pp. 140–141.

21 For a modern edition, see *The Magical Calendar, a synthesis of magical symbolism from the Seventeenth-Century Renaissance of Medieval occultism*, translation and commentary by Adam McLean (Edinburgh: Magnum Opus Hermetic Sourceworks, 1979); revised edition Grand Rapids: Phanes Press, 1994).

22 See I. P. Couliano, *Eros and Magic in the Renaissance* (Chicago: University of Chicago Press, 1987), p. 167.

23 Described by Claudia Rohrbacher-Sticker, "Mafteah Shelomoh: A New Acquisition of the British Library," *Jewish Studies Quarterly*, i (1993/4, pp. 263–270), and "A Hebrew Manuscript of *Clavicula Salomonis*, Part II," *The British Library Journal*, vol. 21 (1995, pp. 127–136).

24 Weyer includes Almadel as one of the "Arab Throng" of "magicians of ill repute," along with Alchindus and Hipocus; see Weyer, *Witches, Devils, and Doctors in the Renaissance*, p. 101.

25 Florence II-iii-24; see Turner, *Elizabethan Magic*, p. 140.

Ars Notoria

The oldest book of the collection, *Ars Notoria*, is a Medieval grimoire of the Solomonic Cycle. Many Latin manuscripts are extant; the oldest date from the 13th century, and possibly earlier. Like *Liber Juratus* (also 13th century), the text centers around an even older collection of orations or prayers that are interspersed with magical words. The orations in *Ars Notoria* and those in *Liber Juratus* are closely related and suggest to me a common oral tradition. The orations in both works are said to have mystical properties that can impart communion with God and instant knowledge of divine and human arts and sciences.

Older manuscripts of the *Ars Notoria* contain exquisite drawings, the "figures" (*notae*) mentioned throughout the text.[26] Their omission adds greatly to the confusion of the text. A Latin edition was printed in the *Opera* of Agrippa von Nettesheim (Lyons, ca. 1620). Robert Turner's English edition (London, 1657) appears to have been translated from the Latin edition. Neither of these two early printed editions include the *notae*.

The *notae* vary considerably in the *Ars Notoria* manuscripts,[27] and individual manuscripts sometimes give alternate versions for the figures as well. Some of these *notae* are symbolic representations of the orations; among these are the first and second notes on the art of grammar. The first note on grammar consists of the oration written in concentric rings; the second consists of the oration written in a diamond-shaped arrangement. Other *notae* seem to be symbolic representations of the arts to be mastered. An example is the "note by which the whole faculty of grammar can be had," which includes various parts of speech in circles. See Appendix 3 for examples of *notae*.

Not all manuscripts of the *Lemegeton* include the *Ars Notoria*. Some list only four books. Those that do contain them are entirely dependent on Robert Turner's 1657 edition.

EDITIONS

Parts of the *Lemegeton* have been published several times in the past. While the following survey is not complete, none of the editions I have reviewed are critical, and most rely only on a single manuscript.

---

26 For examples of the illustrations and an excellent discussion of the *Ars Notoria*, see the articles by Michael Camille and Claire Fanger in Claire Fanger, *Conjuring Spirits, Texts and Traditions of Medieval Ritual Magic* (University Park, PA: Pennsylvania State University Press, 1998), pp. 110 ff. and 216 ff.

27 Fanger, *Conjuring Spirits*, p. 238 n. 12.

Arthur Edward Waite

The Book of Black Magic and of Pacts, (Edinburgh: Privately published, 1898),[28] later revised and published as *The Secret Tradition in Goëtia. The Book of Ceremonial Magic, including the rites and mysteries of Goëtic theurgy, sorcery, and infernal necromancy* (London: William Rider & Son, 1911 [1910], reprinted by New York: University Books, 1961). Waite included the bulk of the *Goetia*, as well as excerpts of the *Pauline Art*, and *Ars Almadel* in his popular compendium of magical texts. When Crowley brought out his own edition of part of the *Goetia* (see below), he included a scathing review of Waite's efforts, but his critique is without substance. Moreover, his argument with Waite was personal and chronic. Unfortunately, Waite's book does, in fact, suffer from many defects. His transcriptions and drawings are not reliable, and his translations are often misleading, inaccurate, and confusing. Waite's intention seems to have been to present the worst examples he could find of magical texts in order to discredit the genre.

Crowley and Mathers

An edition of the first part of the *Lemegeton, Goetia*, was prepared by S. L. MacGregor Mathers and completed by Aleister Crowley (Foyers: Society for the Propagation of Religious Truth, 1904.) It appeared with the title *The Book of the Goetia of Solomon the King. Translated into the English tongue by a dead hand ... The whole ... edited, verified, introduced and commented by A. Crowley....* (pp. ix. 65. 4o). By his own account,[29] Crowley's contribution to the volume was minor, consisting of an essay,[30] a version of the conjurations rendered into John Dee's "Enochian or Angelic language," some minor annotations, a "Preliminary Invocation," prefatory note, and a Magical Square. In the prefatory note, Crowley claims the work is "a translation ... done, after collation and edition, from numerous MSS in Hebrew, Latin, French and English." In reality, Mathers' manuscript sources were all in English, none of which Crowley bothered to check before making the assertion. His assumption was, no doubt, based on the fact that Mathers' edition of the *Key of Solomon* was, in fact, based on numerous manuscripts in the languages mentioned.[31] Crowley's edition in-

---

28 Also published as *The Book of Black Magic* (York Beach, ME: Samuel Weiser, 1972).
29 Aleister Crowley, *The Confessions of Aleister Crowley* (New York: Bantam Books, 1971), p. 378. Crowley's annotations are often merely unconvincing boasts of his prowess in the Goetic practices.
30 "The initiated interpretation of ceremonial magick."
31 Mathers, *The Key of Solomon the King (Clavicula Salomonis)*.

cludes redrawn sigils enclosed in double circles, where the names of the spirits are written in Roman letters. This innovation is similar to the Harley MS, but the latter includes the names in both Roman and Hebrew lettering.[32]

Idries Shah

The Secret Lore of Magic (New York: The Citadel Press, 1970). Shah's work included a transcription of *Ars Almadel* from Sloane MS 2731. He also included an abridged *Goetia* that he split into one chapter and several appendices. Shah also neglected to include key elements in the ritual. Ironically, Shah complained that Waite had not included a verbatim transcript.

Nelson and Anne White

Lemegeton; Clavicula Salomonis: or The Complete Lesser Key of Solomon The King (Pasadena: The Technology Group, 1979). This edition is valuable in that it includes a photocopy (incomplete) of Sloane MS 2731.[33] White provided a transcription of each page, as well as some footnotes primarily based on his experiences as a practitioner of ceremonial magic. The transcriptions are not always reliable.[34] Unfortunately, the poor quality of type and cheap method of reproduction make it almost totally unreadable. It is not known whether these defects were corrected in any subsequent editions.

Mitch Henson

Lemegeton—The Complete Lesser Key of Solomon (Jacksonville: Metatron Books, 1999) Unfortunately, this edition of the *Lemegeton* is also uncritical and indiscriminate in its use of source material. Henson based it initially on the seriously deficient but often cited Sloane MS 2731, but midway through, he silently switched to an inaccurate transcription of Sloane MS 3825 as his chief source. The illustrations have all been redrawn and many were significantly simplified or corrupted.[35] Spelling and punctuation have been par-

---

32   See examples in Appendix 3.

33   In particular, the bulk of *Ars Paulina*, Part 2 was silently omitted.

34   For example, White transcribes "The Little Key" as "The Liffer (Lesser) Key."

35   For example, the Hebrew lettering is omitted from the drawing of the brass vessel. Likewise the Secret Table of Salomon and the seal of Icosiel are simplified, probably because fading ink in the original manuscript was not discernible in Henson's photocopy. The Hexagram, Pentagram, Ring, and Secret Seal were clearly based on

tially modernized, sometimes altering the original meaning, and frequently
introducing new typographic errors. Likewise, the editor took other liber-
ties with the text, presumably in the interests of improving readability and
reducing production costs. Henson arbitrarily omitted all of Book 5, dis-
missing it as showing "no affinity for the listings of spirits that mark the
bulk of" the *Lemegeton*. And, in spite of the title, he silently omitted the
introductory and concluding materials and many other passages, reducing
the text to a slender 95 pages. Nevertheless, it could prove useful for those
who want a low-cost introduction, but those interested in accuracy or in-
tending to practice ceremonial magic may want to use it with caution.

Mathers, who had, himself, changed the drawings. The Magic Circle was based on
Sloane 2731, a particularly bad choice because of crowded corrections written *supra
linea* and misunderstood by Henson's illustrator. Corrections in the Seals of the
Zodiac were similarly misinterpreted.

Lemegeton Clavicula Salomonis

or

THE LESSER KEY OF SOLOMON

Detailing the ceremonial art of
commanding spirits both good and evil

[Preface from Harley 6483]

Liber malorum Spirituum
seu Goetia

This Booke contains all the names, Orders, and Offices of all the spirits Salomon ever conversed with. The seales and characters belonging to each spirit, and the manner of calling them forth to visible appearance.

    Some of these spirits are in Enock's Tables which I have explained, but omitted their seales and characters, how they may be knowne; but in this booke they are at large set forth.

The Definition of Magick

Magick is the highest most absolute and divinest knowledge of Natural Philosophy advanced in its works and wonderfull operations by a right understanding of the inward and occult vertue of things, so that true agents being applyed to proper patients, strange and admirable effects will thereby be produced; whence magicians are profound & diligent searchers into Nature; they because of their skill know how to anticipate an effect which to the vulgar shall seeme a miracle.

    Origen saith that the Magical Art doth not contain any thing subsisting, but although it should yet that must not be evil or subject to contempt or scorne; and doth distinguish the Natural Magick from that which is Diabolical.

    Tyaneus only exercised the Natural Magick by which he performed wonderfull things.

Philo Hebreus saith that true Magick by which we come to the secret works of nature is so far from being contemptible that the greatest monarchs & Kings have studied it. Nay amongst the Persians none might reigne unlesse he were skilfull in this great Art.

This noble science often degenerates, and from Natural becomes Diabolical, from true philosophy turns to Negromancy which is wholly to be charged uppon its followers who abusing or not being capable of that high and mystical knowledge do immediately hearken to the temptations of Sathan, and are misled by him into the study of the black art. Hence it is that Magick lyes under disgrace, and they who seeke after it are vulgarly esteemed Sorcerers. And the fraternity of the Rosy Crucians thought it not fit to stile themselves Magicians, but philosophers, they are not ignorant Empiricks but learned and experienced physicians whose remedies are not only lawfull but divine.

[Introduction]

The little Key of Salomon the King[1] which containeth all the names, orders and offices of all the spirits that ever he hadd any converse with, with the seales or Characters belongeing to Each spirit, and the manner of calling them forth to [visible] appearance, in 5 Parts, called Books viz - - - - -:

- The first part, is a Book of evill spirits, called *Goetia*, shewing how he bound up those spirits and used them in severall things, wherby he obtained great fame.

- The second part is a Booke of [aerial] spirits, partly good and partly evill, wᶜʰ is called *Theurgia Goetia* being all spirits of the ayre.

- The Third part is [a book] of spirits governing yᵉ Planetary houres, and wᶜʰ spirits belong to every degree of the signes and planets in yᵉ signes, and is called *Ars Paulina*.[2]

- The fourth part of this Booke is *called Ars Almadel Solomonis* [sic],[3] contayning 20 cheife spirits wᶜʰ governe the four Altitudes or the 360 degrees of the world & signes [zodiac] &c. These twoo last orders of spirits is of good, and are called the true Theurgia, and it is to be sought affter by divine seeking &c.

- The fifth part is a Booke of orations and prayers that wise Salomon used upon the alter in the Temple which is called *Artem Novam*

---

1   S2 reads, "lemegeton / or CLAVICVLA SALOMONIS: REX: or the Little Key: of / Solomon The King." H omits this introduction.

2   S2: "the pauline art &c."

3   S2: "... called ALMADEE of Solomon."

[sic. *Ars Nova*] The wch was revealed to Salomon by the holy angel of God called Michael, and he also recieved [sic] many breef
Notes written by the fingar of God wch was deliverd[4] to him by y^e
said Angell, with Thunder claps, without w^c Notes [K] Salomon
hadd never obtained to his great knowledge, for by them in short
time he knew all arts and siences both good and badd which from
these Notes [this book] is [also] called *Ars Notoria* .

[100v] In this Booke is contained the whole art of Salomon although
there be many other Bookes that is said to be his yet none is to be
compared with this, for this containeth them all, although they be
titled with severall other names, as the Booke *Helisoe*[5] wch is the
very same as this last [book] is, wch called, *Artem Novam & Ars
Notaria* &c..

These Bookes were first found in the Chaldean & hebrew tongues at
Hierusalem, by a Jewish Rabbi, & by him put into the greeke Language, &
from thence into ye Latine, as it is said &c.

---

4   S2: "declared."
5   S2: "Helisol."

Of The Arte Goetia

[Of the seventy-two infernal spirits evoked and constrained by King Salomon[6]]

The first principall spirit is a king ruling in y[e] East, called **Bael**.[7] he maketh men goe Invisible, he ruleth over 66 Legions of Inferiour spirits, he appeareth in divers shapes, sometimes like a Catt, sometimes like a Toad,[8] sometimes like a man,[9] & sometimes in all these formes at once. he speaketh very horsly.[10] This is his Character w[ch] is to be worne as a Lamen before him who calleth him forth, or else he will not doe you homage.

The second spirit is a Duke called **Agares**, he is under y[e] power of y[e] East and cometh up in the form of a fair Old man riding upon a Crocodill, very

---

6   H heads this section "Lemegeton / Secretum Secretorum." S3 adds the subheading "The first Spirite" (*sec. man.*).

7   S1: "Baell"; W: "Baëll."

8   H: "dog."

9   W: "he appeareth with three heads; the first like a toad ..."

10   H: "... he speaketh hastily and this is his Caracter or Seale which must be worne as a Lamin by the Magician who calls him, on his breast else he will not do you homage."

mildly, carrying a goshawke on his fist. he maketh them runne that stand still, and fetcheth back yᵉ runnawayes. he can teach all Languages or Tongues presently, he hath the power also to destroy dignities, both supernaturall & Temporall; & cause Earthquakes. he was of the order of Vertues; he hath under his government 31 Legions &c: & this is [his] seale or Character wᶜʰ is to be worne as [a] Lamen.

[King Agares (*sec. man.*)]

The Third spirit is a mighty prince, being of yᵉ same Nature as Agares, he is called **Vassago**,[11] This spirit is of a good nature, & his office is to declare things past and to come; and to discover all things hidden or lost &c: he governeth 26 Legions of spirits. This is his seal.

[101r]

The 4ᵗʰ spirit is called **Gamigin**,[12] a great Marquise, he appereth in yᵉ forme of a litle horse or asse and then into humane shape he putteth him- self at yᵉ request of yᵉ Master and speaketh wᵗʰ a horse voice; he teaches all Liberall siences, and giveth and account of yᵉ dead soules of them that dye in sin. & he ruleth over 30 Legions of Inferiors &c. This is his seal, wᶜʰ is to be worne by the Magician when he Invocateth.

---

11   Not found in W.

12   W: "Gamygyn/Gamigin"; C: "Samigina, or Gamigin."

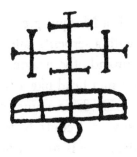

The 5th spirit is called Marbas[13]—he is a great presedent, and appeareth at first in ye forme of a great Lyon: but afterwards putteth on humane shape at ye Request of ye Master. he Answareth truly of Things hidden or secreet, he causeth deseases and cureth them againe & giveth great wisdome & knowledge in mechanicall arts,[14] & changeth men into other shapes. he governeth 36 Legions of spirits. his seal is thus.

The 6th spirit is Valefar[15] — he is a Mighty Duke, & appeareth in ye form of a Lion wh a mans head Lowring,[16] he is a good femiliar, but tempteth those he is femiliar with to steale, he governeth 10 Legions of spirets, this is his seal to worne constantly if you haue his familiarity. Else not.

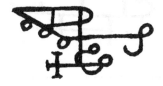

[101v]

---

13   H and W add, "alias Barbas."

14   H and W add, "or Handycrafts."

15   S2, C: "VALEFOR"; W: "Valefar, alias Malaphar." Scot's tr. reads "Valefar, alias Malephar."

16   Lowering, i.e., raging or scowling. S1 reads "with a Mansy heade Lowring" and adds (in margin) "in another copy 'with Amases head Lowing.'" C: "bellowing"; W (tr. Scot): "the head of a theefe." The common element here is the Latin *latronis*, which can mean either barking or thieving.

The 7th spirit is **Amon**.[17] he is a Marquis great in power & most strong, he at first appereth like a wolf with a serpents taile, vomiting out of his Mouth fleames of fire, but at ye command of ye Magician he putteth on ye shape of a man, with dogs Teeth beset in a head like a Raven, or in a Ravens Head, hee telleth [of] all things past & to come, and procureth love,[18] and reconcileth controversies between freinds & foes,[19] & governeth 40 Legions of spirits, his seal is thus, wch is to be worne as afforesaid.

The 8th spirit is called **Barbatos** he is a great duke & appeareth when ye ☉ is in ♐, with four Noble kings and their companions in great troops, he giveth ye understanding of ye singing of Birds, and ye voice of other Creatures and ye [such as] barking of dogs &c, he breaketh hidden treasures open, that have been Laid by ye Enchantment of Magicians, & [he was] of ye order of vertues, [of] which some part beareth rule still &c he knoweth all things past and to come: and reconsileth friends & those that are in power, he ruleth over 30 Legions of spirits, his seal of obedience is this. wch were before you &c.

The 9th spirit in order is **Paimon**; a great king, & very Obedient to Lucifer, he appeareth in ye forme of a man, sitting one a dromedary, wh a

---

17 W: "Amon, or Aamon."

18 C: "feuds."

19 H adds, "He also bringeth to pass, that souls which are drowned in the sea shall take up airy bodies & evidently appear & answer to interrogations at the request of the exorcist."

Crowne most glorious on his head. Three [There] goeth before him a host of spirits like men with Trumpets and well sounding Cymballs, and all other sorts of musicall Instruments &c. he hath a great voice, and roareth at his first comming, and his speech [voice] is such as yᵉ Magician cannot well understand, unless he compelleth him. This spirit can teach all arts and siences, and other secret Things; he can discover wᵗ yᵉ Earth is, and wᵗ holdeth it up in yᵉ waters, & wᵗ yᵉ wind[20] is or where it is, or any other Thing yᵘ desire to know, he giveth dignity and confirmeth yᵉ same, he bindeth or maketh a man subject to yᵉ Magician if he desireth it he giveth good familiars, and such as can teach all arts, he is to be observed towards yᵉ North west,[21] he is of yᵉ order of dominions and hath 200 Legions of spirits under him, one part of them is of yᵉ order of Angells & yᵉ other of Potestates [Potentates], If yᵘ call this spirit Paimon alone yᵘ must make him some offering to him & there will attend him 2 kings called Bebal[22] & Abalam,[23] & other spirits of yᵉ order of Potestates [Potentates] in his host are 25 Legions because all those spirits wᶜʰ are subject to him, are not allwayes wᵗʰ him unlesse yᵉ Magician compelleth them, This is his Character.[24]

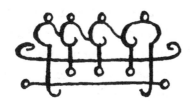

[102r]

The 10ᵗʰ spirit is **Buer**, a great president and appereth in ♐ that is his shape when yᵉ ☉ is there, he teacheth Phylosophy [both] Morall & Naturall, & yᵉ Logicall arts, & yᵉ vertues of all hearbes & plants, & healeth all distempers in Man, & giveth <(familiars)> good familiars, he governeth over 50 Legions of spirits and this is his seale of obediance wᶜʰ you must weare when you call him to apperance.

---

20   C: "Mind."

21   S1 adds (in margin), "in another copy, 'to observed towards the west.'" C: "West."

22   H, S2: "baball"; S1: "Beball"; C: "Labal."

23   C: "Abalim."

24   S2 adds, "which must b [sic] worne as a lamen &c"; S1 adds (in margin) "to be worn as a Lamen."

The 11th spirit is a great & strong duke called **Gusoin**, he appeareth like a Xenophilus he telleth of all things past, present & to come: he sheweth yᵉ meaning of all questions you can ask, he reconcileth friends and giveth honour and dignity to any, and ruleth over 40[25] Legions of Spirits. his seal is this, wᶜʰ weare as aforesaid &c.

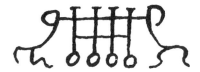

The 12th spirit is **Sitri**,[26] he is a great prince & appeareth at first with a Leopards face, and wings as a griffin. But afterwards at yᵉ command of yᵉ exorcist, he putteth on a humane shape very Beautifull, Inflaming Men with womens Love, and women with mens love, and causeth them to shew themselves Naked, if he [it] be desired, &c. he governeth 60 Legions of spirits, and his seal to be worne is this.

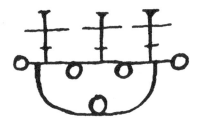

The 13 spirit is called **Beleth** [Bileth[27]], he is a mighty king and terrable, ridding on a pale horse wᵗʰ Trumpets and all other kinds of Musicall In-

---

25 W reads "45," but Scot's translation reads "40," apparently by mistake.

26 W: "Sytry, alias Bitru"; Scot: "Sitri, alias Bitru."

27 W reads, "Byleth," but Scot's tr. reads "Bileth," as does S3 later on. C: "Beleth (or Bileth, or Bilet)."

struments playing before him, he is very furious at his first apperance That is whilest yᵉ Exorcist allay his Courage, for to doe that, he must hold a hazel stick[28] in his hand, streched forth towards yᵉ South & East quarters making a Triangle without yᵉ Circle, commanding him into it by yᵉ vertue of yᵉ Bonds & chaines of spirits hereafter following, & if he doe not come into yᵉ Δ by your Threats, rehearse yᵉ Bounds & chaines before him, and then he will yeild obediance and come into it and do what he is commanded by yᵉ Eorcist [Exorcist], yet he must receive him courteously, because he is a great king & doe homage to him, as the kings and princes doe that attend him, and you must [also] have allwayes a silver Ring on the middle finger of the left hand, held against your face as they do for Amaimon, This king Beleth causeth all yᵉ love that possible may be, both of Men and women till yᵉ Master Eorcist [Exorcist] hath had his mind fullfilled &c. he is of the order of Powers and governeth 85 Legions of spirits, his Noble seal is this wᶜʰ is to be worne before you in the Time of working.   [102v]

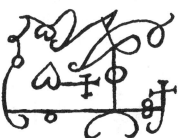

The 14ᵗʰ spirit is called **Leraye** (or Leraje) [written intra linea].[29] he is a Marquize great in power shewing him selfe in yᵉ likeness of an archer, cladd in green carring [carrying] a Bow and quiver, he causeth all great Battles & contests, & causeth yᵉ wounds to putrifie that are [made] wᵗʰ arrows by archers this belongeth to ♐ he governeth 30 Legions of spirits, & his seale of obediance is this.

---

28   W: "hazell bat."

29   S1, S2: "LERAJE"; H: "Leraic"; C: "Leraje, or Leraikha"; W: "Loray, alias Oray"; "Leraie" in Scot's translation.

The 15th spirit is called **Eligor**,30 a great duke, he appeareth in [the] form of a goodly knight carring a lance an Ensigne & a serpent, he discovereth hidden Things & knoweth things to come, & of warres and how the soulders will & shall meet, he causeth the love of Lords and great persons, and governeth 60 Legions of spirits, his seal is thus,31 wch wear or else he will not appear nor obey you &c.

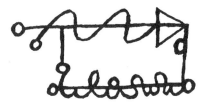

The 16th spirit is called **Zepar**, he is a great duke & appeareth in red apparell & armed like a souldier, his office is to cause women to love Men and to bring them togather in love he also maketh them barren, and governeth [over] 26 Legions of Inferiour spirits, his seal is this, wch he obeyeth when he seeth it.

The 17th spirit is called **Botis**32 a great president and an Earle; he appeareth at ye [first] shew in ye form of an ugly viper Then at ye command of ye Magician he putteth on humane shape, with great teeth, Two horns, carring a sharp bright sword in his hand, he telleth of all Things past and to come and reconcileth friends and foes, he governeth 60 Legions of spirits his seal is this, that he obeyeth when he seeth it.

---

30 W reads "Eligor, alias Abigor"; S2, H, and C read "Eligos"; S1 reads "Eligor," but adds (in margin) "in another copy 'Eligos.'"

31 S2 omits the rest of this sentence.

32 W: "Botis, otherwise Otis."

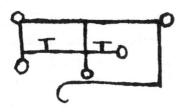

[103r]

The 18th spirit is called **Bathin,** he is a mighty [and] strong duke & appeareth like a strong man wth ye Taile of a serpent, sitting on a ~~plane~~ paile couloured horse33 he knoweth the vertue of hearbes & precious stones, & can transport men suddenly from one Country into an other, he ruleth over 30 Legions of spirits his seal is thus to be made and to be worne before you.

The 19th spirit is called **Saleos** [Sallos34], he is a great and mighty duke, & appeareth in [the] form of a gallant souldier, ridding on a Crocodile, wth a dukes crowne on his head peaceably he causeth ye love of women to men & men to women, he governeth 30 Legions of spirits his seal is this,35 wch must be worne before you.

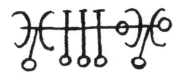

The 20th spirit is called **Purson**36 a great king; he appeareth commonly like a man wth a Lyons face, carring a cruel viper in his hand, and ridding on a Bear goeing before him [are] many Trumpets sounding; he knoweth hid-

---

33   C reads, "[Horse?]" and adds the footnote, "In some of the older Codices this word is left out, in others it is indistinct, but appears to be 'horse,' so I have put the word horse within brackets above. – TRANS. [The Quartos have 'ass.' –Ed]."

34   W: "Zaleos/Saleos"; S3: "Saleos"; H and S2: "Sallos"; C: "Sallos (or Saleos)."

35   S2 omits the rest of this sentence.

36   W: "Pursan, alias Curson"; Scot's translation reads "Purson."

den things and can discover Treasures & tell all Things present past and to come; he can take a Body either humane or aiery, and answareth Truly of all Earthly Things, both secreet & devine, & of yᵉ Creation of yᵉ world, he bringeth forth good familiars, & under his government [power] are 22 Legions of spirits, partly of yᵉ order of vertues & partly of yᵉ order of Thrones, & his mark or seal is this, wᶜʰ he oweth obediance to & [which] must be worne by yᵉ Exorcist in [the] Time of acction.

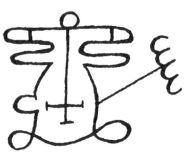

The 21 spirit is called **Morax** [Marax[37]] he is a great Earle and a president, he appeareth like a great Bull wᵗʰ a mans face; his office is: to make men very knowling [sic] in Astronomy, and all yᵉ other Liberall siences; he can give good familiars and [very] wise, wᶜʰ know yᵉ vertues of hearbes & precious stones he governeth 36[38] Legions of spirits, & his seal is to be made Thus and worne [as aforesaid].

The 22ᵈ spirit is called **Ipos**[39]—, he is an Earl and a mighty prince, and appeareth in yᵉ forme of an angel, wᵗʰ a Lions head gooses feet & a haires Taile, he knoweth Things past and to come; he maketh Men witty and bold, and governeth 36 Legions of spirits, his seal or Charecter is This, wᶜʰ must be worne as a Lamen before you.

---

37 H and S2 reads, "Marax." C also reads "Marax," and adds the footnote, "In some of the Codices written Morax, but I consider the above the correct orthography." W: "Morax, alias Foraii."

38 So read S3 and W. H: "3"; S2, C: "30."

39 W: "Ipes, alias Ayperos"; Scot: "Ipos, alias Ayporos."

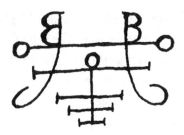

The 23d spirit is called **Aim**,[40] a greatt duke and strong, he appeareth in ye forme of a very handsome man in Body, [but] wth 3 heads, The first like a serpent ye second like a man wth 2 starrs in his forehead, The Third [head] is lik [sic] a Catt; he rideeth on a viper, carring a fire brand in his hand burning, whereth [wherewith] he sets Citties Castles & great places on fire he maketh one witty [in] all manner of wayes, and giveth true answares to privy matters, he governeth 26 Legions of Infernall spirits; his seal is thus to be made, and worne as a Lamen before you.[41]

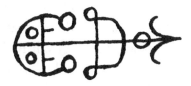

The 24th spirit is called **Naberius**,[42] he is a most valliant Marquiz, & appeareth in ye forme of a Black Crow,[43] fluttering about the Circle, & when he speaketh it is with a hoarse voice; he maketh men cunning in all arts & siences, but especially in ye art [of] Rhetoric; he restoreth lost dignity and honours, & governeth 19 Legions of spirits his seal is this, wch must be worne.

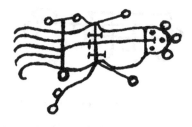

---

40   W: "Aym or Haborym/Haborim."

41   H, S2: "... his seal is this which weare &c."

42   W: "Naberus, alias Cerberus"; Scot: "Naberius, alias Cerberus."

43   C: "Black Crane."

The 25ᵗʰ spirit is called **Glasya Labolas**,⁴⁴ he is a Mighty president & sheweth him selfe in yᵉ forme of a dog wᵗʰ wings like a griffin; he teacheth all arts⁴⁵ in ~~a sudden~~ an Instant, and is an author of Blood shed & Manslaughter, he telleth all Things past & to come, if desired, & causeth love of friends and foes; he can make a Man goe Invisible, & he hath under his rule 36 Legions of spirits, his seal is this, yᵉ wᶜʰ weare [must be worn] as a Lamin.

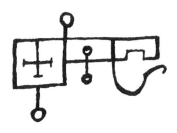

[104r]

The 26ᵗʰ spirit is called **Bune** [or Bime⁴⁶], he is a strong, great & mighty duke, & appeareth in yᵉ forme of a Dragon wᵗʰ three heads, one like a dog, The other like a griffin; The 3ᵈ like a man, he speaketh wⁱᵗʰ a high & comely voice, he changeth yᵉ places of yᵉ dead, & causeth those spirits that are under him, to gather together upon their sepulcheres, he giveth Riches to a man & maketh him wise & eloquent, he giveth true Answards to yʳ demands, & governeth 30 Legions of spirits, his seal is this wᶜʰ he owneth [oweth] obedience to.

first [version]

& Nota he hath another seal or Character wᶜʰ is made Thus. yᵘ may use wᶜʰ yᵘ will, but yᵉ first is best as Salomon saith.⁴⁷

[another version]

---

44   W: "Glasya Labolas, alias Caacrinolaas, or Caassimolar."

45   S1 adds (intra linea) "& sciences." C also reads "Arts and Sciences."

46   S3 and W both read "Bune"; H and S2 both read "Bime." S1 adds (in margin) "in another copy 'Bime.'" C: "Bune, or Bimé.—The Twenty-sixth Spirit is Buné (or Bim)." Mathers' version of the sigil has "BUNE" drawn around it, while his table showing Rudd's Hebrew reads "Bimé."

47   S2: "He hath another seal which is made as the bigest of thes is but the least is best

The 27th spirit is called **Ronove**,[48] he appeareth in ye forme of a Monster, he teacheth y^e art of Rhetorick very well, and giveth good servants knowledge of Tongues, favouer of friends & foes; he is a Marquiz & a great Earle, and there obeieth him [he commandeth] 19 Legions of spirits his seal is this.

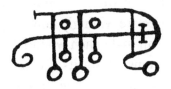

The 28th spirit in order as Salomon bound them, is named **Berith**. he is a Mighty great and terrable duke, he hath two other Names given to him by men of latter Times, viz: **Beal & Bolfry**,[49] he appeareth like a souldier wth red clothing, ridding on a red horse & [having] a Crown of Gold upon his head he giveth True answares of things [concerning the] past present & to come; you [must] use a Ring as is before spoken of [with] Beleth in calling him forth; he can turne all mettals into Gold, he can give dignity & [can] confirm them to Men, he speaketh wth a very clear & subtill voice, he is a great Lyer and not to be Trusted much he governeth over 26 Legions of spirits his seal is this which must be worne as [a] lamin.

&c." The "bigest" evidently refers to the first, which is drawn slightly larger in S2. H omits the note about a second seal, and has only the latter. S1 adds (intra linea) "in another copy 'the least is the best.'" The other copy is evidently S2. C: "the last is the best."

48   W: "Roneve"; Scot: "Ronove"; C: "Ronové."

49   S2: "BEALE & BOFRY"; H: "Beale and Bolfry." S1 adds (in margin) "in another Copy 'Beale & Bofry.'" C: "Beale, or Beal, and Bofry or Bolfry." W: "Of some he is called Beall; of the Jewes Berithi; of Nigromancers Bolfry."

The 29th spirit in order is Named **Astaroth**, he is a Mighty & strong duke, & appeareth in [the] forme of an unbeautifull angel, ridding on an Infernall like dragon, and carring in his right hand a viper (you must not lett him come to neare yᵘ least he doe yᵘ damage by his stinking Breath.) Therefore yᵉ Exorcist must hold yᵉ Magicall Ring⁵⁰ nere to his face and yᵗ will defend him he giveth true answares of things present past & to come & can discover all secreets; he will declare willingly how yᵉ spirits fell, if desired, & yᵉ reason of his own fall. He can make men wounderfull knowing in all Liberall siences; he ruleth 40 Legions of spirits, his seal is as this [shown], wᶜʰ weare as a Lamen before yᵘ, or else he wⁱˡˡ not obey you.

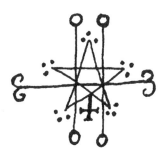

The 30th spirit is called **Forneus**,⁵¹ he is a mighty great Marquiz, & appeareth in yᵉ forme of a great sea Monster, he Teacheth & maketh men wounderfull knowing in yᵉ art of Rhetoric he causeth men to have a good Name, and to have yᵉ understanding of Tongues; he maketh men to be beloved of their foes as well as they be by their Friends; & he governeth 29 Legions of spirits, partly of yᵉ order of Thrones and partly of angels, his seal is this to be made and worne as aforesaid &.

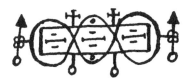

The 31 spirit in order, [as Salomon saith,] is named **Foras**,⁵² he is a mighty great president & appeareth in yᵉ form of a strong man, in humane shape he can give yᵉ understanding to men how they may know yᵉ vertues of all

50   W: "magical silver ring" (annulum argenteum magicum), but "magical ring" in Scot's translation.

51   H: "Forners."

52   W: "Forras vel Forcas"; Scot: "Foras, alias Forcas."

hearbs & precious stones, & [he] teacheth them yᵉ art [of] Logick & Ethicks in All their partes if desired, he maketh men Invisible, witty, Eloquent & to live Long;⁵³ he [can] discover Treasures and recover Things lost, & he ruleth over 29 Legions of spirits, his seale or Character is thus to be made & worne as a Lamen.

The 32ᵈ spirit in order is called **Asmoday**.⁵⁴ he is a great king, strong & powerfull, he appeareth wᵗʰ 3 heads, whereof yᵉ first is like a Bull The second like a Man, The third like a Ram, [he appeareth also] wᵗʰ a serpents Taile, Belching or vomitting up flames of fire⁵⁵ out of his mouth his feet are webed like a Goose, he sitteth on an Infernall dragon carring a Launce and a flagg in his hands, he is yᵉ first & chifiest under yᵉ power of **Amaymon**, & goeth before all others: when the Exorcist hath a mind to call him, lett it be abroad,⁵⁶ and lett him stand on his feet all yᵉ Time of action, wᵗʰ his cap⁵⁷ of [off], for if it be on, Amaymon will deceive him and cause all his doeing to be bewrayed [divulged], But as soone as yᵉ Exorist [Exorcist] seeth Asmoday in yᵉ shape aforesaid, he shall call him by his Name, saying, *thou art Asmoday*, & he will not deny it; & by & by he will bow down to yᵉ ground &c he giveth yᵉ Ring of vertues he teacheth yᵉ art of Arithmitic, geomitry, Astronomy and all

[105r]

---

53   C: "invisible, and to live long, and to be eloquent." He adds the footnote "One or two Codices have 'invincible,' but 'invisible' is given in the majority. Yet the form of appearance of Foras as a strong man might warrant the former, though from the nature of his offices the invincibility would probably be rather on the mental than on the physical plane."

54   W: "Sydonay/Sidonay, alias Asmoday"; H: "Asmodai"; C: "Asmoday, or Asmodai." Asmoday or Asmodeus occurs in *Tobit* 3:8, *New English Bible* (New York: University of Oxford Press. 1971), and is ultimately derived from the Avestan demon *Aeshma-daeva* ("demon of wrath").

55   C: "from his mouth issue Flames of Fire."

56   The translator has evidently read *foris* ("in a foreign land") by mistake; it should read *fit fortis* ("let him be brave"). See W.

57   This follows Scot's "if his cap be on his head," a truly bizarre mistranslation of *si vero coopertus fuerit* ("if he is afraid he will be overwhelmed"). Crowley does it one better by adding "or Head-dress."

[other] handicrafts absolutely; he giveth full & True answares to yr demands, he maketh a man Invisible, he showeth ye place where Treasures layeth, and guardeth it if it be among ye Legion of Amaymon, he governeth 72 Legions of Inferiour spirits, his seal is thus to be made and worne as a Lamen before [thee] on your Breast.

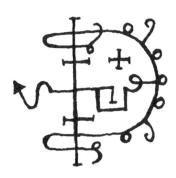

The 33d spirit is **Gaap**.[58] he is a great president & a mighty Prince, he appeareth when ye ☉ is in some of ye Southern Signes, in a humane shape, goeing before 4 great & mighty kings, as if he was a guide to conduct them along in their way. his office is to make men knowing in Phylosophy and all ye Liberall siences; he can cause love or hatred, and make men Insensible[59] he can Teach yu how to consecrate those Things that belong to ye dominion of Amaymon his king & can dilever [deliver] familiers out of the custody of other Magicians; and [he also] answareth Truly and perfectly of Things past present and to come, & can carry and recarry [men] most speedily from one kingdome to another, at ye will and pleasure of [the] Exorcist, he ruleth over 66 Legions of spirits he was of ye order of potestates [potentates]; his seal is thus to be made & worne as a Lamen &c.

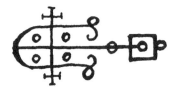

The 34th spirit is called **Furtur** [Furfur[60]], he is a great & mighty Earle, appearing in ye forme of an hart wth a firey [fiery] Taile; he never speaket

[speaketh] Truth, except he be compelled or brought up wthin a Triangle, △ being compelled therein, he will take upon himselfe ye forme
of an angel being bidden; he speaketh with a hoarse voice, & will [can]
willingly make love[61] between man & wife he can raise Thunder, Lightnings, Blasts and great Tempestuous stormes &c he giveth true answares
both of secreet and devine Things if commanded, and ruleth over 26
Legions of spirits, his seal is this which is to be [made &] worne as a
Lamin &c.

[105v]

The 35 spirit is called **Marchosias**,[62] he is a great and mighty Marquiz
appering at first in [the] forme of a wolfe;[63] having griffins wings, and a
serpents Taile, vomiting up fire out of his mouth[64] But afterwards at y^e
command of ye Exorcist, he putteth on ye shape of a man, and is a strong
fighter he giveth true answares to all questions, & is very faithfull to y^e
Exorcist in doeing his Buisness [sic], he was of y^e order of dominations he
governeth 30 Legions of spirits, he Told his chiefe Master wch w^{as} Salomon,
that after 1200 yeares he hadd hopes to returne to y^e 7th Throne &: his seal
is thus, to be made, & worne as a Lamin &c.

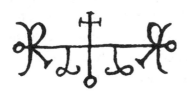

---

61 C: "urge Love."
62 W: "Marchocias," but "Marchosias" in Scot's translation.
63 W: "a cruell shee woolfe." C adds the footnote "In one Codex of the seventeenth
    century, very badly written, it might be read 'Ox' instead of 'Wolf.' – TRANS. [For
    me he appeared always like an ox, and very dazed. -Ed.]."
64 W: "spetting I cannot tell what out of his mouth."

The 36th spirit is called **Stolas**,65 he is a great and powerfull Prince, appearing in ye shape of a Night [mighty]66 Raven at first before ye Exorcist, but afterwards he taketh the image of a man &c; he teacheth the Art of Astronomy, & the vertuses [sic] of hearbs & precious stones, he governeth 26 legions of spirits his seal is thus to be made & worne as a Lamin.

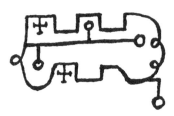

The 37th spirit is called **Phœnix**67 he his [is] a great Marquiz & appeareth like ye [form of the] Bird Phœnix having a Childs voice, he singeth many sweet notes before ye Exorcist, wch he must not regard, but by & by he must bidd him [to] put on a humane shape, Then he will speak Mervellously of all wounderfull siences; he his [sic] a good & excellent Poet, & will be willing to doe yr Request he hath hopes to returne to ye 7th Throne affter 1200 yeares more, as he said to Salomon, he governeth 20 Legions of spirits, his seal is Thus to be made, & worne &c.

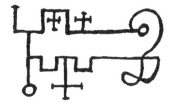

The 38th spirit is called **Halphas**68 he is a great Earle and appeareth in ye forme of a stock dove, and speaketh wth a hoarse voyce; his office is to build up Towers & to furnish them wth ammunition and weapons, and to send men of warre69 to places appointed; he ruleth 26 Legions of spirits; his seal is Thus to be made, & worne as a Lamen &c.70

---

65   H: "Stolus"; C: "Stolas, or Stolos."
66   W: "a nightraven"; S1, H, C: "mighty"; S2: "miaghty."
67   S2: "PHENEX"; H: "Phenix"; C: "Phenex (or Pheynix)."
68   H: "Malthas"; C: "Halphas, or Malthus (or Malthas)."
69   C adds the footnote, "Or, Warriors, or Men-at-Arms."
70   C adds the footnote, "But Malthus is certainly in heaven. See 'Promethius Unbound,' Introduction by P. B. Shelley, a necromancer of note, as shown by the references in his 'Hymn to Intellectual Beauty.' -Ed."

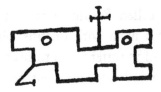

[106r]

The 39th spirit in order is called **Malphas**, he appeareth at first in ye forme like a Crow, But affterwardes will put on a humane shape at ye request of ye Exorcist & speake wth a hoarse voyce; he is a mighty president and powerfull he can Build houses & high Towers & he can bring quickly artificers togather from all places of ye world; he can destroy ye [thy]71 Enemies desires or thoughts, and wt [all that] they have done; he giveth good familiars, & if yu make any sacrifices to him, he will receive it kindly and willingly, But he will deceive him yt doth it; he governeth 40 Legions of spirits; his seal is Thus to be made and worne as a Lamen &c.

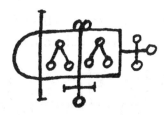

The 40th spirit is called **Raum**,72 he is an Earle, & appeareth at first in ye forme of a Crow but affterwards, at ye command of ye Exorcist he putteth on humane shape his office is to steale Treasures out of kings houses, and to carry it where he is commanded, & to destroy Citties, and ye dignities of men; & to tell all Things past, & wt is, & wt will be; & to cause Love between friends & foes; he was of ye order of Thrones, and governeth over 30 Legions of spirits his seal is Thus, which make and weare as a Lamin before you.

---

71   S2 omits, "quickly artificers ... destroy thy," as does Crowley.
72   W: "Raum, or Raim"; C: "Räum."

The 41 spirit in order is called **Focalor**[73] he is a great duke & strong, & appeareth in y^e forme of a Man with griffins wings; his office is, to kill men, and to drown them in ye waters, and to over throw ships of warre, for he hath power over both winds and seas, but he will not hurt any man or Thing, if he be commanded to y^e contrary by y^e Exorcist; he hath hopes to returne to y^e 7th Throne after 1000 yeares; he governeth 3[74] Legions of spirits, his seal is this wch must be worne as a Lamin.

The 42^d spirit is Named **Vepar**[75] he is a great & strong duke, & appeareth like a Mairmaid, his office is to guide y^e waters, & ships Ladden wth armour thereon[76] he will at y^e [will of the] Exorcist cause ye seas to be rough and stormy, and to appeare full of ships he causeth men to dye in 3 dayes wth putrifying their sores and wounds, & causing wormes in them to bred &c he governeth 29 Legions of spirits, his seal is Thus to be made and worne as a Lamin &c.

[106v]

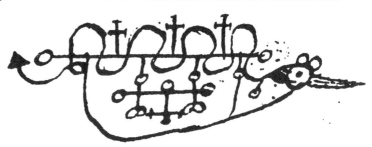

The 43^d spirit in order as Salomon commanded them into y^e Brazen vesel is called **Sabnach** [Sabnack[77]] he is a Mighty great Marquiz, & strong appearing in y^e forme of an armed souldier wth a Lyons head, ridding on a

---

73   H: "Forcalor"; C: "Focalor, or Forcalor, or Furcalor."

74   C reads, "30", but adds the footnote "Three is given instead of 30 in several Codices; but 30 is probably the more correct."

75   W: "Vepar, alias Separ"; C: "Vepar, or Vephar."

76   C reads, "... laden with Arms, Armour, and Ammunition, etc., thereon" and adds the footnote "In several Codices this passage reads: 'His Office is to Guide the Waters and Ships laden with Armour thereon.'"

77   S1: "'Sabnack', in another copy 'Sabnock'"; S2, H: "SABNOCK"; C: "Sabnock, or Savnok"; W: "Sabnac, alias Salmac"; in Scot: "Sabnacke, alias Salmac."

pale couloured horse, his office is to build high Towers, Casteles and Citties, and to furnish them wth armour, & to afflict men severall dayes wth wounds & rotten sores full of wormes; he giveth good familiars at y^e command of y^e Exorcist he commandeth 50 Legions of spirits, his seal is Thus to be made, and worne as a Lamin &c.

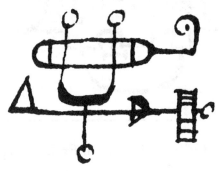

The 44th spirit in order is named **Shax,**[78] he is a great Marquize & appeareth in y^e forme of a stock dove,[79] speaking wth a hoarse & subtill voyce. his office is to take away y^e sight, hearing & understanding of any man or woman at ye command of ye Exorcist, & to steal money out of kings houses & carry it againe in 1200 yeares, if commanded, he w^ill fetch horses or any Thing at ye Request of ye Exorcist, but he must be commanded into a Δ Triangle first or else he will deceive him, & tell you many lyes, he can discover all Things that are hidden & not kept by wicked spirits, he giveth good familiars sometimes, he governeth 30 Legions of spirits his seal is thus to be made, and worne as a Lamin &c.

The 45 spirit is called **Vine,**[80] he is a great king & an Earle, & appeareth in y^e forme of a Lyon[81] ridding on a Black horse wth a viper in his hand his office is to discover Things hidden, witches, and Things present past & to

[107r]

---

78   W: "Chax, alias Scox." In Scot's translation, "Shax, alias Scox."

79   W: "storke."

80   C: "Viné, or Vinea."

81   C (footnote): "Or, 'with the Head of a Lion,' or 'having a Lion's Head,' in some Codices."

come. he, at y^e command of y^e Exorcist, w^ill build Towers, Throw down great stone walls, make waters rough wth stormes &c, he governeth 35^82 Legions of spirits, his seal is this, wch make and wear as a Lamin &c.

The 46th spirit is called **Bifrons**,[83] he is an Earle and appeareth in y^e forme of a Monster at first but after a while at y^e command of y^e Exorcist he putteth on y^e shape of a man, his office is to make one knowing in Astrology & geomitry & other arts & siences, & Teacheth ye vertues of all hearbs, precious stones & woodes, he changeth y^e dead Bodyes & putteth Them into one another [anothers'] places, & lighteth candeles seemingly upon y^e graves of y^e dead he hath under his command 6^84 Legions of spirits, his seal is this, wch he w^ill owne and submit unto &c.

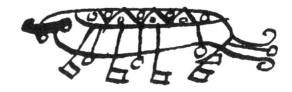

The 47th spirit is called **Vual** [Vuall^85]. he is a great & mighty strong duke, he appeareth in y^e forme of a mighty dromedary at first, but after a while he putteth on humane shape, and speaketh in y^e Egyptian Tongue, but not perfectly;[86] his office is to procure ye love of women, and to tell

---

82   S1, C: "36."

83   S2: "BIFROVS"; S1 adds (in margin) "in another copy 'Bifrous.'"; C: "Bifrons, or Bifröus, or Bifrovs."

84   W: "six and twentie"; C (footnote): "Should probably be 60 instead of 6."

85   W: "Wal/Vuall"; S1, S2, and H all read, "Vuall"; C: "Uvall, or Vual, or Voval."

86   This again seems to be a mistranslation of Weyer's Latin *linguam sonat Ægyptiacam graviter* ("he sounds out in the Egyptian language in a deep voice", which Scot translates "he soundeth out in a base voice the *Ægyptian* toong.") Crowley adds the footnote, "He can nowadays converse in sound though colloquial Coptic. -Ed."

Things past, present and to come, and also to procure friendship betweene friends & foes, he was of the order of Potentates [potestates]; he governeth 37 Legions of spirits; his seal is Thus to be made and worne as a Lamin before you &c.[87]

The 48th spirit is called **Haagenti**, he is a great president appearing in the forme of a mighty Bull wth griffins wings at first, But afterwardes at ye command of the Exorcist, he putteth on humane shape &c his office is to make men wise and to Instruct them in divers Things & to Transmute all mettales into gold, & change wine into water, & water into wine; he commandeth 33 Legions of spirits; his seal is Thus made, & to be worne as a Lamin &c.

[107v]

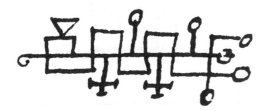

The 49th spirit is named **Procel** [Crocell[88]], he appeareth in ye forme of an angel, he is a great & strong duke, speaking somthing mystically of hidden Things; he Teacheth ye art of geometry & ye Liberall siences, he at ye command of ye Exorcist, will make great Noises, like ye running of great waters, allthough there be none he warmeth waters and distempereth [discovereth] Bathes &c he was of ye order of potestates [potentates][89] (as he declared to Salomon) before his fall, he governeth 48 Legions of spirits, his Character or Marke is Thus to be made, & worne as a Lamin before you.

---

87   H adds, "Note that a Legion is 6666. Read Cardanus & Jamblicus."

88   W: "Procell"; S2, H: "CROCELL"; S1: "'Procel', in another copy 'Crocell.'" C: "Crocell, or Crokel."

89   C: "Potestates, or Powers."

The 50th spirit in order is called **Furcas**, he is a knight & appeareth in ye forme and similitude of a cruel old man wth a long Beard and a hairy head, sitting on a pale colloured horse, wth a sharpe weapon in his hand; his office is to teach ye art of Phylosophy, astronomy [astrology90], Rhetorick, logick, Chyromancy & Pyromancy in all their partes perfectly, he hath under his power 20 Legions of spirits, his seal or Mark is this wch make & weare as a Lamin.

The 51 spirit in order is **Balam**,91 he is a Terrable, great & powerfull king, appearing wth 3 heads, The first is like a Bulls, The second like a Mans, & ye Third like a Rams head he hath a serpents Taile, & Eyes flaming; riding upon a furious Beare, carrying a goshawke on his fist, he speaketh wth a hoarse voyce, giving True answares of Things past present & to come, he maketh men to goe invisible & witty he governeth 40 Legions of spirits his seal is Thus [to be] Made, & to be worne as a Lamin &c.

---

90   S2, H, C.
91   C: "Balam, or Balaam."

The 52d spirit [in order] is called **Alloces**[92] — he is a great & mighty strong duke, appearing in yͤ forme of a souldier[93] ridding on a great horse; his face is like a Lyons, very redd, having Eyes flaming, his speech is hoarse & verry Bigg; his office is to teach yͤ art of Astronomy, & all yͤ Liberall siences, he Bringeth good familiars & ruleth 36[94] Legions of spirits, his seal is Thus made, & [is] to be worne, &c.

The 53d spirit is called **Caim** [Camio[95]], he is a great president & appeareth in yͤ forme of a Bird called a Thrush at first, but after a while he putteth on yͤ shape of a man carring in his hand a sharp sword; he seemeth to answare in Burning ashes, he is a good disputer, his office is to give men yͤ understanding of all Birds, loweing of Bullocks, Barking of doggs & other Creatures, and also yͤ Noise of waters, and [he] giveth very true answares of Things to come; he was of yͤ order of angels, & now Ruleth 30 Legions of Infernall spirits; his seal is This, wͨͪ wear as a Lamin.

The 54th spirit in order is called **Murmur** [Murmus[96]], he is a great duke & an Earle, & appeareth In yͤ forme of a souldier ridding on a griffin with a dukes Crown on his head, there goeth before him two of his Ministers, wͭͪ great Trumpets sounding, his office is to teach Phylosophy perfectly, &

---

92 W: "Alocer/Allocer"; C: "Alloces, or Alocas."

93 C (footnote): "Or Warrior."

94 H: "30."

95 W: "Caym." S3 and W/Scot: "Caim"; S2 and H: "Camio"; S1: "'Caim', in another copy 'Camio.'"; C: "Camio, or Caïm."

96 S3 and W: "Murmur"; S2 and H: "Murmus"; S1: "'Murmur', in another copy 'Murmus.'"; C: "Murmur, or Murmus, or Murmux."

to constraine soules discesed [deceased] to come before yᵉ Exorcist to answare those things yᵗ he shall aske them, if he desireth, he was partly of yᵉ order of Thrones & partly [of the order] of angels, & [he] Ruleth now 30 Legions of spirits, his seal is this, wᶜʰ is to be worne as a Lamin &c.

The 55ᵗʰ spirit is called **Orobas**, he is a mighty great prince, appearing at first like a horse, But afterwards at yᵉ command of yᵉ Exorcist he putteth on yᵉ Image of a man,[97] his office is to discover, all Things past, present & to come and to give dignities & places & yᵉ favour of friends & foes, he giveth true answares of divinity & of yᵉ Creation of yᵉ world, he is faithfull to yᵉ Exorcist & wⁱˡˡ not suffer him to be Tempted by any spirit he governeth 20 Legions of spirits,[98] his seal is this, wᶜʰ must be made & worne as a Lamin &c.

[108v]

The 56 spirit is called **Gemory**,[99] he is a strong and powerfull duke appearing in The forme of a Beautifull woman, wᵗʰ a Dutches [Duchess] Crownett Tyed about her middle,† ridding on a great Camell, his office is to tell of all Things past present & to come, and of Treasure hidden and wᵗ it layeth in, & procureth yᵉ love of women, both young & old, he governeth 26 Legions of spirits, his seal is Thus made, & worne as a Lamin before yᵉ Exorcist in [the] Time of working.

97 W: "a mans idol."

98 H: "26."

99 S2: "GREMORY"; S1: "Gemory," in another copy "Gremory"; C: "Gremory, or Gamori"; W: "Gomory."

†   W reads, "*ducali cingitur corona*," literally, "a duchess' crown (or coronet) encircling" (the head or body).

The 57 spirit is called Ose,[100] he is a great president & appeareth like a Leopard at first, But after a little Time he putteth on yᵉ shape of a man, his office is to make one cunning in yᵉ Leberall [liberal] siences & to give True answares of devine & secreet Things, and to change a man in [to] any shape that yᵉ Exorcist desireth so that he that is so changed will not thinck any other Thing but that he is that Creature or Thing, he is Changed into, he governeth 3 Legions of spirits,[101] his seal is This, wᶜʰ wear as a Lamin.

The 58ᵗʰ spirit is called [named] Amy,[102] he is a great president, & appeareth at first in yᵉ forme of a flaming fire, But after a while he putteth on yᵉ shape of a man, &c: his office is to make one wounderous [wonderfully] knowing in Astrology & all yᵉ Leberall [liberal] siences; he giveth good familiars & can bewary [divulge] Treasures, wᶜʰ are kept by spirits; he governeth 36 Legions of spirits, [&] his seal is This, wᶜʰ wear as a Lamin &c.

[To make sense of the attempted corrections, compare with the version given in Sloane 2731:]

---

100 H: "Oso"; C: "Oso, Osé, or Voso."

101 W does not give the number of legions. C (footnote): "Should probably be 30. For these 72 Great Spirits of the Book Goetia are all Princes and Leaders of numbers."

102 H: "Auns"; C: "Amy, or Avnas."

The 59 spirit is named **Orias**,[103] he is a great Marquiz and appeareth in yᵉ forme of a Lyon,[104] riding on a mighty horse, wᵗʰ a serpents Taile, holding in his right hand 2 great serpents hissing, his office is to Teach yᵉ vertues of yᵉ starres and to know yᵉ Mansions of yᵉ planets, and how to understand their vertues, also he Transformeth men & giveth dignities and places [prelacies], and confirmations, & yᵉ favour of friends & foes, he governeth 30 Legions of spirits, his seal is This, to be made & worne &c.

[109r]

The 60ᵗʰ spirit is called **Vapula**,[105] he is a great mighty & strong duke, appearing in yᵉ forme of a Lyon, wᵗʰ griffins wings; his office is to make men knowing in all handicraft proffecsions [professions] also in Phylosophy & other siences &c he governeth 36 Legions of spirits, his seal or Character is Thus made, and is to be worne as a Lamin &c.

The 61 spirit is called **Zagan**,[106] he is a great king & president, and appeareth at first in yᵉ forme of a Bull wᵗʰ griffins wings, But afterwardss he putteth on humane shape, he maketh men witty, and can turne wine into water & Blood into wine,[107] and also water into wine he can turne all mettals into Corne [coin] of that dominion yᵉ mettles are of & can make foolls wise he governeth 33 Legions of spirits; his seal is Thus made & wᵒʳⁿᵉ as a Lamin.

---

103 C: "Oriax, or Orias."

104 C (footnote): "Or, 'with the Face of a Lion.'"

105 H: "Nappula"; C: "Vapula, or Naphula."

106 W: "Zagam"; Scot: "Zagan."

107 W: "oil"; Scot mistakenly reads "wine."

The 62d spirit is called **Valac**,[108] he is a mighty great president & appeareth like a Boy[109] wth angels wings, ridding on a 2 headed Dragon; his office is to give True answares of hidden Treasures, and to tell where serpents may be seene, wch he will bring & dilever [deliver, discover] to ye Exorcist without any force or strengeth, he governeth 30 Legions of spirits,[110] his seal is This wch must be made & worne as a Lamin &c.

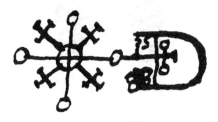

The 63 spirit is called **Andras**, he is a great Marquiz appearing in ye forme of an angell wth a head like a Black night Raven, ridding upon a strong black woolf, wth a sharpe bright sword flourishing in his hand, his office is to sow discords, if ye Exorcist hath not care he will kill him and his fellows, he governeth 30 Legions of spirits his seal is Thus to be [made, and] worne as a Lamin before [thee] on your Breast.

[109v]

The 64th spirit is named **Flauros** [Haures[111]], he is a great duke, and appeareth at first like a mighty Terrable and strong Leopard but afterwards at ye command of ye Exorcist he putteth on ye shape of a man wth fiery Eyes and a Terrable Countenance; he giveth True answares of all Things past present & to come, but unless he be commanded into a [the] Triangle, he will Lye in all those things and deceive or beguile ye Exorcist in other Things or Buisness [sic], he will gladly talke of divinity, and of ye Creation

108 W: "Volac"; Scot: "Valac"; H: "Valu"; C: "Volac, Valak, or Valu, or Ualac."

109 C: "child."

110 So S3, W, S1, S2, and C all read, "38."

111 S2, H: "Haures"; S1: "'Flauros', in another copy 'Hauros.'"; C: "Haures, or Hauras, or Havres, or Flauros."

of ye world, and of his and all other spirits fall [falls], he destroyeth and burneth those That are ye Exorcist [Exorcist's] enimies if he Requesteth it, and will not suffer him to be Tempted by any spirit or otherwise; he governeth 36 Legions of spirits,[112] his seal is Thus to be made, & w^orne as a Lamin &c.

The 65 spirit is called **Andrealphus**,[113] he is a Mighty great Marquiz appearing at first in ye forme of [a] Peacock, w^ith great Noises but afterwards he putteth on humane shape, he can teach perfectly geomitry, & all Things belonging to measuring, [&] also Astronomy, he maketh men very subtile and cunning therin, he can Transforme a Man into ye likness of a Bird & he governeth 30 Legions of spirits his seal is This, wch is to be worne as a Lamin &c.

The 66th spirit is called **Cimeies**[114] he is a mighty great Marquiz strong & powerfull appearing like a valiant souldier, riding on a goodly Black horse; he ruleth over all spirits in ye part of Africa, his office is to Teach perfectly grammar Rhetoric [&] logick and to discover Treasures & Things lost or hidden, he can make a man seeme like a souldier of his own likeness, he governeth 20 Legions of cheefe [chief] spirits, but more Inferior [than] himself his seal is Thus made, & worne as a Lamin &c.

---

112 H: "three."

113 W: "Androalphus"; Scot: "Andrealphus."

114 W, H: "Cimeries"; C: "Cimejes, or Cimeies, or Kimaris."

The 67th spirit in order is called **Amduscias**,[115] he is a strong & great duke appearing at first like an Unicorne, But afterwards at ye Request of ye Exorcist he standeth before him in humane shape causing Trumpets and all manner of Musicall Instrument to be heard But not seene also [causing] Trees to bend and Incline according to ye Exorcist [Exorcist's] will; he giveth Excellent familiars & ruleth 29 Legions of spirits his seal is Thus formed and is to be worne as a Lamin &c.

[110r]

The 68th spirit is called **Belial**, he is a mighty king and powerfull; he was Created next after Lucifer, & is of his order; he appeareth in ye forme of a Beautiful angel[116] sitting in a Charriot of fire, speaking wth a comly voice, declaring that he fell first & amongst ye worthier & wiser sort wch went before Michael & other heavenly angels; his office is to distribute preferments of senatorships, and to cause favour of friends & foes, he giveth Excellent familiars & governeth 80 Legions of spirits.[117] Note this kink [king] Belial must have offerings sacrafices & gifts presented to him, by ye Exorcist or else he will not give True answares to his demands; But then he Tarryeth [will tarry] not one hour in ye truth except [unless] he be constrained by devine power & his seal is Thus wch is to be worne as a Lamin, before ye Exorcist &c.

115 S2: "AMDVSIAS"; S1: "'Amduscias,' in another copy 'Andusias,'" but the sigil is labelled "Anduscias"; C: "Amdusias, or Amdukias."

116 S1 adds (in margin): "another copy 'he appeareth in the form of 2 beautifull Angels.'" C also reads "Two Beautiful Angels."

117 C (footnote): "Perhaps an error for 30. -Trans. The actual number is 50; at least it was in 1898. -Ed." H adds (intra linea): "partly of the order of vertues partly of Angels."

The 69 spirit is called **Decarabia**,[118] he appeareth in yᵉ forme of a starre in yᵉ Pentacle ✦ at first, but afterwards at yᵉ command of yᵉ Exorcist, he putteth on yᵉ Image of a man, his office is to discover yᵉ vertues of hearbs[119] and precious stones; and to make yᵉ similitude of all Birds to fly before yᵉ Exorcist, & to Tarry wᵗʰ him, singing and Drinking as Naturall Birds doe, he governeth 30 Legions of spirits, being himselfe a great Marquiz, his seal is Thus to be made, and worne as a Lamin before yᵉ Exorcist &c.

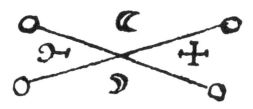

[110v]

The 70ᵗʰ spirit in order is called **Seere** [Seer[120]], he is a Mighty Prince and powerfull under Amaymon, king of yᵉ East he appeareth in yᵉ forme of a Beautifull Man, riding on a strong horse wᵗʰ wings: his office is to goe & come, and to bring all Things to pass on a sudden & to carry & recarry any Thing where Thou wilt have it, or have it from for he can pass over yᵉ whole world in yᵉ Twinckling of an Eye, he maketh a True relation of all sorts of Theft and of Treasures hidd, and of all other things, he is Indifferent good Natured, willing to do any thing yᵉ Exorcist desireth; he governeth 26 Legions of spirits, his Mark or seal is Thus made, and is to be worne as a Lamin &c.

The 71 spirit is called **Dantalion**,[121] he is a great & Mighty duke appearing in yᵉ forme of a Man wᵗʰ many faces, all like men & women, & a

---

118   W: "Decarabia or Carabia."

119   S1: "birds."

120   This spirit is not found in W, nor are Dantalion or Andromalius. S2, H, S1: "'Seere', another copy 'Seer'"; C: "Seere, Sear, or Seir."

121   H: "Dantaylion."

Booke in his right hand; his office is to Teach all arts and siences to any-one, and to declare ye secreet Councelles of anyone, for he knoweth ye Thoughts of all men and women, and can change them at his will, he can cause love and shew (by vision) y^e true similitude of anyone lett them be in w^t place or part of y^e world they will, he governeth 36 Legions of spirits his seal is This, wch is to be worne as a Lamin.

The 72^d spirit in order is called **Andromalius** he is a great and Mighty Earle appearing in y^e form of a Man, holding a serpent in his hand, his office is to bring a theefe & goods y^t are stolen, Back; and to discover all wickedness, and understand dealings, & to punish Theives [thieves] & other wicked people, & to discover Treasure that is hidd, &c, he ruleth 36 Legions of spirits his seal is This, wch make & wear as a Lamin in time of acction &c.

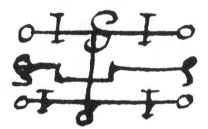

These be the seaventy two Mighty kings or Princes wch King Salomon commanded into a vesall [vessel] of Brasse wth their Legions, of whome **Belial Bileth**[122] **Asmoday & Gaap** wear the Cheefest, & it is supposed it was for their pride, for Salomon never declared why he thus bound them; & when he hadd bound them up & sealed ye vesel, he by ye devine power cast Them all into a deep lake or hole in Babilon [Babylon], & the

---

122 S2: "baleth."

[111r] Babilononians [Babylonians] woundering to see such a thing there, they went wholy into ye lake to brake [break] ye vesel open, suspecting to find a great Treasure; but when they hadd broken it open out flew all ye cheefe spirits Immediately, and their Legions followed them, and they were restored againe to their former places; But only Belial who entered Into a certaine Image, and there gave answares to those whome [who] did offer sacrifice unto him as ye Babilonians did; for they offered sacrafices, & worshiped that Image as a God &c.

Observations[123]

[First] Thou art to observe first ye Moones age for y^r working. The best dayes are when y^e ☽ is 2, 4, 6, 8,[124] 10, 12 or 14 dayes old, as Salomon sayeth, and no other dayes are profitable &c.

The seals of those 72 kings are to be made in Mettalls, The cheefest King in ☉, Marquisses in ☽, Dukes in ♀. Prelates in ♃, knights in ♄, & Presidents in ☿, & Earles in ♀ & ☽ equally alike &.[125]

These 72 kings are under the power of **Amaymon, Corson,**[126] **Ziminiar,**[127] **& Goap** [Gaap] wch are kings ruling in ye 4 quarters[128] East, West, North, & south, and are not to be called forth except it be upon great occasions But Invoked & commanded to send such & such spirit as are [is] under their rule and power, as is shewed in ye following Invocations, or [rather] conjurations &c.

---

123 At this point, H inserts the characters of the angels of the 7 days from de Abano's *Heptameron*. He then jumps to the section titled, "The Conjuration for to call forth any of the forsaid spirits."

124 S1: "'9', other copy instead as '9' is '8.'"

125 Gold, silver, copper, tin, lead, mercury, copper + silver respectively. Noticeably absent is Mars (=iron).

126 W: "Gorson."

127 W, S2: "Zimimar"; S1: "Ziminar"; C: "Zimimay or Ziminiar."

128 C adds, "or Cardinal Points" and adds the footnote: "These four Great Kings are usually called Oriens, or Uriens, Paymon or Paymonia, Ariton or Egyn, and Amaymon or Amaimon. By the Rabbins they are frequently entitled: Samael, Azazel, Azäel, and Mahazael."

The chife [chief] kings may be bound from 9 to 12 of yᵉ Clock at noone & from 3 till sunset.129 Marquizes may be bound from 3 of yᵉ Clock in yᵉ after Noon till nine at night and from 9 at nᵗ [night] till sunrising.

Dukes may be bound from sunrising till Noonday in clear weather.

Prelates may be bound in any hour of the day.

Knights may be bound from yᵉ dawning of yᵉ day till sunrising or from four of yᵉ Clock till sunset.

Presidents may be bound in any hour of yᵉ day, Except Twilight, at Night, or [if] the king whome he is under, be also Invocated &c.

Counts or Earles may be bound in any hour of the day so [if] it be in woods or any other place where Men resort Not, or where No Noise is &c.

[111v]
[112r]

[The Magical Circle]

[The circle of Salomon is to be made nine feet across, & the divine names are to be written around it, from **Eheye** to **Levanah**.130]

---

129 H: "5."

130 S2: "This Cirkel is to be made 9 foot ouer & thes names Round in it in one line begining at Eheie & so goe on tel you come Round to [Jehouah] Levanah S ☽" In the Mathers/Crowley edition, the letters around the perimeter of the circle are transcribed into Hebrew letters within a coiled serpent (in accordance with "one private codex"). In a footnote, he adds, "In English letters they run thus, ... + Ehyeh Kether Metatron Chaioth Ha-Qadesh Rashith Ha-Galgalim S.P.M (for 'Sphere of the Primum Mobile') + Iah Chokmah Ratziel Auphanim Masloth S.S.F. (for 'Sphere of the Fixed Stars,' or S.Z. for 'Sphere of the Zodiac') + Iehovah Elohim Binah Tzaphquiel Aralim Shabbathai S. (for 'Sphere') of Saturn + El Chesed Tzadquiel Chaschmalim Tzedeq S. Jupiter + Elohim Gibor Geburah Kamael Seraphim Madim S. of Mars + Iehovah Eloah Va-Daäth Tiphereth Raphaël Malakim Shemesh S. of the Sun + Iehovah Tzabaoth Netzach Haniel Elohim Nogah S. of Venus. + Elohim Tzabaoth Hod Michaël Beni Elohim Kokav S. of Mercury + Shaddaï El Chai Iesod Gabriel Cherubim Levanah S. of the Moon +." S1 (outer ring) reads "+ Jehovah Elohim Binah Aralim Zabbathi. S. ♄. El hesed Hasmalim Zedeck, ♃, Elohim Giber Geburah Seraphim Camael Madim, ♂. Eloha Tiplareth, Malachim, Raphl Shemes, ☉. Jehovah Sabaoth Nezah Elohim haniel nosa ♀." S1 (inner ring) reads "+ Benelohim, Mikel Cockab ☿, Sadai Jesod, Cherubin, Gabrill Levanh ☽, Eheie. Kether, Haioth Hakados, Metattron, Restchith, Hagallatin P.M. Jod Jehovah Hochmah, Ophanim, Jophiel, Masloth, S. Z." and in margin, "in another copy was writ Round beginning thus: Jehovah Elohim Binah Aralim Sabbathi. S. ♄. El Hesel Hasmalim Zeleck S. ♃ + Eheie Kether Haioth Hakados Methraton Reschith Hagallatin P.M. Jod Jehovah hochmat ophanim S. Z. here end the first Round. Elohim Giber Seraphim Camael Madim S. ♂. Eloha Tetragrammaton Raphiel Schemes S. ☉. Jehovah Sabaoth neza (?) elohim haniel Noza S. ♀. Elohim Sabaoth hod Ben Elohim Michael Cochab S. ☿. Sadai Jesol Cherubin Gabril Zeranah S. ☽."

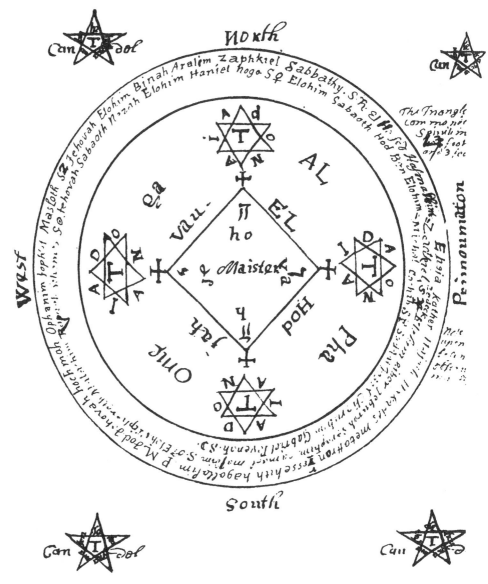

Figure 1. The Circle of Salomon.

A figure of the Circlel [Circle] of Solomon [Salomon], that he made for to preserve himselfe from The malice of those evill Spirits &c.

[The Triangle]

[This is the forme of] The Triangle that Salomon commanded the disobedient spirits into; it is to be made two foot [feet] of [out] from the Circle and 3 foot [feet] over [across].

Note this △ is to be placed upon [towards] that Coast [quarter] [that] the spirit belongeth [to] &c. Observe the moon in working, &c.

Figure 2. The Triangle of Salomon.

Solomons sexangled [hexagonal] ffigure

This figure is to be made on parchment made of a calfes Skin and worne at the Skirtt of yᵉ white vestment, and covered wᵗʰ a lennen [linen] cloath to [sic] yᵉ which is to be shewed to the spirits when they are appeared that they may be compelled to be obedient and take a humane shape &c.

[112v]

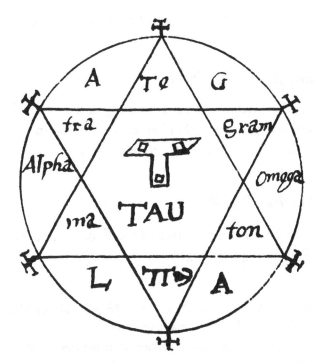

Figure 3. The sexangled [hexagonal] figure of Salomon.

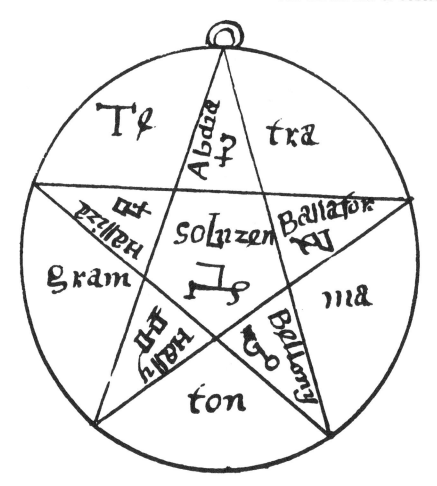

Figure 4. The pentagonal figure of Salomon.

The Pentagonall ffigure of Solomon

This figure is to be made in ☉ or ☽ and worne upon the brest with the seal of the spirit on one [the other] side of itt. it is for to preserve [the Exorcist] from danger, and allso to command by &c.

[113r]   ### *[Solomon's Magical Ring131]*

This Ring is to be held before the face of the Exorcist to preserve him from The stinking fumes of spirits &c.132

---

131 S1, S2. "Solomons Magicall Ring"; C: "The Magic Ring or Disc of Solomon." According to Weyer, it should be made of silver.

132 Note that the requisite hazel stick, mentioned in the description of Bileth, is not mentioned here.

Figure 5. The Ring of Salomon.

The Secret Seal of Salomon.

by which he bound and sealed up the aforsaid spirits with their legions in [into] a Brazen Vesel &c.

Figure 6. The secret seal of Salomon.

This secreet seal is to be made by one that is cleane both Inward and outward, and hath not defiled himself by any woman in the space of a Month; but hath with fasting and prayers to God desired pardon of all his sins, &c: Itt is to be made on a Tuesday or Saturday night at 12 of the Clock, written with the Blood of a Black Cock which never trode hen, on virgins parchment, Note, on those nights the ☽ must be encreasing in ♍, when it [is] so made, fume it with Allum, Raisins of the Sun, dates, Cedar & lignum Aloes, by this seal Salomon compelled the aforesaide spirits into a Brass vessel, and sealed it up with the same, he by it gained the love of all Manner of persons, and overcame in Battle, for neither weapon fire nor water could hurt him.

[113v]

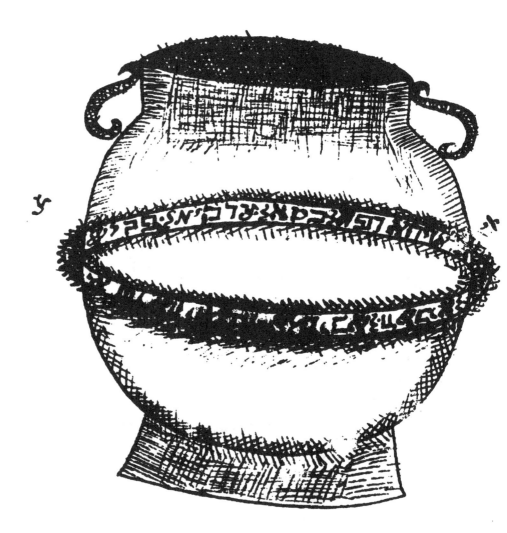

Figure 7. The brass vessel for containing spirits.

The fforme of the brasse vessel that Salomon shut Those spirits In.

The priuie [secret] seal aforesaid was made in Brasse,[133] to cover This vessel with at ye Top &c.

The other materialls is [are] a sceptre or sword; a miter or cap, a long white Robe of Linnen, with shoes and [the] other Clothes for ye purpose[134] also a girdle of Lyons skin 3 Inches broad, with all the names about it as is about the uttermost round [part of the] Circle, & also perfumes and a chafin [chafing] dish of Charcoles kindled to put the fumes into; to smoke or perfume ye place appointed for action. also annoynting oyles to anoynt yr Temples & Eyes wth; & fair water to wash yrselves in. & in so doeing yu are to say as david said (viz)

> Thou shalt purge me wth Hysop o Lord, & I shall be cleane; Thou shalt wash me & I shall be whiter than snow &c.

& at ye Garments putting on, you must say:

[Oration]

> by ye figurative Mystery of these holy vestures or vestments, I will cloath me with ye armour of Salvation in ye strength of ye highest, **Ancor Amacor Amides Theodonias**[135] **Anitor**, That my desired End may be Efected Through ye strength [of] **Adonay** To whome ye praise and glory will forever & ever belong. Amen.

[114r]

After yu have so done, make prayers to God according to your worke, as Salomon hath commanded. The formes that Salomon used for any perticular art is shewed in ye 5th part of this Book wch is called *Artem Novam* [*Ars Nova*] &c.

---

133 S2 omits, "in Brasse." The Hebrew letters as given in the Mathers / Crowley edition read (lower arc, read right to left): "AShR AHIH: GBRIAL: MIKAL: HANIAL" and in upper arc read left to right with letters reversed: "ARARIThA: ChShMLIM: AL: TzDQIAL." The editor adds: "or in some Codices: ARARIThA: RFAL: KMAL: TzDQIAL: and TzFQIAL." S1 reads (in Hebrew letters, lower arc, read right to left: "AShAHIH. GBRIAL. MIKAL. HANIAL," and upper arc, also read right to left: "ARARIThA. RFAL. KMAL. TzRQIAL [sic] TzFQIAL."

134 C (footnote): "In many codices it is written 'a sceptre or sword, a mitre or cap.' By the 'other garments' would be meant not only under-garments, but also mantles of different colours."

135 S2: "Theodonas."

The Conjuration for to call forth any of the forsaid spirits

I Invocate and conjure you spirit N. & being wth power armed from ye supreame Majesty, I throughly [thoroughly] command you by Be^ralanensis [Beralanensis], **Baldachiensis, Paumachiæ & Apologiæ-Sedes**136 and ye most powerfull princes **Genio Liachidi**137 ministers of ye Tartarean seat, Cheefe princes of of [sic] ye seat of **Apologia**, in ye Ninth Region; I exorcise & powerfully command you spirit N, in and by him that said ye word, & it was done, and by all ye holy and most glorious Names of ye most holy and true God, and by these his most holy Names **Adonai** [Adonay], **El, Elohim, Elohe, Zebeoth** [Zebaoth138], **Elion** [Elyon], **Escerchie,**139 **Jah, Tetragrammaton Saday** That you forthw^th appear and shew y^rselves here unto me before this Circle, in a fair and humane shape, without any deformity or ugly shew and without delay, doe ye come, from all parts of ye world to make & make [sic] rationall answares unto all Things wch I shall ask of you; and come yee peacebly, visibly and afably without delay, manifesting w^t I desire, being conjured by ye Name [Names] of ye Eternall liveing and true God **Helioren** I conjure you by ye especiall and true Name of your God that ye owe obediance unto and by ye Name of y^r king, wch beareth rule over you, That forthwith you come without Tarring [tarrying], and fullfill my desires, and command, and persist unto ye End, & according to my Intentions and I conjure y^u by him ^by whome all Creatures are obediant [unto] and by this ineffeble name **Tetragrammaton Jehovah** [Jehova], wch being heard, ye Elements are overthrown; The aire is shaken, The sea runneth back, The fire is quenched, The Earth Trembleth and all ye hosts of Celestialls, Terrestialls [terrestrials] & Infernalls doe Tremble, and are troubled and confounded togather. that [come] you visibly and affebly, speak unto me with a Clear voice Intelligible, and without any ambiguity, Therefore come ye in the Name **Adonay Zebeoth** [Zebaoth140]; **Adonai** [Adonay], **Amiorem**, com com141 why stay [tarryieth] you? hasten: **Adonay Saday**, the Kinge of kings commandeth you:

Say this as often as you please. And if they com not then say as ffolloweth

---

136 S2, H: "Paumachie & apologiæ."

137 S2: "Liachida"; H: "Liachiæ"; S1: "Liachidæ."

138 H, S1. S2: "Zabaoth."

139 In marg: "Eskerie."

140 H, S1. S2: "Zabaoth."

141 S2: "com ye com ye."

[The Second Conjuration]

[114v]

I Invocate, conjure and command you spirit N, to appear and shew y^rselfe visibly to me, before this Circle, in fair and comly shape, without any deformity or Tortuosity, by ye Name & in ye name Y & U wch Adam heard & spoake, & by the name **Joth** wch Jacob heard from ye angel wrestling with him, and was delivered from ye hands of Esau his Brother; and by ye name of God **Agla**, wch Lot heard and was saved with his family; and by ye name **Anaphexaton** [Anepheneton[142]] wch Aron [Aaron] heard and speak [spake] and became wise, & by the names **Schemes-Amathia**[143] which Joshua called upon and ye sun stood still, and by ye name **Emanuel** wch ye 3 Children Sedrach [Shadrach] Mesach [Masach] and Abednego, sung in ye midst of ye fiery furnace, and were delivered; and by the name **Alpha & Omega** which Daniel named & Destroyed the Bell [Bel] & ye Dragon; & by the name **Zebaoth**[144] which Moses named & all the Rivers & waters in the land of Ægypt ware turnd into blood & by the name **Escerchie Oriston**, wch Moses named & all the Rivers Brought forth froggs, & they went into ye houses of ye Egyptians, Distroying all things; & by the name **Elion** wch Moses called upon & there was great haile, such as never was [seen] sence the Creation of the world to that Day; & by the name **Adonay** wch Moses named And there came up Locust Thrueout all the land of Egypt and devoured all that the Haill at [had] left; and by the name **Hagios**, and by the seal[145] of **Adonay** and by **Otheos, Iscyros, Athenatos, Paracletus**[146] and by these [3] holly and sacred names **Agla, On, Tetragrammaton** and by the dreadfull Judgement of god; and by the uncertaine sea of glass: which is before the face of the divine Majesty, who is mighty and most powerful. And by the four beasts before the throne, haveing Eyes before and behind, and by the ffire round about the throwne, and by the holly angells of heaven; and by the Mighty Wisdom of god, & by the seal of **Baldachia** [Basdathea[147]], and by this name

---

142 S1, S2, H. C: "Anaphaxeton," and adds the footnote, "Or, Anapezeton."

143 S2: "Schemes Amatia"; H: "Scemes Amathia"; S1: "Schems Amathia"; C: "Schema Amathia."

144 C: "Zabaoth," and adds the footnote "Or, Tzabaoth."

145 C (footnote): "In some 'By the Seat of Adonai' or 'By the Throne of Adonai.' In these conjurations and elsewhere in the body of the text I have given the divine names as correctly as possible."

146 S2: "Otheos: Icyros: Athenaros: peracletos"; H: "O Theos Iscyroa Athanatos Paracletos"; S1: "Otheos: Ictros: Athenaros: peracletos."

147 S1, S2, H. Note the *Clavicle* and *Heptameron* give "Baldachia"; C: "Basdathea Baldachia."

Primeumaton[148] which Moses named and the Earth opened and swallowed up Chora, Dathan & Abiram, [I command] That you make true and faithfull answers, to all my demands, and to performe all my desiers, so farr as in office you are capaple [capable] to performe therefore come ye paecable [peaceably], vissible and affable now without delay, to manifest what I desire speaking with a perfect and clear voyce, Intelligible unto my understanding &c.

if [somehow] they do not come at the rehearsing of these 2 fforegoeing Conjurations (but without doubt they [normally] will) say one [on] as ffolloweth, it being a constraint.

[The Constraint]

I conjure the [thee] spirit N. by all the most glorious and Effacius [efficacious] names of the most great and Incomprehensible Lord god of Host [Hosts], that you comest quickly without delay ffrom all parts and places of the world: [wherever thou mayest be,] to make rationell answers to my demands and that visible and affably speakeing with a voice Intellegible to my understanding as aforesaid, I conjure and constrain you spirit N., by all aforesaid and by these seven names by wch wise Salomon bound thee and thy fellows in a vessel of Brass. **Adonay, Prerai Tetragrammaton; Anephexeton [Anaphexeton[149]], Inessenfatall, Pathatumon, & Itemon.**[150] That you appeare hear before this Circle, to fullfill my will in all things, that shall seeme good unto me and if you be disobedient and refuse to come I will in the power and by the power of the name of ye supream and Everliving god, Who created both you and me and all the whole world in six days and what is contained in it **Eye-Saray,**[151] and by the power of his name **Primeumaton;** which commandeth the whole hoste of heaven, curse you and deprive you, from all your office, Joy & place, and binde you in the debth [depth] of ye Bottomless pit There to remaine unto the day of the last Judgement, and I will bind you into Eternall fire & into the lake of fire and Brimstone, unless you come forthwith and appeare heere before this Circle to doe my will in all things. Therefore com [thou!] in and

[115r]

---

148 S2: "primumaton."

149 H: "Anepheneton." *Liber Juratus* also reads "Anepheneton."

150 S2: "Adnaij: preyai: Tetragram^maton: Anepheneton: Inessenfatoal: Pathatumon: & Itemon"; S1: "Adonaÿ Preyai Tetragrammaton Anepheneton Inessenfatoal Pathtumon & Itemon"; C: "Adonai, Preyai or Prerai, Tetragrammaton, Anaphaxeton or Anepheneton, Inessenfatoal or Inessenfatall, Pathtumon or Pathatumon, and Itemon."

151 C: "Eie, Sarayé."

by these holly names **Adonay, Zebeoth** [Zebaoth], **Adonay, Amiorem;**[152] come yee, **Adonay** commandeth you.

If you come so farr, and he yet doth not appeare you may be sure he is sent to some other place by his king, and cannot come and if it be so Invocate the king as followeth to send him, But if he doth not come still, Then you may be sure he is bound in chains in hell: and he is not in the Custody of his king: So if you have a desier to call him ffrom thence, you must rehearse the spirits Chaine &c.

For to Invocate the Kinge say as ffolloweth[153] -

O you great mighty and Powerfull kinge **Amaymon**, who beareth rule by the power of thy supreame god **El** over all spirits both superior and Inferiour of the Infernal order in the Dominion of the Earth [East], I invocate and command you by the especial and truest name of your god and by god that you worship and obey, and by the seal of ye Creation, & by the most mighty & powerfull name of god **Jehovah Tetragrammaton**, who cast you ought [out] of heaven with all other of the Infernall spirits and by all ye most powerfull and great names of god who created heaven, Earth & hell, and all things contained in them, and by their power and vertue, & by ye name **Primeumaton** who commandeth the whole host of heaven, that you cause, enforce & compell N. to come unto me hear before this Circle in a fair & comely forme, without doeing any harme to me or any other Creature, and to answere truely & faithfull to all my Requests, That I may accomplish my will and desiers, in knowing or obtaining any matter or thing wch by office you know is proper for him to performe or to accomplish, threw [through] the power of god **El** who createth and disposeth of all things both celestiall, ayerall [aerial], Terrestiall [terrestrial] and Infernall.

After you have Invocated the king in this manner twise or thrice over, then conjure ye spirit you would have calld forth by the aforsaid conjurations rehearsing them severall times together, and he will come without doubt if not at ye first or second time rehearsing. But if he doth not come, add the

---

152 C: "Adonai, Zabaoth, Adonai, Amioran."

153 C (footnote): "It will depend on the quarter to which the Spirit is attributed, which of the four chief kings is to be invoked."

spirits Chaine to the end of yᵉ afforsaid Conjuration and he will be forced
to come even if he be Bound in chains: for the chaines will break of [off]
from him and he will be at liberty &c.

[115v]   **The generall Curse, called the spirits Chaine against all spirits that Rebell.**

> O thou wicked and disobedient spirit, because thou hast rebelled and not
> obeyed nor regarded my words which I have rehearsed They being all
> most glorious and Incomprehensible names of yᵉ true god Maker and
> creator of you and me and all the world, I by the power of those names
> wᶜʰ no creature is able to resist doe curse you into the debts [depths] of yᵉ
> Bottomless Pitt, There to remaine untill yᵉ day of doom in chaines of fire
> and Brimstone unquenchable, unless you dost forthwith appear before
> this circle in This Triangle Δ To doe my will; Therefore come paceably
> [peaceably] and quietly [quickly] in & by these names — **Adonai**
> [Adonay], **Zebaoth, Adonay, Amioram;**¹⁵⁴ come come why stay you,
> **Adonay** comandeth you.

When you have read so farr and he doth not come, Then write his name
and seal in [on] virgins parch [parchment] and put it into a black Box with
Brimstone aquafateda [asafetida] and such things that have a stincking strong
smell and bind the Box round with a wire and hang it on yᵉ swords point
and hold it over the fire of Charcoles, and say to the fire first [as followeth]
(it being placed toward that quarter the spirit is to come)

[The Conjuration of the fire]

> I conjure ~~thee~~ you [O] fire by him that made thee and all other good crea-
> tures in the world that you Torment Burne and consume this spirit N. ever-
> lastingly. I condem [condemn] thee thou spirit N. into fire everlasting, be-
> cause thou art disobedient and obeyd not the command, nor kept the precepts
> of the lord thy god, neither wilt thou appeare to me nor obey me nor my
> invocations, haveing thereby called you forth, [I] who am the servant of yᵉ
> most high and Imperiall Lord, god of hosts **Jehovah,** and dignified and forti-
> fied by his Celestiall power and Permission, Neither comest thou to answer
> to these my Proposalls hear made unto you, for wᶜʰ your averseness and con-
> tempt you are gilty [guilty] of grand disobedience and Rebellion, and there-
> fore I shall excommunicate you and destroy thy name and seal wᶜʰ I have

---

154 S1, S2, and H all read, "Amiram," but *Heptameron, Theurgia Goetia,* and *Ars Paulina*
all read "Amioram."

hear enclosed in this black Box, and shall burne thee in immortall fire and bury thee in Immortall oblivion, unless thou Immediately comest & appearest visibly, affably, frendly, & curteously hear unto me before this Circle in this Triangle, in a faire and comly forme and in no wise terrible, hurtfull or frightfull to me or any other creatures whatever upon the face of the Earth and make rationel Answers to my requests and performe all my desiers in all things that I shall make unto you &c.

If he cometh not yet, say as followeth:

[The curse[155]]

Now o thou spirit N. since thou aft still pertonalius [pernicious] and disobedient and will not appear unto me to answer to such things as I shoulde have desiered of you or would have been satisfied in &c, I doe in the name and by the power and dignity of the omnipotent Immortall Lord god of host **Jehovah Tetragrammaton,** The only creator of heaven Earth and hell and all that in them is who is the marvellious disposser of all things both visible and Invisible Curse you and deprive you from all your offices Joy and place and do bind the [thee] in the debtts [depths] of yᵉ Bottomless Pitt, There to remaine untill the day of the last Judgement; I say into the lake of Fire & Brimstone which is prepared for all rebellious disobedient obstinate & pertinacious [pernicious] spirits, let all the Holy company of heaven curse thee, The ☉, ☽ and starrs, the light and all yᵉ hoste of heaven Curse thee, I curse thee into the fire unquenchable, & torments unspeakable, and as thy name and seal is contained in this box, chained and bound up and shal be choacked in sulphurous & stincking substance and burnt in this material fire, so I in the name **Jehovah,** and by the power and dignity of these three names **Tetragrammaton, Anaphexeton** [Anepheneton[156]], **& Primeumaton,**[157] cast thee, o thou disobediant spirit N. into that lake of fire which is prepared for thee damned and cursed spirits and there to remain untill the day of doome and never more to be remembered of before the face of god wᶜʰ shall come to Judge the quick and the dead and the world by fire.

[116r]

Here the Exorcist must put the box into the fire and by and by he will come. But as soone as he is come quickly quench the fire that the Box is in

---

155 C has the heading, "The Greater Curse" and adds the footnote "In some codices this is called 'the Curse' only; but in one or two the 'Spirit's Chain' is called 'the Lesser Curse,' and this the 'Greater Curse.'"

156 So read H, S1, and S2; Crowley reads, "Anaphaxeton."

157 S2: "pimumaton."

and make a sweet perfume and give him a kind entertainment shewing him the pentacle that is at yᵉ bottom of yᵉ vesture covered with linnen cloath, saying.

[The address unto the spirit upon his coming]

Behold your conclusion [confusion] if you be disobedient. Behold the Pentacle of Salomon which I have brought heare before thy presence: Behold the person of the Exorcist who is called **Octinomos**, in the midst of the Exorcism, who is armed by god & without fear, who potently invocateth you and called you to appeare, Therefore make rationall answers to my demands and be obedient to me your master in the name of yᵉ Lord **Bathat** rushing upon **Abrac Abeor** coming upon **Aberer**.[158]

Then they or he will be obedient and bid you ask what you will for they are subjected by god to fullfill your desiers and demands, and when they or he are appeared and shewed themselves humble and meek, Then you are to say [as followeth]:

[The welcome unto the spirit]

Welcom [thou] [spirit N. or] spirits or most noble king or kings I say you are welcome unto me because I called you through him who created both heaven & Earth & Hell and all that is contained therein and you have obeyed allso by the same power that I called you forth [by] I binde you that you remaine affably and vissibly hear before this circle (or before this circle in this Δ) so constant and so long as I haue ocasion for you and not to depart without my leasure[159] until you haue faithfully and truely performed my will without any fallacity &c.

---

[158] S2: "Bathal rushing upon abrack Abeor coming upon Aberer"; H: "Bathal Rushing upon Abrack coming upon Aberer"; S1: "Bathal rushing upon a brack Abeor coming upon a Berer"; C: "Bathal or Vathat rushing upon Abrac! Abeor coming upon Aberer!" and adds the footnote "In the Latin, 'Bathal vel Vathat super Abrac ruens! Abeor veniens super Aberer!'" The Latin is found in both *Heptameron* and in *Le Grimoire du Pape Honorius* (Rome [Paris], 1800).

[159] S2: "lisence." C also adds, "Then standing in the midst of the Circle, thou shalt stretch forth thine hand in a gesture of command and say, 'By the Pentacle of Solomon have I called thee! Give unto me a true answer.' Then let the exorcist state his desires and requests. And when the evocation is finished thou shalt license the Spirit to depart thus." Note none of the manuscripts ever use the word "evocation," so this may be an innovation of Mathers'.

The licence to depart

> O Thou spirit N. Because thou hast very dilligently answered my de-
> mands and was ready and willing to come at my first call I doe hear
> licence thee to depart unto thy proper place without doeing any Injury or
> danger to any man or beast depart I say and be ever reddy to come at my
> call being duly Exorcised and conjured by ye sacred rites of Magicke. I
> charge thee to withdraw peacebly and quietly, and the peace of God be
> ever continued between me and the [thee]. Amen.

After you have given the spirit licence [to depart] you are not to go out of
ye Circle till they be gone and you have made prayers unto god ffor the
great blessing he hath bestowed upon you in granting you your desiers and   [116v]
delivering you from the malice of the Enemy the devill.

Nota [Note] you may command these spirits into the Brazen vessell as
you doe into the Triangle saying That you forthwith appeare before this
Circle in this vessell of Brasse in a faire and comely shape &c as is shewed
before in the forgoing Conjurations &c.160

The End of the First Part which is called Goetia

---

160 Here H inserts the bulk of the *Heptameron*.

Here beginneth the second Part called

the Art Theurgia Goetia

of Kinge Salomon

In this following Treatise you have 31 names[1] of cheife spirits with severall of the ministering spirits which are under them with their seals and characters which are to be worne as a lamin on your breasts; for without that the Spirit that has appeared will not obey you, to do your will &c.

The offices of these spirits is all one, for what one can doe the other [others] can doe the same. They can shew and discover all things that is hidd and done in the world: and can fetch and carry or doe any thinge that is to be done or is contained in any of the four Elements Fier, ayre, Earth and water &c allso [they can discover] the secrets of kings or any other person or persons let it be in what kinde it will.

These spirits [being aerial] are by nature good and evill That is, one part is good, and the other part Evill. They are governed by their princes, and each prince hath his place of abode in the points of the compass—as is shewed in the following figure; Therefore when you have a desire to call any of the kings or any of their Servants, you are to direct yourselfe to that point of the compass the Kinge hath his mansion or please [place] of abode, and you cannot well erre in your operations.

Note: every prince is to observe his conjuration, yet all [are] of one forme, except the name and place of the spirit [being varied], for in that they must change and differ allso the seal of the spirits is to be changed accordingly. as for the garments and other materiall things they are [the same as] spoken of in the Booke *Goetia*.

The form of the figure which discovereth the order of the 31 kings or princes wth their servant ministers for when the king is found his subjects are Easy to be found out &c.

---

1   S1, S2: "the names."

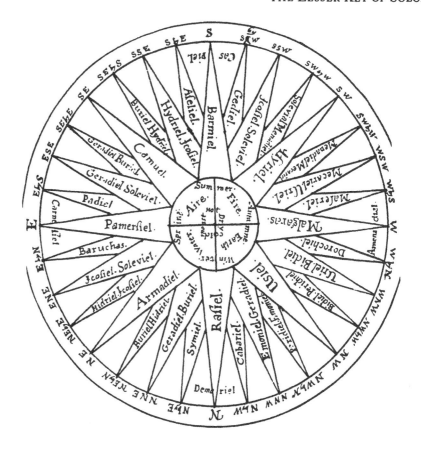

Figure 8. The thirty-one kings and princes and their mansions.

You may perceive by this figure that 20 of these kings have their first mantions [mansions] and continue in one place, and that yͤ other 11 are moveable [mobile] & are sometimes in one place sometime in another, and in some other times [they are] together more or less: therefore its no matter which way you stand with your face, when you have a desier to call any of them forth or their servants.

[118r] *[The Art Theurgia Goetia: Of the thirty-one aerial spirits evoked and constrained by King Solomon.]*

Carnesiell [Carnesiel[2]] is the most great and Cheefe Emporor Ruling in The East who hath, 1000 great Dukes and a 100 lesser Dukes under him,

---

2   See T1.17. T and H both read, "Carnesiel," as does S3 in the label of the sigil; S1, S2: "Carnefiel"; H: "Carmasiel."

besides 50000000000000[3] of ministering spirits which is more Inferior then
the Dukes, whereof [wherefore] we shall make no mention [of these], but
only 12, of the Cheefe Dukes and their seals, because they are sufficient for
practise.

Carnesiel his Seal.

His dukes.

Myrezyn,[4] Ornich,[5] Zabriel, Bucafas, Benoham, Arifiel,[6] Cumeriel, Vadriel,
Armany, Capriel, Bedary,[7] Laphor.[8]

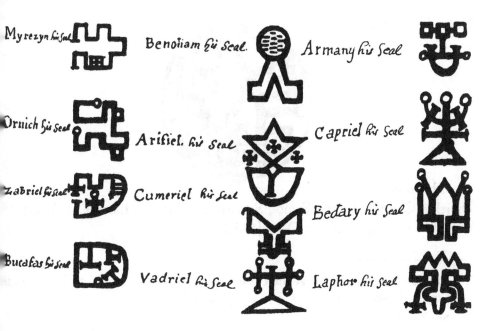

---

3   H: "60000000000000."

4   T: "Myresyn."

5   S1: "Orvich"; S2: "Orrich"; H: "Orich."

6   T: "Arisiel."

7   T: "Bedarys."

8   H: "Lapor."

Note, Carnesiel, when he appears, day or night, [there] attends him 60000000000000 Dukes [spirits] but when you call any of these Dukes there never attend above 300 and sometimes not above 10 &c.

The Conuration [Conjuration] of Carnesiel as followeth[9]

Wee Conjure thee O thou mighty & potent Prince Carnesiel who is the Emperour & cheife Comander, ruling as King in the dominion of the East who beares rule by the power of the supreame God El, over all Spirits &c.

[118v] Caspiel[10] is the Great and Cheefe Emperor Ruling in the South who hath 200 great Dukes and 400 lesser Dukes under him, besides 1000200000000 ministering spirits, which are much Inferiour &c. whereof wee (Salomon saith) shall make noe mention, but only of 12 of the Cheefe Dukes and their seales, for they are sufficient for practise.

Caspiel his Seal.

12 of his dukes.
Ursiel,[11] Chariel, Maras, Femol, Budarim,[12] Camory, Larmol,[13] Aridiel,[14] Geriel,[15] Ambri, Camor,[16] Oriel [Otiel].[17]

---

9   The conjuration is added at the bottom of the page by a second hand. S2 reads simply: "I coniure Thee &c = The Conguration."

10   See T1.18.

11   S1, S2, H: "Usiel."

12   S1, S2, H: "Femel, Budarÿm."

13   S2: "Larmel"; S1: "Camorr, Larmel."

14   S1: "Ariaiel."

15   T: "Geriol."

16   H: "Camorÿ."

17   T, S1, S2, H.

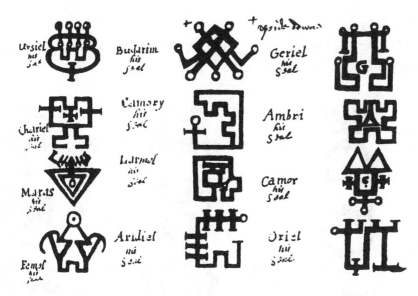

These 12 Dukes have 2660 under [lesser] Dukes a peece [each] to attend them, whereof some of them comes along with him when he is Invocated [invoked], but they are very Stuborne and Churlish &c.

The Conjuration of Caspiel

Wee Conjure thee O thou [Great] Mighty and Potent Prince Caspiel &c.

[119r]

Amenadiel[18] is the Great Emperor of the west, who hath 300 great Dukes, and 500 lesser Dukes, besides 40000030000100000 other ministering spirits more Inferiour to attend him, wheof [whereof] we shall not make any mention but only of 12, of the cheefe Dukes and their seales which is sufficient for practice.

Amenadiel his Seal.

---

18   See T1.19. H: "Ameradiel."

12 of his dukes.
Vadros,[19] Camiel, Luziel,[20] Musiriel, Rapsiel,[21] Lamael, Zoeniel, Curifas, Almesiel,[22] Codriel, Balsur, Nadroc.[23]

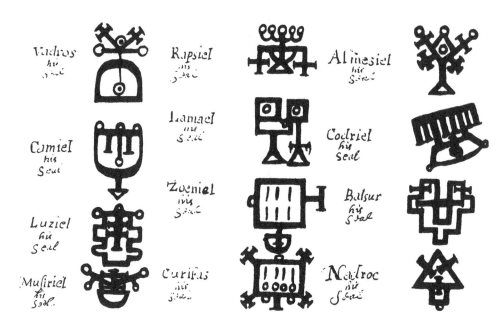

Note Amenadiel may be called at any hour of the day or night, but his dukes (who hath 3880[24] servants a peice to attend them) Are to be called in Certaine houres, as Vadros he may be called in the 2 first hours of the day, Camiel in the second 2 houres of the day and so [on] successively till you come to Nadroc who is to be called in ye 2 last houres of the night, And then begin againe at Vadros &c. The same Rule is to be observed in calling the Dukes belonging to Demoriel the Emperor of the North.

The Conjuration

Wee Conjure the [thee] O thou mighty & potent Prince Amenadiel who is the Emperour & cheife King ruling in the dominion of the West &c.

---

19   S1, S2, H: "Vadras."
20   H: "Luriel."
21   S1, S2: "Rapsel."
22   S1, S2: "Amesiel"; H: "... Currifas, Alinesiel."
23   H: "Madrock."
24   S1, S2: "3000."

Demoriel[25] is the Great and Mighty Emperor of the North, who hath 400 great Dukes and 600 lesser Dukes with 70000080000900000 [700,000,800,000,900,000] servants under his Command to attend him, whereof we shall make mention but of 12 of the cheefe Dukes and their seales, which will be sufficient for practice.

[119v]

Demoriel his Seal.

12 of his dukes.

Arnibiel, Cabarim, Menador,[26] Burisiel, Doriel,[27] Mador, Carnol,[28] Dubilon, Medar,[29] Churibal, Dabrinos, Chamiel [Chomiel].[30]

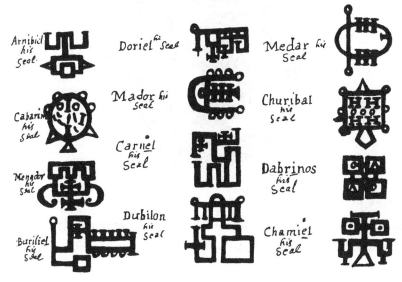

---

25   See T1.20.

26   S1, S2: "Armbiel, Cab^arym, Menander."

27   S1, S2: "Diriel"; H: "Burifiel, Diriel."

28   S3 reads "Carnel," corrected to "Carnol." T, S1, H: "Carnol."

29   S1, S2: "Meder"; H: "Medal."

30   T, S1, S2, H.

Note, Each of those Dukes hath 1140 Servants whoe attends [to attend] them as need Requireth for when that Duke yee call for have [hast called forth hath] more to doe then ordenary, he hath the more Servants to attend him.

The Conjuration of Demoriel

Wee Conjure thee O thou &c.

[120r]   **Pamersiel**[31] is the First and Cheefe spirit in the East, under Carnesiel, who hath 1000 spirits under him which are to be called in the day time, but with great care for they are very Lofty and stuborne whereof we shall make mention but of a [sic] 11 [eleven] as followeth.

Pamersiel his Seal.

[His dukes.]
Anoyr, Madriel, Ebra, Sotheano,[32] Abrulges, Ormenu, Itules, Rablion, Hamorphiel,[33] Itrasbiel, Nadrel.[34]

---

31   See T1.1.

32   S1, S2: "Sotheans."

33   S1, S2: "Hamorphel."

34   S2: "Madres." In S1 and S2, this spirit appears before Abrulges. H reads (UR to LL) "Sotheans, Itules, Madres, Rablion, Anoyr, Abrulge, Hamorphiel, Madriel, Ormenus Itrasbiel, Ebras."

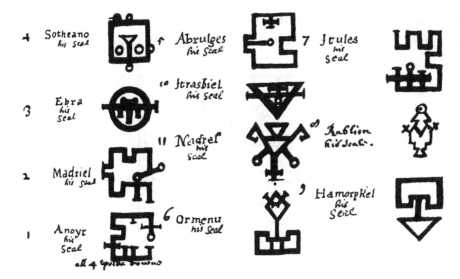

4 Sotheano his Seal

3 Ebra his Seal

2 Madriel his Seal

1 Anoyr his Seal

5 Abrulges his Seal

10 Jtrasbiel his Seal

11 Nadrel his Seal

6 Ormenu his Seal

7 Jtules his seal

8 Anblion his Seal.

9 Hamorphel his Seal

all 4 ...

Note These Spirits are by Nature Evill, and verry false, [and] not to be trusted in secrett things but is [are] Excellent in driving away spirits of Darkness from any place, or house that is haunted &c.

To call Forth Pamersiel, or any of these his servants,[35] chuse the uppermost [uttermost] private or secrett and most tacit† Rome in the house, or in some Certaine Island wood or Grove or the most occult and hidden place [removed] from all commers and goers, that noe one chanc by, may (if possible) happen that way ([into your] Chamber or what soever place else, you Act yr Concerns in) observe that it be very Ayery because these spirits that is in this part are all of the Ayer,[36] you may call these spirits into a Crystall stone or Glass Receptacle, [this] being an Ancient & usuall way of Receiveing & binding of spirits, This Cristall stone must be four Inches Diameter[37] sett on a Table of Art made as followeth [according to the following figure] wch is truly called the secrett Table of Salomon, & having the seale of the spirit on your Breast, and the Girdle about your wast [waist][38]

[120v]

---

35 H adds, "make a Circle in the forme as is shewed in the Book *Goetia* foregoing in the upper room..."

†   Corrected from "Picitt."

36 In S1 and S2, this paragraph reads, "to call forth pamersiel or any of thes his seruants make a cirkel in the forme as is shewed in the book Goetia before going in the uper roome of your house or in a place that is ayry becase thes spirits that is in this part are all ayry."

37 S2: "you may call thes spirits into a cristal stone 4 inches diameter."

38 S2 adds, "as is shewen in the book Goetia."

and you cannot erre, the forme of the Table is Thus, as this present figure
doth here represent & shew, behold the [thee] the figure

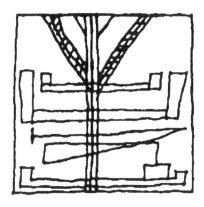

when you have thus prepared what is to be prepared, Rehearse the conjuration following severall times that is whilst the spirit come, for without dout
he will come, note the same method is to be used in all the following part
of this Booke as is here of Pamersiel and his servants. Also the same in
calling the king and his servants &c.[39]

The Conjuration of Pamersiel.

We Conjure thee O Pamersiel, a Cheefe Spirit. Ruling in the East, &c.[40]

The Second Spiritt in order under the Emperor of the East is called **Padiel**,[41]
he Ruleth in the East and by South as King, and governeth 10000 spirits
by day and 20000, by night,[42] besides severall Thousands under them, They
are all good by nature and may be trusted. Salomon sayeth that these spirits
have noe power of them selves but [only] what is given unto them by their
prince Padiel. Therefore he hath made noe mention of any of their names
because if any of them is called they cannot appear without the Leave of
their prince as others can doe &c you must use the same method in calling
this prince Padiel, as is declared before of Pamersial; the seale of Padiel, is
this.

---

39   S2, H: "calling the 4 Kings & ther seruants aforesaid &c."

40   S1, S2: "I coniure thee o thou & potent prince pamersiel who ruleth as King in the
     domminian of the East &c."

41   See T1.2.

42   T, S1: "200000."

Padiel his Seale.

The Coniuration

Wee Conjure thee o thou Mighty and Potent Prince Padiel, who rules as a cheife Prince or king in the dominion of the East & by South, We Invocate Camand & compell you, by the especiall name of yoʳ God &c.

The Third Spirit placed and Ranked In order under the Cheefe Mighty great   [121r]
and potent King of the East is called **Camuel**[43] who Regneth Ruleth and governeth as King in the South East part of the world & hath many & severall spirits under his Goverment & command whereof wee shall only make mention but of 10 that appertaineth & belongeth to the day & 10 to yᵉ night. And Each of these have 10, servants to attend on ~~them~~ each except Camyel, Sitgara, Asimiel,[44] Calym, Dobiel and Meras,[45] for they have 100 a peice to attend them, but Tediel, Moriel & Tugaros, they have none at all, They appear all in A verry Beautifull forme,& verry Courteously, And in yᵉ night as well as in yᵉ day &c They are as followeth wᵗʰ their Seales.

Camuel his Seal.

---

43 See T1.3.

44 S2: "Citgara Asmiel"; S1: "Citgaras Asmiels"; H: "Citgara, Apuiel."

45 H: "Maras."

10 of his Servants belongs to yͤ day & will appear in the night.
Orpemiel [Orpeniel], Omyel, Camyel, Budiel, Elcar, Citgara, Pariel, Cariel, Neriel, Daniel.[46]

Ten of his servants belonging to the Night & will appʳ in the day.
Asimiel, Calim,[47] Dobiel, Nodar, Phaniel, Meras, Azemo,[48] Tediel, Moriel, Tugaros.[49]

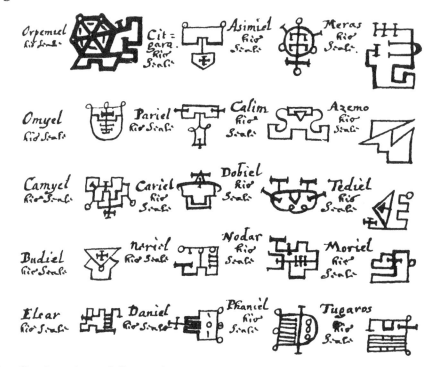

The Conjuration of Camuel,

> Wee Coniure the O thou &c: Camuel who rules &c. in the South East part of the World, We Invocate &c.[50]

---

46   T: "Orpeniel, Camyel, Budiel, Elcar, Citgara, Pariel, Cariel, Neriel, Daniel, Omyel"; H: "Camÿvel, Orpeniel, Budiel, Elear, Dobiel, Nodar, Cariel, Neriol, Daniel, Omiel"; S1: "Orpeniel, Camÿel, Budiel, Elcary, Citgara, Pariel, Cariel, Neriel, Daniel, Omiel."

47   T: "Calym"; S2: "Asniel, Calÿm."

48   T, S2: "Azimo."

49   S2: "Tuaros"; H: "Asniel, Calÿm, Tugaro, Phaniel, Meras, Azino, Tediel, Moriel, Citgaras, Pariel"; S1: "Asniel, Calÿm, Dobiel, Nodar, Phaniel, Meras, Azimo, Tediel, Moriel, Tuaros."

50   S2: "The Conjuration. I coniure thee o thou mighty & potent prince &c." At this point, S2 inserts an alchemical formula titled "Tincture universalis" that occupies 2 full pages, followed by a blank page, before resuming with "the 4th spirit."

The Fourth Spirit in order is called **Aseliel**[51] he governeth as King under Carnesiel, in the South and by East he hath 10 cheefe spirits belonging to ye day, and 20 to the night, under whome are 30 principall spirits,[52] and under those as many, whereof wee shall make mention, but of, 8 of ye cheefe presidents belonging to the day, And as many belonging to the night, And every one hath 20 servants at his command, they are all very courtious and Loving, and beautifull to behold &c They are as followeth with their seales.

Aseliel his Seale.

8 of his Servants belonging to the day.
Mariel, Charas, Parniel, Aratiel, Cubiel, Aniel, Asahel, Arean.[53]

8 of his Servants belonging to the Night.
Asphiel, Curiel, Chamos, Odiel, Melas, Sariel, Othiel, Bofar [Bufar].[54]

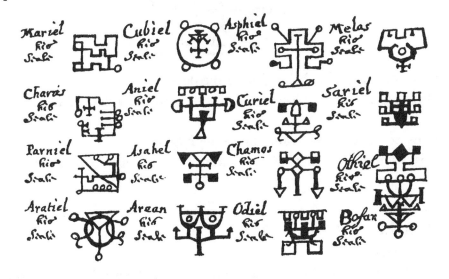

---

51 See T1.4. S2: "Ascliel"; H: "Aschiel"; S1: "Asteliel."

52 S1: "3."

53 S1: "... Otiel, Othiel"; H: "Mariel, Charas, Parniel, Aratiel, Sariel, Cubiel, Aniel, Asahel."

54 T: "Bufar"; S2: "bupar"; H: "Asphiel, Othiel, Arean, Curiel, Chamos, Odiel, Melos, Bufar"; S1: "Sariel, Asahel, Aream, Euriel, Chomos, Asphiel, Bufar, Melas."

The Coniuration of Aseliel as followeth.

Wee Conjure thee O thou Mighty & potent prince Aseliel, who rules as a cheif prince or King under Carnesiel, in the South & by East, &c.

[122r]

The fift [fifth] spirit in order is called **Barmiel**;[55] he is the first and cheefe spirit under Caspiel, The Emperour of the South [He ruleth] as king [of the South] under Caspiel, and hath 10 Dukes for the day: And 20 for the night to attend him to doe his will, the which is all very good, and willing to obey the Exorcist, whereof wee shall make mention but of 8 that belongs to the day, and as many for the night, with their seals for they are sufficient for practice, Note Every one of these Dukes hath 20 servants apiece to attend him when he is called, Excepting the 4 last that belongs to the night, for they have none, They are as followeth with their Seales.

Barmiel his Seale.

8 of his servient dukes belonging to the day.
Sochas, Tigara, Chansi, Keriel, Acteras,[56] Barbil, Carpiel,[57] Mansi.[58]

8 of his Servants ^dukes belonging to the Night.
Barbis, Marguns,[59] Caniel, Acreba, Mareaiza,[60] Baaba, Gabio,[61] Astib.[62]

---

55   See T1.5.

56   T: "Acterar"; S2: "Kiriel, acterer."

57   S2: "Carpid."

58   S1: "Sochas, Tigara, Cleansi, Kiriel, Acterer, Barbil, Carpid, Mansi"; H: "Sochas, Tigara, Chansi, Marquis, Achereba, Astib, Acterer, Barbill."

59   T: "Marquus."

60   T: "Marciaz"; S1: "Morcaza."

61   T: "Gabir."

62   S2: "berbis, marquus, Camel, acereba, mercaiza, Baabal, Gabus, Astib"; S1: "Berbis,

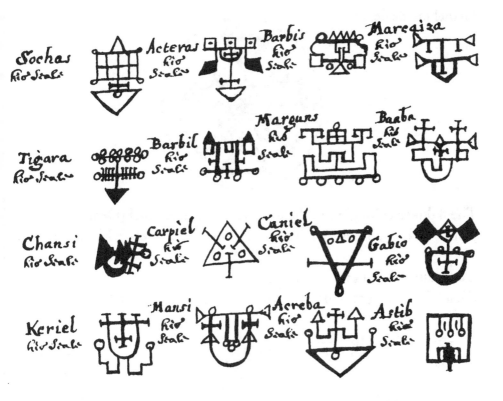

The Coniuration of Barmiel as followeth:

Wee Coniure thee O thou mighty & potent Prince Barmiel, who rules as
a cheife Prince or King in the South under Caspiel, &c:

The sixth spirit in order, but the second under the Emperour of the   [122v]
south is called **Gediel**;[63] who Ruleth as a kinge in the South & by West
who hath 20 cheefe spirits to serve him in the day, & as many for the
night, and they have many servants at their commands whereof wee
shall make mention, but of 8 of the cheefe spirits that belonge to the
day, And as many of those belonge to the night: who hath 20 servants
apiece to attend them when they are called forth to appearance, they are
very willing, loving and courteous to doe your will, &c whose names &
seals is as followeth:

Marquus, Camel, Acereba, Mercaza, Baabal, Gabir, Ashib"; H: "Mansi, Barbis, Caniel,
Baabal, Keriel, Carpiel, Marcaiza, Gabir."
63   See T1.6.

Gediel his Seale.

The 8 dukes belonging to the day that is under Gedial [Gediel].
Coliel,[64] Naras, Sabas, Assaba, Sariel, Ranciel [Rantiel[65]], Mashel, Bariel.[66]

The 8 dukes belonging to the night.[67]
Reciel, Sadiel, Agra, Anael, Aroan,[68] Cirecas, Aglas, Vriel.[69]

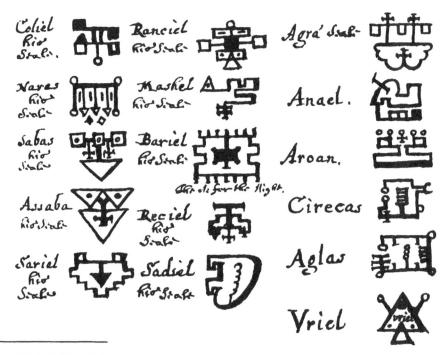

---

64   S1, S2: "Cotiel."

65   T, S1, S2: "Rantiel."

66   S1: "Cotiel, Reciel, Sadiel, Naras, Sabas, Assaba, Agra, Anael"; H: "Coliel, Naras, Sabas, Affaba, Seriel, Rantiel, Bariel, Mashel."

67   S1: "here followeth the names & seals of the 8 dukes that is under Gediel & Reciel by night."

68   S2: "Ayoan."

69   S1: "Sariel, Rantiel, Miskel, Aroan, Cirecas, Bariel, Aglas, Vriel"; H (read down starting UL): "Reciel, Sadiel, Agra / Anael, Arons, Circea / Aglas, Vriel."

The Coniuration of Gedial [sic] as fol:

Wee~~I~~ conjure thee O thou mighty & potent prince Gediel, who ruleth as King in the South & by West, We Invoke constraine comand &c.

The seventh spirit in order, but the third under the great Emperour of the South is called **Asyriel**, he is a mighty kinge, Ruling in the South West part of the world and hath 20 great Dukes to attend him, in the day time, and as many for the nights, who hath under them severall servants to attend them &c here wee shall make mention [but] of 8 of the cheefe Dukes that belongs unto the day, And as many that belong to the night, because they are sufficient for practice: And the first 4 that belongs unto the day: And the first 4 that belongs to the night hath 40 servants apiece to attend them: And the last 4 of the day, [have] 20, and the last 4 of ye Night [have] 10 apiece: they are all good natured & willing to obey, [Note] those that is of the day, is to be called then [in the day], And those of the night in the night: &c these be their names & Seales that followeth:

[123r]

Asyriel his Seale.

The 8 dukes y^t belonge to y^e day under Asyriel.
Astor,[70] Carga, Buniel, Rabas, Arcisat, Aariel,[71] Cusiel,[72] Malguel.[73]

---

70 S2: "Aitor."

71 T: "Adriel."

72 S2: "Ariel, Cubiel."

73 H (read down starting UL): "Aitor, Cargo, Buniel / Rabas, Arcifat, Nariel / Cusiel, Malguels"; S1: "Olitor, Carga, Buniel, Rabas, Arisat, Ariel, Cuopiel, Malugel."

The 8 for the night.
Amiel, Cusriel,[74] Maroth, Omiel, Budar,[75] Aspiel, Faseua,[76] Hamas.[77]

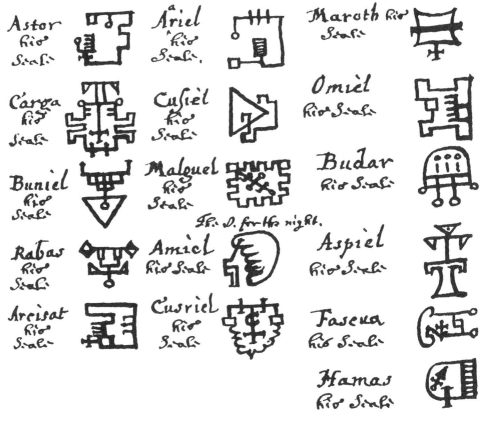

The Conjuration

[123v]

Wee Conjure thee &c: who rules as a cheife king in the South West &c.

The eighth spirit in order But the fourth under the Emperour of the South is called **Maseriel**,[78] Who Rulleth as king in the Dominion of yᵉ West, and by South, and hath a great number of princes & servants under him, to attend him, whereof we shall make mention of 12 of the cheefe [Dukes] thatt attend him in the day time, and 12 that attend

---

74   T: "Cusiel"; S2: "Cusrel."

75   S2: "Onuel, Buder."

76   T: "Fassua"; S2: "Fascua."

77   H (read L to R): "Amiel, Cusriel, Onuel / Aspiel, Maroth, Budar / Fascua, Hamas"; S1: "Amiel, Cusrel, Marott, Onuel, Buder, Aspiel, Fascua, Hamas."

78   See T1.8.

him to doe his will in the night time, which is sufficient for practice, they are all good by nature & willingly will doe your will in all things: those that is for the day, is to be called in the day, And those for the night in the night, they have every one 30 servants apiece to attend them & their names and seales is as followeth.

Maseriel his Seale.

The 12 that belonge to the day under Maseriel.
Mahue, Roriel,[79] Earviel, Zeriel, Atniel,[80] Vessur,[81] Azimel, Chasor,[82] Patiel, Assuel,[83] Aliel, Espoel.[84]

These 12 following belong to the Night.
Arach, Maras, Noguiel, Saemiel,[85] Amoyr, Bachiel,[86] Baros, Eliel, Earos,[87] Rabiel, Atriel, Salvor.[88]

---

79   T: "Rouiel"; S2: "Mayhuc, Roniel."

80   T: "Fariel, Zerael, Athiel."

81   S2: "armel, vescur."

82   S2: "Claros."

83   T: "Potiel, Alsuel."

84   H: "Leriel, Myhuc, Requiel / Earuiel, Atmiel, Vessur / Vazimel, Nogeiel, Atiel / Espoel, Ariel, Assuel"; S1: "Mayhuc, Roviel, Earviol, Zeriel, Atmel, Vescur, Azimel, Charos, Patiel, Assuel, Aliel, Espoel."

85   T: "Noquiel, Sarmiel"; S2: "Mras, Nogeiel, Sarmiel."

86   T, S2: "Badiel."

87   T: "Paras"; S2: "Ewas, Eliel." It also adds, "The seale of Eliel shold haue ben placed before Ewas."

88   T: "Saluar"; S2: "Solvar"; H: "Arach, Maras, Charos / Patiels, Sarmiel, Amoyor / Badiel, Baros, Eliel / Earo, Rabiel, Solvar"; S1: "Arach, Naras, Nogeiel, Sarmiel, Amoyr, Badiel, Baras, Eliel, Eras, Rabiel, Atriel, Solvar."

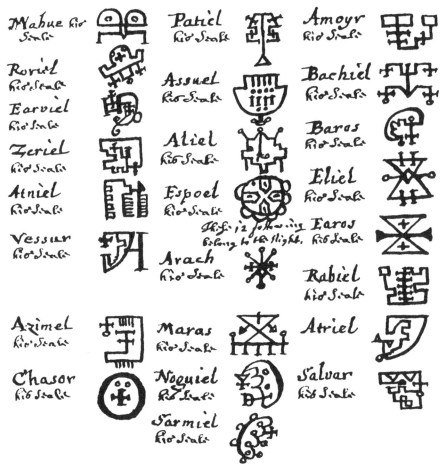

The Coniurat:

Wee Coniure thee &c: Maseriel who rules as cheife Prince or King in the
dominion of West & by South &c.

[124r]   The ninth spirit in order, but the first under the Emperour of the West
          is called **Malgaras**[89]—he Rulleth as king in the Dominion of the West,
          and hath 30 Dukes under him to attend him, in the day, and as many
          for the night, and several under them againe; whereof wee shall make
          mention of 12 Dukes that belongs to the day, and as many as belongs to
          the night, And every one of them hath 30 servants to attend on them
          Excepting **Misiel**,[90] **Barfas**, **Aspar**,[91] & **Deilas**,[92] for the [they] haue but

---

89   See T1.9.

90   S1: "Miliel."

91   S1, S2, H: "Asper."

92   H: "Dilas."

20 and **Arois & Basiel,**[93] they have but 10: &c. They are all very courteous and will appear willingly to due your will, they Appear 2 & 2 at a
time wth their servants, They th[t] are for the day is to be called in the
day and those for the night in the night. Their Names and seals is as
followeth:

Malgaras his Seale.

The 12 dukes that belonges to the day.
Carmiel,[94] Meliel, Borasy,[95] Agor, Casiel, Rabiel, Cabiel, Udiel, Oriel,
Misiel,[96] Barfas,[97] Arois.[98]

12 dukes for the night.
Aroc,[99] Dodiel,[100] Cubi, Libiel,[101] Raboc, Aspiel, Caron, Zamor, Amiel,
Aspar [Aspor],[102] Deilas, Basiel.[103]

---

93   H: "Aroias Basir."

94   S1, S2: "Carimiel."

95   T: "Borass"; S1: "Boras."

96   S1, S2: "Alisiel."

97   S2: "Barface"; H: "Carmiel, Meliel, Baras / Agor, Casiel, Rabiel / Gabiel, Vdiel,
     Oriel / Alisiel, Barface, Aroias."

98   T: "Aroiz."

99   S2: "Arois."

100 T: "Dobiel."

101 S2: "libieli."

102 T, S2: "Aspor"; S1: "Asper."

103 H: "Aroc, Dodiel, Cubis / Libiel, Raboc, Aspiel / Caron, Zamor, Amiel / Aspor,
     Delias, Basiel."

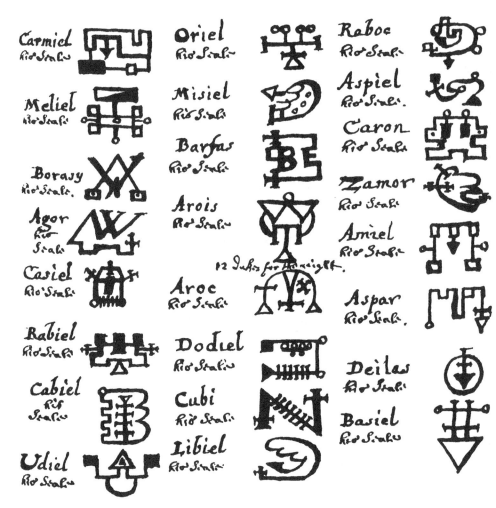

Carmiel Rio Scale · Oriel Rio Scale · Raboc Rio Scale · Meliel Rio Scale · Misiel Rio Scale · Aspiel Rio Scale · Barfas Rio Scale · Caron Rio Scale · Borasy Rio Scale · Arois Rio Scale · Zamor Rio Scale · Agor Rio Scale · Amiel Rio Scale · Casiel Rio Scale · 12 Dukes for the night · Aroc Rio Scale · Aspar Rio Scale · Rabiel Rio Scale · Dodiel Rio Scale · Deilas Rio Scale · Cabiel Rio Scale · Cubi Rio Scale · Basiel Rio Scale · Udiel Rio Scale · Libiel Rio Scale

The Coniuration &c.

Wee Coniure thee &c: Malgaras who ruleth &c: in yᵉ West &c.

[124v] The tenth spirit in order, But the second under the Emperour of the West is called **Dorochiel**,[104] who is a mighty prince bearing Rule in the West, and by North, and hath 40 Dukes to attend [on] him in the day time, and as many for the night, with an Innumerable company of servants spirits, whereof wee shall make mention of 24 Cheefe dukes that belongs to the day, and as many for the night, with their seales as followeth. Note the 12 first that belonge to the day, and yᵉ 12 first that belongs to the night hath 40 servants apiece to attend on them: And the 12 last of both the day, and of the night hath 400 apiece to Attend on them when they appeare, &c

---

104 See T1.10. H reads, "Darochiel" here, but "Dorochiel" below.

Allso those of the day is to be called in the day and those of the night in the night: Observe the planetary motion in calling, for yᵉ 2 first that belongs to the day are to be called in yᵉ first planetary hour of yᵉ day: and the 2 next in yᵉ second planetary hour of the day, and soe successively on till you have gone quite threw yᵉ day and night, till you come to the 2 first againe &c. They are all of a good nature and will willingly obey &c. Their names and seales is as followeth:

Dorochiel [his Seale]

The 24 dukes belongs to yᵉ day, 12 before noone.
Magael, Artino, Efiel, Maniel/Efiel, Suriel/Maniel, Carsiel/Suriel, Carsiel, Fabiel, Carba, Merach, Althor, Omiel.

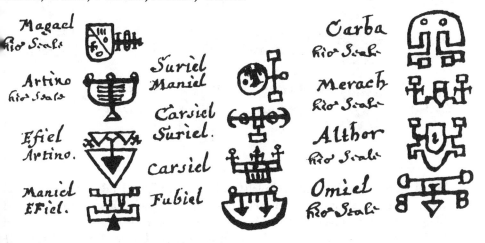

Heere followeth the 12 dukes, afternoone.
Gudiel, Asphor, Emuel, Soriel, Cabron, Diviel Abriel, Danael, Lomor, Casael, Busiel, Larfos.[105]

---

[105] T: "Mugael, Choriel, Artinc, Efiel, Maniel, Suriel, Carsiel, Fubiel, Carba, Merach, Althor, Omael, Gudiel, Asphor, Emuel, Souiel, Cabron, Diuiel, Abriel, Danael, Lomor, Cesael, Busiel, Larfos"; S2: "Margael, Choriel, Artino, Efiel, Mamel, Suriel, Carciel,

[125r]

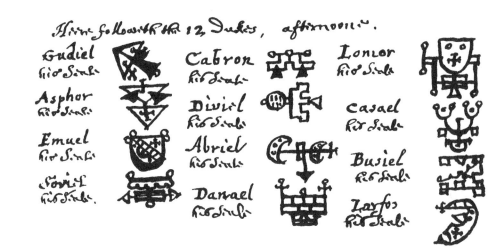

The 24 Dukes that belong to the night under Dorochiel &c. These 12 before Mightnight [midnight].

Nahiel, Ofisiel,[106] Bulis, Momel, Darbori, Paniel, Cursas, Aliel,[107] Aroziel, Cusyne, Vraniel, Pelusar.[108]

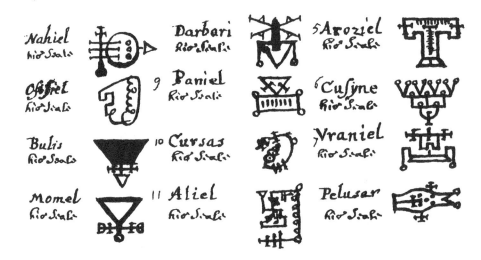

Tubiel, Corba, Merach, Alshor, Omiel, Gudiel, Asphor, Emuel, Soriel, Cabron, Diriel abriel, Danael, Lomor, Casael, Buciel, Lorfos"; H: "Magaels, Choriel, Artino / Efiel Mamel, Arsiel / Tubiel, Corba, Merach / Alshor, Omiel, Carfas / Liel, Mosiel Gudiel / Asphor, Emuel, Soviel / Uriel, Diviel, Abriel / Danael, Lemor, Casael"; S1 "Magael, Choriel, Artino, Efiel, Mamel, Suriel, Carciel, Tubiel, Corba, Merach Alshor, Omiel, Gudiel, Asphor, Emuel, Soviel, Cabron, Diviel, Abriel, Danael, Lomor Casael, Buciel, Lorfos."

106 S2: "Naliel, Ofisel."

107 S2: "Curfas, Liel."

108 H: "Maziel, Phutiel, Aroziel / Buchiel, Laefo, Naliel / Ofisiel, Bulis, Moinel / Pasiel Cabron, Geriel"; S1: "Naliel, Ofisel, Budis, Momel, Pasiel, Gariel, Soriel, Darbori Paniel, Curfas, Liel, Maziel."

These 12 after midnight.
Pafiel,[109] Gariel, Soriel, 12 Maziel, 1 Futiel [Putiel],[110] 2 Cayros, 3 Narsial,
4 Moziel,[111] 9 Abael, 10 Meroth, 11 Cadriel, 12 Lodiel [Lobiel[112]].

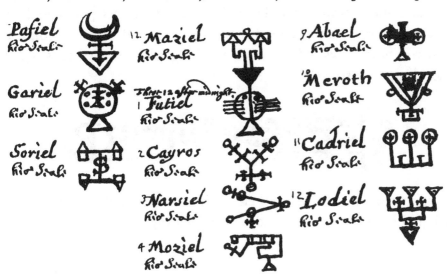

The Coniuration of Dorochiel as followeth:

Wee Coniure thee O thou mighty &c: Dorochiel, who ruleth as King in
the West & by North, wee Invocate &c:

The eleventh spirit in order, But the third under the Emperour [125v]
Amenadiel is called Usiel,[113] who is a mighty prince Ruleing as king in
the North West. he hath 40 Dyurnall [diurnal], and 40 nocturnall Dukes
to attend on him in the day and the night, whereof wee shall make
mention of 14 that belongs to yᵉ day and as many for yᵉ night which is
sufficient for practice, the first 8 that belongs to the day hath 40 servants a piece And the other 6 hath 30. And the first 8 that belongs to yᵉ

---

109 S2: "Pasiel."

110 S2: "Putiel."

111 S2: "Narfiel, Mosiel."

112 S2: "lobiel"; T: "Nachiel, Ofisiel, Bulis, Moniel, Pafiel, Gariel, Soriel, Darbori,
     Paniel, Curfas, Aliel, Maziel, Phutiel, Cayros, Narsyel, Moziel, Aroziel, Cusync,
     Vraniel, Pelusar, Abael, Meroth, Cadriel, Lobiel"; H: "Vraniel, Soriel, Darbori /
     Paniel, Cayros, Narsiel / Cusÿne, Merorh, Abac / Cadriel, Blusar, Lobiel"; S1:
     "Putiel, Cayros, Narsiel, Mosiel, Aroziel, Cusÿne, Vraniel, Pelusar, Abael, Meroth,
     Chadriel, Lobiel."

113 See T1.11.

night hath forty Servants a piece to attend on them, And the next 4 Dukes 20 servants, And the last 2 [of the night] hath 10 a piece, and they are very obedient and doth willingly appeare when they are called, they have more power to hide or discover Treausures [treasures] then any other spirits (saith Salomon) that is contained in this Booke, and when you hide, or would not have anything taken away that is hidden, make these four seals[114]

in virgins parchment and lay them with ye Treasury, where the Treasury lyeth and it will never be found nor taken away. The names and seals of these spirits is as Followeth.

Usiel his Seale.

The 14 dukes yt belong to the day.
Abariel, Ameta, Arnen,[115] Herne, Saefer, Potiel, Saefarn, Magni,[116] Amandiel, Barsu, Garnasu, Hissam, Fabariel, Usiniel [Usimel[117]].

---

114 From right to left: the seals of Adan, Ansoel, Magni, and Abariel.

115 S2: "Abaris, Amel, annen."

116 S2: "Saefer, Mapni."

117 T: "Abaria, Ameta, Arnen, Herne, Saefer, Poriel, Saefar, Maqui, Amandiel, Barsu, Garnatu, Hissam, Fabariel, Vsiniel"; S2: "Barfu, Garnafu, Hisiam, Fabariel, Usimel"; H: "The names & Seales of Usiels Eight Diurnal ~~Nocturnal~~ / Dukes / Saefor, Potiel, Abaria / Saefar, Ameta, Arnew / Herne, Maqur / The names & Seals of Vsiels six ^Diurnal ~~Nocturnal~~ / Dukes / Amandiel, Barfies, Garfus / Hissam, Fabariel, Usiniel"; S1: "Abaris, Ameta, Amen, Herne, Sadfar, Potiel, Seafar, Mapui, Amandiel, Barfu, Garnafu, Hisiam, Fabariel, Vsimel."

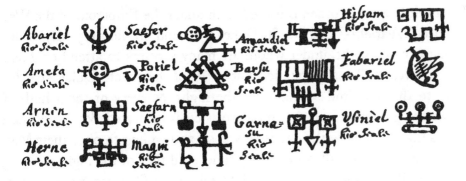

The 14 dukes that belong to the Night.
Ansoel,[118] Godiel, Barfos, Burfa, Adan, Saddiel, Sodiel, Ossidiel, Pathier,[119]
Marae, Asuriel, Almoel, Las Pharon,[120] Ethiel.[121]

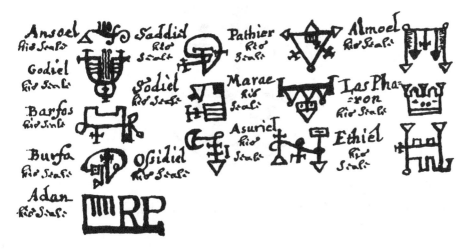

The Conjuration of Usiel as fol:

Wee Conjure thee O thou mighty &c: Usiel who ruleth as cheif Prince or   [126r]
King under Amenadiel in the North West &c.

---

118 S2: "Anfol."

119 S2: "Ofsidiel, Pathir."

120 S2: "Lasphoron."

121 T: "... Sobiel, Ossidiel, Adan, Asuriel, Almoel, Lapharon, Pathyr, Marae, Ethiel";
     H: "The Names and Seales of Vsiel's / Eight ~~Diurnal~~ Dukes - Nocturnal /
     Ansoel, Godiel, Barfos / Burfas, Lasphoron, Sodiel / Offidiel, Adan / The Names
     and Seales of Vsiels 6 ~~Diurnal~~ / Dukes. Nocturnall / Asuriel, Minoel, Pathir /
     Saddiel, Marcie, Ethiel"; S1: "Anfol, Godiel, Barfos, Burfa, Saddiel [sc Sodiel],
     Ofsidiel, Adan, Asurel, Almod, Pathir, Narad, Lasphoron, Ethiel, Saddiel." This
     second Saddiel has the further annotation ,"This seal should haue been between
     Burfa & Saddiel [sc Sodiel]."

The twelfth spirit in order, But the fourth under the Emperour of the West is called **Cabariel**;[122] he hath 50 Dukes to attend on him in yᵉ day[123] and as many in the night, under whom are many servants to attend on them, whereof wee shall make mention but of 10 of the cheefe Dukes that belongs to the day, And as many for the night, & every of them hath 50 servants to give attendance when their masters is Invocated, &c. Note Those Dukes that belongs to the day is very good and willing to obey their Master, and is ^are to be called in the day time, And they of the night is ^are by nature Evill & Disobedient, and will deceive you if They can &c they are to be called in the night: The names and seales of them all are as followeth:

Cabariel his Seale:

The 10 yᵗ belongs to yᵉ day:
Satifiel, Parius, Godiel, Taros,[124] Asoriel,[125] Etimiel,[126] Clyssan,[127] Elitel, Aniel, Cuphal.[128]

The 10 dukes for the Night.
Mador, Peniel, Cugiel, Thalbus, Otim,[129] Ladiel, Morias, Pandor, Cazul,[130] Dubiel.[131]

---

122 See T1.12. S1 adds, "who is a mighty prince Ruling in the west & by North."

123 S1, S2: "5" (erroneously).

124 S2, H: "Tarof."

125 S1: "Aforiel."

126 T: "Etymel"; H: "Alsoriel, Elimiel."

127 S1: "Elÿsam."

128 S2: "Cupher or ..l"; H: "Yssan, Elitel, Aniel / Gupharort." Note this appears to indicate a misreading of S2 and thus some common prototype. S1: "Cupher or Cuphir."

129 T: "Thalbos, Orym"; S1, S2: "Ugiel, Thalbor, Orijm."

130 S1: "Cazsul."

131 H: "Mador, Pandor, Dubiel / Peniel, Vgiel, Thalbor / Orÿm, Ladiel, Morias / Cazul."

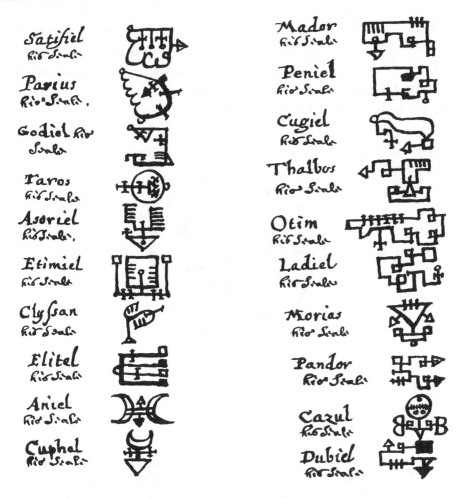

Satifiel Rio Scale

Pavius Rio Scale.

Godiel Rio Scale

Taros Rio Scale

Asoriel Rio Scale.

Etimiel Rio Scale

Clyssan Rio Scale

Elitel Rio Scale

Ariel Rio Scale

Cuphal Rio Scale

Mador Rio Scale

Peniel Rio Scale

Cugiel Rio Scale

Thalbus Rio Scale

Otim Rio Scale

Ladiel Rio Scale

Morias Rio Scale

Pandor Rio Scale

Cazul Rio Scale

Dubiel Rio Scale

The Coniuration of Cabariel as followeth.

We Conjure thee O thou mighty & potent Prince Cabariel &c: who ruleth
as king in the North & by West &c.

The 13th Spirit in order But the first under Demoriel: the Emperour of the   [127r]
north is called **Raysiel**,[132] he ruleth as King in the north, & hath fifty
dukes for the day, [133] and as many for the night to attend him, & they have
many servants under them againe—for to doe there will &c. where of these
we shall make mention of 16 cheife dukes that belong to the day, because
they are by nature good & willing to obey, & but [only] 14 that belong to
the night, because they are by nature evill & stubborne & disobedient, &

132 See T1.13. S1 and S2 read, "Rasiel" here, but the seal is labelled "Raÿsiel." H reads,
     "Rasiel" throughout.

133 H: "150."

will not obey willingly—all those dukes that belong to the day have 50 servants a peece,[134] exceping the 6th Last, for they have but 30 a peece & the 8 first that belonge to the night have 40 sarvants [sic] a peece excepting the 4 next following for they have but 20 a peece, & the last 2 have but 10 a peece, there names & seales are as followeth vixt—

Raysael[135] his seale.

The 16 dukes that belong to ye day.
Baciar, Thoac,[136] Sequiel, Sadar, Terath, Astael, Ramica, Dubarus, Armena, Albhadur, Chanaei,[137] Fursiel, Betasiel, Melcha, Tharas,[138] Vriel.[139]

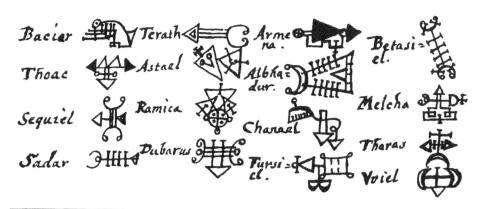

---

134 H: "5."

135 S1, S2: "Raÿsiel"; H: "Rasiel."

136 S2: "Bacier, Phoca."

137 T: "Chanael."

138 S2: "Albadur, Chanoel, Furciel, Betasid, Milcha."

139 T: "Vuiel"; H: "Basiar, Phocas, Sequiel / Melchas, Sadar, Astael / Dubarus, Albahadur / Fursiel, Tharas, Feruh / Ramica, Armena, Chanoel / Betasiel, Vuiel"; S1: "Baciar, Thoac, Chanael, Fursiel, Betasiel, Melcha, [Lazaba, Aleasy, Sebach, Quibda, (These are the 5th 6th 7th and 8th 'spirit of the night misplac't'] Sequiel, Sadar, Terach, Astael (corrected from Astiel), Ramica, Dubarus, Armena, Alhadur, Tharas, Vuiel."

The 14 dukes that belong [to the] night.

Thariel, Paras, Arayl,[140] Culmar, Lazaba, Aleasi,[141] Sebach, Quibda, Belsay, Morael,[142] Sarach, Arepach, Lamas, Thurcal.[143]

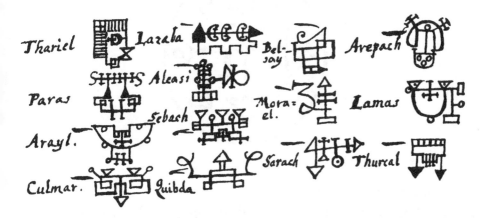

The Coniuration of Raysael as fol:

Wee Coniure thee &c.

The 14th spirit in order, But the second under the Emperour of the North   [127v]
is called **Symiel.**[144] who ruleth as King in the North & by Easte who hath
10 dukes to attend him in the day & a 1000 for the night & every one of
these have a certaine number of sarvants; whereof we shall make mention
of the 10 that belong to the day, & 10 of those that belong to the night &
those of the day are very good & not disobedient, as are those of the night
for they are stubborne & will not appeare willingly &c allsoe those of the
day have 720 sarvants amongst them to doe there will, & the rest of the
night have 790 servants to attend on them as occasion sarveth, the names
of these 20 are as followeth, with theire seales & number of sarvants &
[&c.]

---

140 S2: "Arayel."

141 S2: "Aleasÿ."

142 S2: "Belsag, Morad."

143 T: "... Quibda, Lamas, Belsay, Moraei, Thurcal, Sarach, Arepach"; S2: "Arepath, Lamas, Thurcall"; H: "Thariel, Arayl, Lazabas / Quibdas, Sarach, Thurcal / Paras, Culmar / Aleasi, Belsag, Arepach / Sebach, Morae, Lamas"; S1: "Thariel, Paras, Arayl, Culmar, [Lazaba, Aleasy, Sebach, Quibda,] Belsay, Morael, Sarach, Arepach, Lamas, Thurcal."

144 See T1.14. H reads, "Symiel" here, but "Simiel" on the seal.

Symiel his Seale.

The 10 dukes that belong to yᵉ day.
Asmiel 60, Chrubas 100, Vaslos 40,[145] Malgron 20, Romiel 80, Larael 60, Achot 60,[146] Bonyel 90,[147] Dagiel 100,[148] Musor 110.[149]

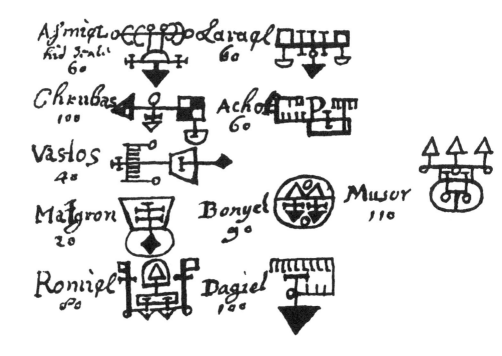

---

145   T: "Vastos"; S1, S2: "Vafros."

146   S2: "Achet."

147   T: "Banier 90"; S1, S2: "Boniel 90."

148   S2: "Dagael"; S1: "Dagiel 105."

149   H: "Asmiel 60, Larael 60, Boniel 90 / Chrubas 100, Vastra 40, Achol 60 / Dagael 100, Romiel 80, Malgrom 20 / Musor 110."

The 10 dukes that belong to the night.
Mafrus 70, Apiel 30, Curiel 40, Molael 10, Arafos 50, Marianu 100, Narzael 210,[150] Murahe 30,[151] Richel 120, Nalael 130.[152]

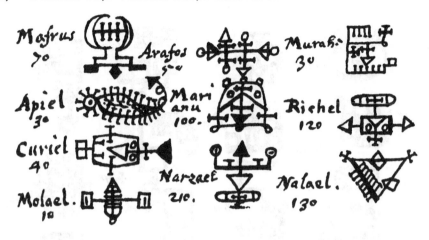

The fiteenth [sic] spirit in order, But the third under the Emperour of the North is called **Armadiel**,[153] who rulleth as king in the North East part, and haue many dukes under him besides other servants, whereof we shall make mention of 15 of the cheefe Dukes who have 1260 servants to attend him [on each of them].[154] these dukes are to be called in yᵉ day and night dividing yᵉ same into 15 parts beginning at sun rising with yᵉ first spirit and so on till you come to yᵉ last spirit and last division of the night, these spirits are good by nature and willing to doe your will in all things. These be there names and seals &c.

[128r]

Armadiel his Seale.

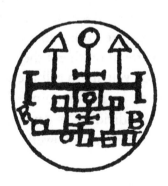

---

150 S1: "20."

151 S2: "Narzal, Marale."

152 H: "Mafrus / 79, Arafo 50, Richel 120 / Apiel 30, Curiel 40, Maliel 10 / Marianus 100, Nalaels 130, Narzal 201, Marahe 30." Note the invocation does not appear for this spirit.

153 See T1.15.

154 S2, H: "260"; S1: "'1260' other copy '260.'"

Fifteene of his dukes.

Nassar, Parabiel, Lariel, Calvarnia,[155] Orariel, Alferiel, Oryn, Samiel, Asmaiel, Jasziel, Pandiel, Carasiba, Asbibiel, Mafayr, Oemiel.[156]

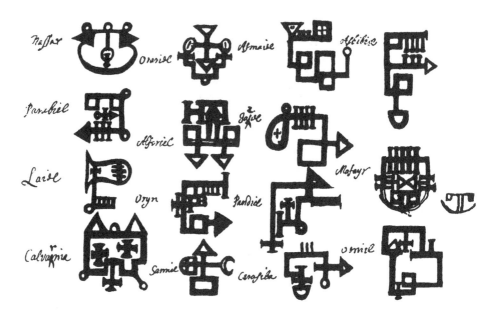

The Conjuration

I conjure thee o thou mighty and potent prince Armadiel &c.

[128v]

The 16th spirit in order, But the fourth under the Emperour of the North is called **Baruchas**[157]—who rulleth as [a] king in the East and by North and hath many Dukes and other several spirits to attend him whereof we shall make mention of 15 of the cheefe Dukes that belong to the day and night who have 7040 servants to attend on them: they are all by nature good and are willing to obey [you,] &c. you are to call these spirits in the same manner as Ishewed [is shewed] in ye foregoing Experiment [example] of Armadiel and his Dukes: vizt dividing ye day and night into 15 parts and &c. the names and seales of these as followeth—

---

155 S2: "Massak, Parabiel, Laiel, Catvarnia."

156 T: "Massar, Parabiel, Laiel, Caluarnya, Alferiel, Orariel, Oryn, Samiel, Asmael, Iaziel, Pandiel, Carasiba, Asbibiel, Mafayr, Oeniel"; H: "Massax, Parabiel / Laiel, Carasiba / Olniel, Calvarnia / Alfevil, Orariel / Candiel, Asbibiel / Samiel, Asmael / Joziel, Masayr / Caudiels"; S1: "Alferiel, Orariel, Orin, Samiel, Massar, Parabiel, Asmael, Iaziel, Pandiel, Carasiba, Laiel, Caluarnia, Asbibiel, Mafayr, Oeniel."

157 See T1.16.

Baruchas his Seale.

Fifteene of his dukes.
Quitta,[158] Sarael, Melchon, Cavayr,[159] Aboc,[160] Cartael, Janiel, Pharol, Baoxas, Geriel, Monael, Chuba [Chubor[161]], Lamael, Dorael,[162] Decaniel.[163]

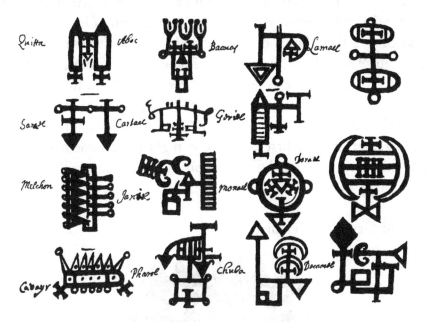

The Conjuration of Barachus

I conjure Thee o thou mighty and potent prince Barachus &c.[164]

---

158   T, H: "Quita"; S2: "Quinta"; S1: "'Quita', other Copy 'Quinta.'"

159   T, S1: "Couayr"; H: "Cavayx."

160   S2, H: "Aboce."

161   T, S1: "Chubor"; S2: "Chubar."

162   T1, S2, H, and S1 all read, "Dorael." Note, the seal of Cartael is badly drawn and crossed out in Sloane 3825. A replacement is drawn in the margin, but it is faint to the point of being almost unreadable. I supply the version from Harley MS 6483 instead.

163   H: "Lamaels, Cartael / Geriel, Dorael, Janæl / Monael, Pharol, Chubor / Decaniel."

164   S2 adds, "The End of the / Seales of the Pinces [sic] / and Dukes of the / four Empires."

[Here followeth the wandering dukes]

In this place we are to giue you the understanding of all of a [the] mighty[165] and potent princes with their servants wch wander up and down in ye Aire and never continue in one place, &c. whereof one of the Cheefe and first [of the wandering spirits] is called **Geradiel**,[166] who hath 18150 servants to attend him, for he hath no Dukes nor princes. Therefore he is to be Invocated alone, but when he is called there cometh a great number [many] of his servants with him, but more or less according to [with] the hour of ye day and hour or night he is called in, for in [the] 2 first hours of the day according to ye planatary motion, and the two second hour [sic] of the night there cometh 470 of his servants with him and in the 2 second hours of ye Day, and ye 2 third hours of ye night there cometh 590 of his servants with him and in ye 2 third hours of the day and ye 2 fourth hours of ye night there cometh 930 of his servants with him and in ye 2 fourth hours of ye day and ye 2 fifth hours of ye night there cometh 1560 of his servants &c and in ye 2 fifth hours of ye day and the 6th 2 hours of ye night there cometh 13710 of his servants and the 6th 2 or last 2 hours of y^e day there cometh 930 and In the 2 first houres of y^e night there cometh 1560 of his servants &c. they are all indifferent good by nature and will obey in all things willingly &c.

The Seal of Garadiel [Geradial].

The Conjuration of Garadiel [Geradiel]

I conjure thee o thou mighty and potent prince Garadiel [Geradiel] who wandereth hear and there in the Aire with thy servants I conjure the

[129r]

---

165 S2: "... understanding of all mighty."

166 See T1.21. The manuscript has "Geradiel" here, but "Garadiel" below. S1, S2, and H read "Geradiel" in both places.

Garadiel that thou forth with appeareth with thy attendance in this first hour of yᵉ Day here before me in this Crystall stone or here before this Circle &c.

The next of these wandring princes is called **Buriel**,[167] who hath many Dukes & other servants which doe attend on him to doo his will they are all by nature evill and are hated by all other spirits. They they [sic] appeare Rugish [roguish] and in the form of a serpent with a virgins head and speak with a mans voice: They are to be called in the night, because they hate the day and in the planetary houres, whereof wee shall mention 12 of the cheefe Dukes that answereth to the 12 planetary houres of the night who [each] have 880 servants to attend on them in the night amongst them their names and seales are as followeth with the name of Buriel.

[129v]

Buriel his Seale.

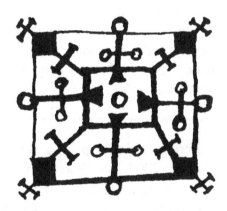

The 12 dukes are as followeth.
Merosiel,[168] Almadiel, Cupriel,[169] Sarviel, Casbriel, Nedriel, Bufiel, Futiel,[170] Drusiel, Carniel, Drubiel, Nastros.[171]

---

167 See T1.22.

168 S2: "Marosiel."

169 S2: "Eupriel."

170 S2: "Busiel, futid."

171 H: "Cupriel, Bufiel, Dribiel / Sarviel, Casbriel, Futiel / Merosiel, Almadiel, Nedriel / Drusiel, Carniel, Nastros"; S1: "Merosiel, Saruiel (corrected from Sarniel), Drusiel, Almadiel, Cupriel, Bufiiel, Casbriel, Nedriel, Futiel, Carniel, Drubiel, Nastros."

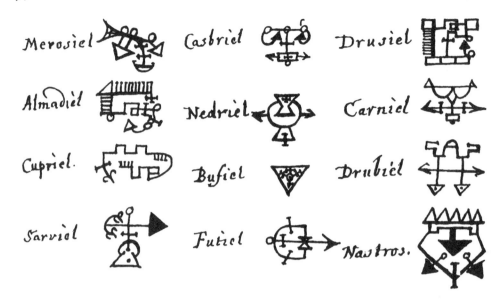

Merosiel   Casbriel   Drusiel

Almadiel   Nedriel   Carniel

Cupriel.   Bufiel   Drubiel

Sarviol   Futiel   Nastros.

The Conjuration

I conjure[172] Thee o thou mighty and potent prince Buriel who wandereth here and therre in the Aire with the [thy] Dukes and other thy Servient Spirits I conjure thee Buriel that thou fore with appeare with thy attendance in the first hour of ye night, here before me in this crystall stone (or here before this Circle) in a fair and comly shape to doe my will in all things that I shall desier of you &c:

[130r]   The third of these wandering spirits or princes is called **Hydriel**,[173] who hath 100 great Dukes besides 200 lesser Dukes and servants without number under him, whereof we shall mention 12 of the Cheefe Dukes which hath 1320 servants to attend them: They are to be called in ye Day as well as in ye night according to the planetary motion. The first beginneth with the first hour of ye day or night and so succesfully [successively] on till you come to the last, they [also] appeare in the forme of a serpent, with a virgins head and face: yet they are very courteous and willing to obey, they delight most in or about waters and all moist grounds. There names and Seales are as followeth:

---

172 S2 reads, "The Coniuration / I coniure thee O thou mighty Prince Buriel &c. / I coniure..."

173 See T1.23. S1: "Hidriel."

Hydriel[174] his Seale.

The 12 dukes are as followeth.

Mortaliel, Chamoriel, Pelariel, Musuziel, Lameniel, Barchiel, Samiel, Dusiriel, Camiel, Arbiel, Luciel, Chariel.[175]

The Conjuration

I conjure Thee o thou mighty and Potent prince Hydriel. &c.

---

174 S2 reads "Hidriel" here and in the conjuration below, but "Hÿdriel" above. S1 reads "Hidriel" throughout.

175 T: "Mortaliel, Chamoriel, Pesariel, Musuziel, Lemeniel, Brachiel, Samiel, Dusiriel, Camael, Arbiel, Lusiel, Chariel"; S2: "Mortaliel, Chamorid, Pesariel, Musuziel, Leminid, Brachiel, Samiel, Dusiriel, Camael, arbiel, Luciel, Chariel"; H: "Chamoriel, Pesariel, Mortaliel / Musiel, Lemeniel, Beachiel / Samiel, Dusiriel, Camael / Arbiel, Luciel, Chariel"; S1: "Mortaliel, Chamoriel, Pesariel, Musuziel, Laminiel, Brackiel, Samiel, Dusiriel, Camiel, Arbiel, Lusiel, Chariel."

[130v] The fourth[176] of these wandering princes in order is called **Pirichiel**,[177] He hath no princes nor Dukes under him But knights: whereof we shall mention 8 of them They being sufficient for practice who have 2000 servants under them, They are to be called according to y^e planetary motion. They are all good by nature, and will doe your will willingly. Theire Names and Seales are as followeth.

Pirichiel his Seale.

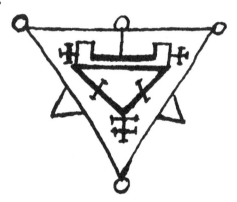

his eight Knights.
Damarsiel, Cardiel, Almasor, Nemariel, Menariel, Demediel, Hursiel, Cuprisiel.[178]

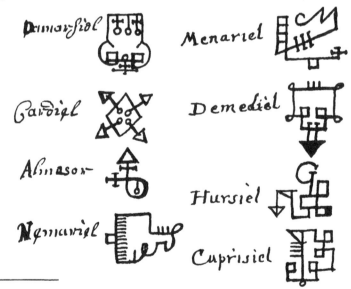

---

176   S2 adds, "spirit."

177   See T1.24. T and H read, "Pyrichiel"; S2 reads, "Pÿrichiel" throughout; S1 and S2 read, "Pirichiel."

178   S2: "… namariel, Merariel, Demediel, Hursiel, Cupriciel"; H: "Cardiel, Menariel Cupirsiel / Almator, Demediel, Darmarsiel / Nemariel, Husiel"; S1: "Damarsiel Cardiel, Almasor (with Almariel written above it), nemariel, Menaziel, Demediel Hursiel, Cuprisiel."

The Conjuration

I conjure Thee O thou mighty and potent prince Pirichiel; who wandreth
&c.

The 5th wandering prince is called **Emoniel**,[179] who hath a hundred
princes and cheef Dukes, besides 20 under [lesser] Dukes and a multitude of servants to attend him whereof wee shall mention 12 of the
cheef Princes or Dukes—who have 1320 Dukes & other Inferiour Servants to attend them They are all by nature good and willing to obey: it
is said they Inhabit most in the woods: they are to be called in the day
as well as in the Night, and according to ye Planetary order. Their names
and seales are as followeth,

[131r]

Emoniel his Seale.

His 12 dukes are as followeth.
Ermoniel, Edriel, Carnodiel, Phanuel, Dramiel, Pandiel, Vasenel, Nasiniel,
Cruhiel, Armesiel, Caspaniel,[180] Musiniel.[181]

---

179 See T1.25.

180 S2: "Caspaniet."

181 S2: "Ermoniel, Edriel, Carnodiel, Dramiel, Pandiel, Vasenel, Nasiniel, Cruhiel,
     Armesiel, Panuel, Caspaniet, Musiniel," and adds the note, "Panuel Seale shold
     haue ben placed third"; H: "Phamiel, Ermoniel, Edriel / Carnodiel, Dramiel,
     Pandiel / Nasiniel, Cruhiel, Armesiel / Caspaniel, Musiniel, Vasenel"; S1: "(1.
     Emoniel) 2 Ermoniel, 3 Panuel, 4 Edriel, 5 Carnodiel, 6 Dramiel, 7 Pandiel, 8
     Vasenel, 9 Nasinel, Cruhiel, Armisiel, Caspaniel, Musiniel." On folio 32r, S1
     gives another version: "Ermoniel, Cruhiel, Carnodiel, Dramiel, Pandiel, Vasenel,
     Nasiniel, Caspaniel, Panuel, Edriel, Musiniel. Panuel seal should have been placed
     third."

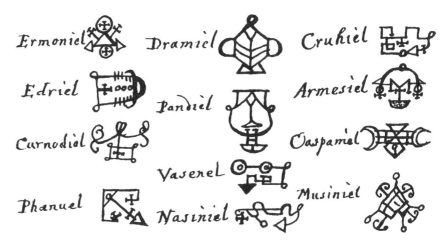

Ermoniel   Dramiel   Cruhiel
Edriel   Pandiel   Armesiel
Curnodiel   Oaspamiel
Vasenel
Phanuel   Nasiniel   Musiniel

The Conjuration

I conjure Thee o Thou mighty and Potent Prince Emoniel: who wandereth &c.

The sixth of these wandring princes is called **Icosiel**,[182] Who hath a 100
Dukes & 300 companions besides other servants which are more Inferiour
whereof we have taken 15 of yᵉ Cheefe Dukes for Practice they being sufficient, &c. they haue 2200 servants to attend them.[183] They are all of a
good nature and will doe what they are commanded. They appear most
commonly in houses because The [they] delight most therein. They are to
be called in the 24 houres of the day and night: That is to devide the 24
houres into fiveteen parts according to the number of the spirits, begining
with the first at Sunrise and with the last at Sun riseing next day &c. Their
names and Seales are as followeth.

[131v]

Icosiel his Seale.

182 See T1.26.
183 S1: "2000" both here and in an alternate version on fol. 32r.

His 15 dukes are as followeth.

Machariel, Pischiel [Psichiel], Thanatiel, Zosiel, Agapiel, Larphiel, Amediel, Cambriel, Nathriel, Zachariel, Athesiel, Cumariel, Munefiel, Heresiel, Urbaniel.[184]

The Conjuration

I conjure Thee O thou mighty and Potent Prince Icosiel, &c.

The 7th of these is called **Soleviel**,[185] who hath under his command 200   [132r]
Dukes, and 200 Companions who change every year their places, They have many servants to attend them They are all good and very obedient &c. here we shall mention 12 of the Cheefe Dukes whereof the first 6 are Dukes one year, and the other 6 the next following and so rulling in order to serve there prince. They have under them 1840 servants to attend on

---

184 T: "Machariel, Psichiel, Thanatiel, Zosiel, Agapiel, Larphiel, Amediel, Cambriel, Zachriel, Nathriel, Athesiel, Vrbaniel, Cumariel, Heresiel, Munefiel"; S2: "Machariel, Psichiel, Tanatiel, Zosiel, asapiel, Lerphiel, Amediel, / The ... (illeg) dukes followeth with thre [sic] names & Seales / Cambriel, Nathriel, Zachariel, Athesiel, Urbaniel, Cumariel, Heraciel, Munefiel"; H: "Zosiel, Cambriel, Machariel / Agapiel, Zachariel, Psichiel / Lerphiel, Nathriel / The Names and Seales of Icosiels seven / other Dukes / Thanaliel, Amediel, Athesiel / Vrbaniel, Cumariel, Heresiel / Munefield"; S1: "Machariel, Psichiel, Tlanatiel, Zosiel, Acapiel, Lerphiel, Amediel, Tianabriel, Zachriel, Nathriel, Athesiel, Vrbaniel, Cumariel, Heraciel, Munetiel," and in an alternate version on fol. 32r: "Machariel Tlanatiel Acapiel Psichiel Zosiel Lerphiel Amediel Tyanabriel Nathriel Vrbaniel Zachariel Athesiel Cumariel Heraciel Munetiel."

185 See T1.27. S1: "Soleriel."

them they are to be called in the day as well as in the night: according to the planetary hours or motion. Their names and seales are as followeth.

Soleviel his Seale.

his 12 dukes.
Inachiel, Praxeel, Moracha, Almodar, Nadrusiel, Cobusiel, Amriel, Axosiel, Charoel, Prasiel, Mursiel, Penador.[186]

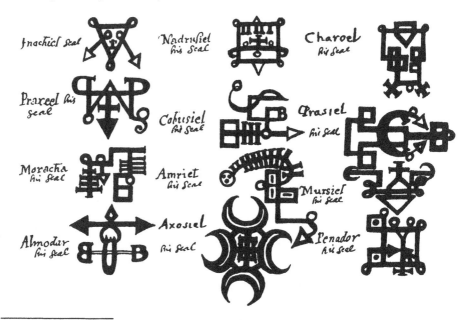

---

186 T: "Inachiel, Praxeel, Morucha, Almodar, Nadrusiel, Cobusiel, Amriel, Prasiel, Axosiel, Charoel, Mursiel, Penador"; H: "Maruchas, Amodar, Nadrusiel / Cobusiel, Inachiel, Amriel / Prasiel, Proxel, Axosiel / Charoel, Mursiel, Penador"; S2, S1: "Inachiel, Proxel, Marucha, Amodar, Nadiusiel, Cobusiel, Amriel / Amrel, Prasiel, axosiel, Caroel, Mursiel, Penader." Note that S1 and S2 label the seal of Amriel as though it were two seals, the "amriel seale" (the top half) and "Amrel his Seale" (the bottom half), which yields thirteen seals, even though the section is titled "the 12 dukes folloeth & ther seals." In an alternate version on fol. 32v, S1 gives, "4 Marucha Amriel Caroel 2 Inachiel Amodar Proxel." The seal for Proxel was never rendered and the manuscript breaks off at this point.

The Conjuration

I conjure Thee O thou mighty and Potent Prince Soleviel who wandereth &c.

The eighth of those wandering princes is called **Menadiel**,[187] who hath 20 Dukes & 100 companions and many other servants. They being all of a good nature and very obedient. here wee have mentioned 6 of the cheefe Dukes and 6 of ye under [lesser] Dukes or companions, they haue 390 servants to attend them: Note you must call these according to ye planetary motion [with] a Duke in ye first hour and a companion in the next [hour] and so succesfully [sucessively] on through all the houres of ye day or night. whose names and seales are as followeth:

[132v]

Menadiel his seale.

his 12 dukes.

The 6 cheife dukes.
Larmol, Drasiel,[188] Clamor,[189] Benodiel, Charsiel, Samyel.[190]

The 6 under dukes.
Barchiel, Amasiel,[191] Baruch, Nedriel, Curasin,[192] Tharson.[193]

---

187 See T1.28.
188 T: "Drassiel"; S2: "Brafsiel"; S1: "Brassiel."
189 S1: "Chamor."
190 S1: "Samiel"; H: "Clamor, Samÿel, Larmol / Drassiel, Benodiel, Charsiel."
191 S1: "Armasiel."
192 T: "Curasyn"; S2, S1: "Curaÿn."
193 H: "Nedriel, Barchiel, Baruch / Amasiel, Curaÿn, Tharson."

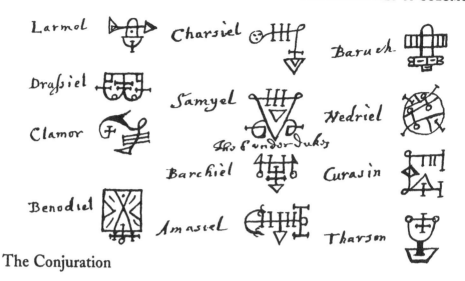

Larmol   Charsiel   Baruch

Drassiel   Samyel   Nedriel

Clamor   The 6 under Dukes

Barchiel   Curasin

Benodiel   Amasiel   Tharson

The Conjuration

I conjure thee O thou mighty and potent Prince Menadiel, who wand:

[133r] The 9th spirit in order that wandereth is called **Macariel**,[194] who hath 40 Dukes besides a very many other Inferiour Servants to attend on him, whereof wee shall mention 12 of the Cheefe Dukes who have 400 servants to attend them.[195] They are all good by nature & obedient to doe yᵉ will of yᵉ Exorcist. They appear in divers formes but most commonly in yᵉ forme of a dragon with virgins heads: These Dukes are to be called in the day as well as night according to yᵉ planetary order. Their names and seales are as followeth.

Macariel his Seale.

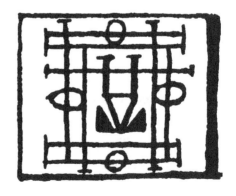

---

his 12 dukes.

Claniel, Drusiel, Andros, Charoel, Asmadiel, Romyel, Mastuel,[196] Varpiel, Gremiel, Thuriel, Brufiel, Lemodac.[197]

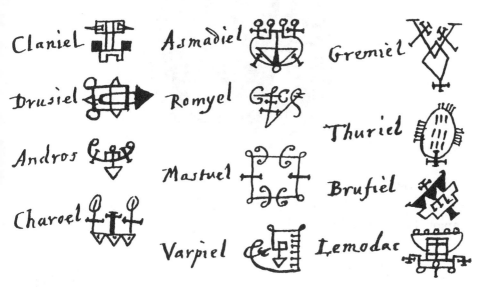

The Conjuration

I conjure Thee O thou mighty and potent prince Macariel (who wandereth &c.

[133v]

The 10th spirit in order that wandereth or great prince is called Uriel,[198] who hath 10 cheef Dukes and 100 under [lesser] Dukes with many servants to attend him. They are by nature Evill and will not obey willingly and are very false in their doings. They appear in the form of a serpent with a virgins head and a face: whereof we shall mention but ye 10 cheefe Dukes who haue 650 Companions & servants to attend them &c There names and seales are as followeth—

---

196 T: "Nastuel."

197 S2: "Chaniel, Drusiel, Andros, Caroel, Amadiel, Remÿel, naustuel, Verpiel, Gerniel, Thirciel, Burfiel, Albenusÿ"; H: "Asmadiel, Varpil, Brusiel / Claniel, Andros, Romÿel / Gremiel, Aldrusÿs, Drusiel / Charoel, Nastuel, Thuriel"; S1: "Chaniel, Drusiel, Andros, Caroel, Amadiel, Remÿel, Naustuel, Verpiel, Germel, Thirsiel, Burfiel, Aromusÿ."

198 See T1.30.

Uriel his Seale.

His 10 Dukes:

Chabri, Drabros,[199] Narmiel, Frasmiel, Brymiel,[200] Dragon, Curmas, Drapios, Hermon, Aldrusy.[201]

The Conjuration

I conjure thee O Thou mighty and potent prince Uriel, who wandereth &c.

---

199 T: "Drabos."

200 T: "Byrmiel."

201 S2, S1: "Chabri, Darbos, Narmiel, Frasmiel, Brymiel, Dragon, Curmis, Darpios, Hermon, Adrnsis." In S2 the latter name might also be, "Adrnsÿ"; H: "Chabris, Darbo, Dragon / Hermon, Brimiel, Drapias / Narmiel, Frasmiel, Curmas / Aldrusÿ."

The 11th and last prince of this wandering order is called Bidiel[202] who hath under his command 20 Dukes and 200 other Dukes wch are more Inferiour, besides very many servants to attend him. These Dukes change every year their office and place. They are all good and willing to obey the Exorcist in all things &c They appear very Beautifull and in a humane shape whereof wee shall mention 10 of ye Cheefe Dukes who have 2400 servants to attend them, their Names and Seales are:

[134r]

Bidiel his Seale.

his 10 great dukes.
Mudirel, Cruchan, Bramsiel, Armoniel, Lameniel, Andruchiel, Merasiel, Charobiel, Parsifiel, Chremoas.[203]

---

202 See T1.31. T reads, "Bydiel"; S2 reads, "Bÿdiel" here and in the seal below, but "Bidiel" in the conjuration. S1 reads, "Bÿdiel" in all three places.

203 T: "... Lameniel, Charobiel, Andrucha, Merasiel, Parsifiel, Chremoas"; S2: "... Lemeniel, Charobiel, Andrucha, Manasael, Persifiel, Chremo"; H: "... Lemeniel, Charobiel / Mevasael, Parsifiel, Andruchas / Chremoas"; S1: "Mudriel, Chrucham, Bramsiel, Armoniel, Lemeniel, Charobiel, Andrucha, Manasael, Persifiel, Chremo."

The Conjuration to the wandring Princes

I conjure Thé o Thou mighty and potent prince Bidiel, who wandereth hear and there in the aire with thy Dukes and other of thy Servants spirits, I conjure Thee Bidiel that thou forthwith come and appeare with attendance in this first hour of yᵉ day here before me in this Cristall stone (or here before this Circle) in a fair and comly shape to do my will in all things that I shall desier of you &c. *[& note this marke * in the conjuration following & go on there as it followeth there204]

[134v]

The Conjuration to the princes that Govern the points of the compass:

I conjure thee o thou mighty and potent prince N. who ruleth as a cheefe prince or king in the dominion of the East (or &c) I conjure thee N205 that thou fortwith appeareth with Thy attendance in this first hour of yᵉ day here before me in this cristall stone (or hear before this Circle in a fair and comely shape to doe my will in all things that I shall desier of you &c *)

[The Conjuration to the 4 Empires [Emperors]206

I coniure thee o thou great & mighty & potente prince Carnasiel207 who is the Empire [Emperor & Cheif King208] ruling in the dominion of the East I coniure thee Carnatiel [sic] that thou forth with appear, & obserue this marke △ and go on ther in the folling coniureation &c.]

To the Dukes that wander209

I conjure thee O thou mighty and potent duke N. who wandereth hear and there [in the aire] with thy Prince N. and others of his & Thy servants in yᵉ Aire. I conjure Thee N. that thou forwith [forthwith] appeareth &c. △

---

204 S2, S1, and H.

205 S1: "I conjure thee o thou mighty & Potent Prince Pamersiel who Rulest as King in the dominion of the East under the great Emperor Carnatiel I conjure thee Pamersiel..."

206 This section is in S2, S1, and H. H puts "The Conjuration to the 4ᵗʰ Empire" after the conjuration, "I conjure thee O thou great Mighty & potent Prince Carnasiel..." etc.

207 S1: "Carnatiel."

208 S1.

209 S2 and S1 add, "To the wandering dukes how to call them forth or any other dukes that doth not wander only leaueing out 'wandering here & ther' and only for 'prince' say 'duke.'"

To the Dukes that governeth the Point of the Compasse with their Prince.

I conjure Thee O thou mighty and Potent Duke N. who ruleth under thy prince or king N. in the dominion of the East (or &c) I conjure thee N. that thou forthwith appeareth △, allone (or with [thy[210]] servants) [of the air] in this first (or second) houre of the day, here before me in this cristal stone (or here before this circle) in a fair and comely shape, to doe my will in all things that I shall desire or request of you *. I conjure and powerfully command of you N. By him who said the word and it was done: and by all the holy and powerfull names of god and by the name of the only creator of heaven, Earth, and hell and what is contained in them **Adonay, El, Elohim, Elohe, Elion, Escerchie** [Escherie[211]], **Zebaoth, Jah, Tetragrammaton, Saday.** The only lord god of the hosts, That you forthwith appearth unto me here in this Cristall stone (or here before this circle) in a fair and comely humane shape: without doeing any harme to me or any other creature that god **Jehovah** created or made; But come ye peacibly, vissibly and affably, now without delay manifesting what I desiere, being conjured by the name of yᵉ Eternall Liveing and true god: **Helioren, Tetragrammaton, Anephexeton** [Anepheneton[212]], and fulfill my commands and persist unto the end; I conjure command and constraine you spirit N. by **Alpha and Omega**. By the name **Primeumaton,** which commandeth the whole host of heaven and by all those names which Moses named when he by the power of those names brought great plagues upon Pharao [Pharoah], and all the people of Ægypt. **Zebaoth, Escerchie, Oriston, Elion, Adonay, Primeumaton** and by the name of **Schemes. Amathia,**[213] with [which] Joshua called upon and the sun stayed his course, and by the name of **Hagios,** and by the **Seal of Adonay** and by **Agla, On,**[214] **Tetragrammaton.** To whome all creatures are obedient and by the dreadfull Judgement of the high god and by the holly angells of heaven and by the mighty wisdome of the great god of hosts That you come from all Parts of yᵉ world and make rational answers unto all things I shall aske ~~thee~~ of you, and come you peaceable vissible and affable speaking unto me with a voyce Intelligible and to my understanding Therefore come, come yee in the name of **Adonay, Zebaoth, Adonay, Amioram,**[215] Come, why stay you, hasten. **Adonay, Saday** the king of kings commandeth you.

[135r]

---

210 S1.

211 S1: "Escerchis."

212 S2, S1, H.

213 S1: "Schemeta Mathia."

214 S1: "Aglaon."

215 S1: "Aamioram."

When he is appeared shew him his seal,[216] and the Pentacle of Salomon, saying [as follows:]

[The Address unto the Spirit upon his coming]

Behold the Pentacle of Salomon which I have brought before your presence &c

as is shewed in the first Booke *Goëtia*, at the latter end of the conjurations: allso when you haue had ye desier of the Spirits: licence them to depart as is shewed there &c.

And so ends the second Book
called Theurgia Goetia

Note The above written conjurations doe onely differ in the first part as is shewed there untill you come to these markers Δ and *. But from thence forward they are to be all one and ye same.

Nota, wheresoever in this Booke *Theurgia Goetia* in some parts of the Seales I haue used these fine strokes ///////. That part of the seal is to be all black which I did not doe because this paper is to course and thine &c.[217]

---

216 S2, S1, H: "shew him the seale."

217 These notes are only found in S3.

The Art Pauline of   [135r]
King Salomon

This [book] is divided into two parts, the first containing [dealing with] the Angells of the hours of the day and night: The second part [with] the Angells of yᵉ signs of the Zodiac as hereafter followeth &c.[1]

    The Nature of these 24 [four and twenty] Angells of the day and night changeth every day: and their offices is to doe all things that are attributed to the 7 planetts. But that changeth every day also: as for example you may see in the following Treatise That Samuel[2] The Angell rulleth the first houre   [135v] of the day beginnig [sic] at Sunn Rising, supose it be on a munday in the first hour of yᵉ day (that houre is attributed to the ☽) That you call Samuel or any of his Dukes; There offices in that houre is to doe doe all things that are attributted to the ☽. But if you call him or any of his Servient Dukes on Tuesday Morning at Sunn Riseing: being the first hour of the day: Their offices are to doe all things that are attributed to ♂, and so the like is to be observed in the first houre of every day: and the like is to be observed of the Angells and their servants that Rule any of the other hours: either in the day or night: allso againe there is an observation to be observed in makeing the Seales of these 24 Angells according to the time of the years Day and hour that you call the Angells or his servants in to doe your your [sic] will: But you cannot mise [miss] therein if you doe well observe the Example That is laid down in the following worke: They being all fitted for

---

1   S2: "The King (this deuides into to partes the first) parte the angels of the hours of the day and night the angels of the signes of Zodiack as hereafter folloeth &c."; S1: "Here beginneth ye Book called the Art Pauline of solomon the King & this is divided into two parts the first the Angels of the hours of the Day & Night The Second the Angels of the Signs of the Zodiak as hereafter followeth."

2   S1 reads, "Samael" here and below.

the 10th day of March Being one [on] a wednesday in the year 1641 according to the old account[3] &c and as for to know what is attributed to the planetts, I doe referr you to the books of Astrology whereof large volumes have been written. &c.[4]

[Concerning the chief spirits of the hours, and their servants and seals.]

[Of the hours of the day.]

The first houre of any Day is ruled by an [the] angel called **Samuel** [Samael],[5] who hath under his command many Dukes and servants: wherof whe shall mention 8 of the cheefe Dukes which is sufficient for practice: who have 444 servants [apiece] to attend them. Theire Names are as Followeth: **Ameniel, Charpon,[6] Darosiel, Monasiel, Brumiel, Nestoriel, Chremas, Meresyn.** Now for to fitt or make a seal for any of these 8 Dukes or the cheefe prince Samuel doe as followeth—first write the Character of yᵉ lord of the ascendent secondly the ☽ afterwards the Rest of the planets, and after then the characters of yᵉ signe that ascendeth on the 12 house in that hour that is shewed in this sigill which is fitted for the 10th Day of March in the year 1641 being on a wednesday in the first house &c:[7]

---

3   In other words using the Julian calendar. The Gregorian calendar was adopted throughout Europe in 1582, but not in England until 1752. Many documents of the time carry both dates, or, as in this case, specified which calendar they were following.

4   The subsequent instructions are confused by the fact that they are scattered throughout the text. S1 rearranges things a little here. It starts with "When the seal is made according to the former [sic] Directions Lay it on the table of Practice upon that part of the table that it Notes with the Character that the Lord of the Ascendant is off then Lay your hand on the Said seal & say the Conjuration that is at the latter end of this third part for it serveth for all only changing the Names according to the Time you work." This is followed by the "Table of Practise" drawing, then "The Perfumes is to be made of such Things as is attributed to the 7 Planets &c. / Note Mars is lord of the Ascendant every first hour of the Day whilst the sun goes through Aries & Scorpio so is Venus Lady of the Ascendant every first hour whilst the Sun goes through Taurus & Libra so the like of the Rest. / The 24 hours of the day & night / The first houre. . . ." Note that the wording "the former Directions" makes it clear that this is not the original order.

5   See T2.1. T, H, and S1 all read "Samael."

6   H: "Charpen."

7   S1: "... Wednesday & the first hour of the Day."

This seal being thus made lay it on the Table of practice, Lay your hand on it and say The Conjuration that is written at the latter end of this first part for it serveth for all onely the names are to be changed according to the time you work in &c.

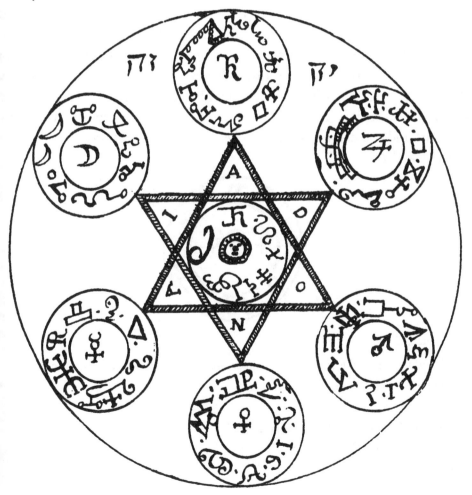

Figure 9. The Table of Practice

Nota[8] lay the seal on the Table or that of the table that is notted wth that charecter [sic] as lord of the ascendent is of, as ♂ is lord of the ascendent in the above said seal therefore it is to be laid upon the characters of ♂ in the table of practice: &c: doo the like with all other seales &c.

The perfumes are to be made of such things as are attributed to the same planetts &c.

The second hour of the day is called **Cevorym,**[9] The Angell that governeth that hour is calld **Anael,** who hath 10 cheefe Dukes[10] and 100 lesser Dukes[11] to attend him whereof we shall mentione 9: But the thre first are of ye cheefe [greater], and the other 6 of the under [lesser] Dukes. They haue 330 [of their own] Servants [apiece] to attend them. Those 9 [in order] are as followeth vizt: **Menarchos,**[12] **Archiel,**[13] **Chardiel,**[14] **Orphiel, Cursiel, Elmoym, Quosiel, Ermaziel,**[15] **Granyel.** When you haue a desier to worke in the second hour of wednesday on the 10th day of March make a seal as followeth on any clean paper or parchment writting first the characters of ye Lord of the ascendent—Then the Rest of the Planetts, and the signe of ye 12th house as you may see in this following sigill and when it is made lay it upon the part of y^e table as is noted with the same charrecter as the lord of the ascendent is. Observe this same rule in all the following part of this first part and you can not Eare &c Then say the conjuration as is written at y^e latter end &c.

---

8   S2 adds, "when the seales [sic] is made according to the former directions,..."
9   See T2.2. S2, S1, H: "Sevormi."
10   H: "70."
11   S2 and S1 omit, "and 100 lesser dukes."
12   S1: "Menerchos."
13   S1: "Sarchiel."
14   S2, S1: "Cardiel."
15   S2, S1: "Ermoziel"; H: "Ermosiel."

The 3d hour of any day is called **Dansor,**[16] and the Angell that rulleth that hour is called **Vequaniel,**[17] who hath 20 cheefe Dukes and 200 lesser Dukes, and a great many other servants to attend him, whereof wee shall mention 4 of the cheefe Dukes and eight of the lesser [Dukes] who hath 1760 servants to attend them there names are as followeth vizt **Asmiel,**[18] **Persiel, Mursiel, Zoesiel;**[19] and **Drelmech, Sadiniel,**[20] **Parniel, Comadiel, Gemary, Xantiel,**[21] **Serviel, Furiel.**[22] These being sufficient for practice. Make a seal sutabble to the day hour and year as this is for the time before mentioned and you cannot Erre, then say the Conjuration.

The 4th hour of any day is called **Elechym,**[23] and the Angell thereof is called **Vathmiel,**[24] who hath 10 cheefe Dukes and 100 under [lesser] Dukes, besides many servants whereof wee shall mention 5 of the cheefe and 10 of the under [lesser] Dukes; who have 1550 servants to attend them.[25] Their names are as followeth: viz **Armmyel,**[26] **Larmich, Marfiel, Ormyel, Zardiel, Emarfiel, Permiel, Queriel, Strubiel, Diviel, Jermiel, Thuros [Thuroz**[27]**],**

---

16 See T2.3. T: "Danzur."

17 H: "Vegvaniel."

18 S2, S1: "Ansmiel."

19 S2, S1: "Zoetiel."

20 S1: "Sadimel."

21 S1: "Xautiel."

22 H: "Lossiel, Drelmech, Sadmiel, Parniel, Comadiel, Gemarÿ, Xautiel, Serviel, Furtiel, Ansmiel, Persiel, Mursiel."

23 See T2.4. S1, H: "Elechin."

24 S1, H: "Vachmiel."

25 H: "155."

26 T: "Ammyel."

27 T: "Thuroz."

Vanesiel, Zasviel, Hermiel.[28] These being sufficient for practice. Make a seal suitable to this hour as is before directed and you can not erre: the form [of] it will be as this is heare, for the time aforsaide, &c when it is made: doe as before directed: and say The conjuration:

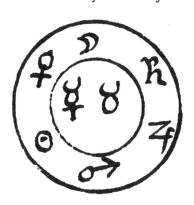

[137r]

The 5th hour of every day is called **Fealech** [Tealech[29]], and the angel thereof is called **Sasquiel**. He hath 10 Dukes cheefe, and 100 lesser Dukes and very many servants whereof wee shall mention 5 of the cheefe Dukes and 10 of y[e] the lesser [Dukes] who have 5550 servants to attend [on] them whose names are as followeth, viz[t]: **Damiel, Araniel, Maroch, Saraphiel, Putisiel; Jameriel, Futiniel,[30] Rameriel, Amisiel, Uraniel, Omerach, Lameros, Zachiel, Fustiel, Camiel,[31]** These being sufficient for ^to practice: then make a seal suetable for the time as I here giue you an Example of for the day before spoken of in the year 1641 and when you haue made it lay it upon the Table as you was before shewed and say the conjuration:

---

28   S2: "Armmyel, Larmiel, Marfiel, Ormÿel, Zardiel, Emerfiel, Permiel, Queriel, Serubjel, Daniel, Jermiel, Thuzoz, Vanesiel, Zasuiel, Harmiel"; S1: "Ammiel, Larmiel, Marfiel, ormÿel, Zardiel, Emerfiel, Permiel, Queriel, Serubiel, Daniel, Jermiel, Thuzez, Vanesiel, Zasviel, Harmiel"; H: "Armmiel, Larmiel, Marfiel, Ormiel, Zardiel, Emarfiel, Permiel, Queriel, Strubiel, Daniel, Jermiel, Thuzoz, Vanesiel, Lasaiel, Harmiel."

29   S2, S1: "Tealeach"; H: "Tealech."

30   T: "Maroch, Sarapiel, Putifiel."

31   S2: "Damiel, Aramiel, Maroch, Sarapiel, Putrsiel; Jameriel, Futuniel, Rameziel, Amisiel, [Uraniel,] Omerach, Lameros, Zathiel, Fustiel, Bariel"; S1: "Damiel, Aramiel, Maroch, Serapiel, Putrsiel; Jameriel, Futuniel, Ramesiel, Amisiel, [Uraniel,] Omezach, Lameros, Zathiel, Fustiel, Bariel"; H: "Damiel, Aramiel, Maroch, Sarapiel, Putrsiel; Jameriel, Futiniel, Ramesiel, Amisiel, [Uraniel,] Omezach, Lameros, Zathiel, Fustiel, Bariel."

The 6th houre of the day is called **Genapherim**,[32] and the Angell rulling that houre is called **Saniel**,[33] who hath 10 cheefe Dukes and 100 lesser Dukes besides many other Inferiour servants whereof wee shall mention 5 of the cheefe and 10 of the lesser [Dukes] who have 5550 servants to attend them: whose names are as followeth vizt: **Arnebiel, Charuch, Medusiel, Nathmiel, Pemiel, Gamyel, Jenotriel, Sameon, Trasiel, Xamyon, Nedabor,**[34] **Permon, Brasiel, Camosiel, Evadar.**[35] They being sufficient for practice in this houre of the day. Then make a seal sutable to the time of the day year and hour as here is made one for the time aforesaid Then lay it on the Table as you was before directed and you cannot erre. Then say the conjuration &c.

The 7th houre of the day is called **Hamarym**,[36] and the Angell that governeth the same is called **Barquiel**,[37] who hath 10 cheefe dukes and a 100 under [lesser] Dukes besides servants which are very many whereof wee shall mention 5 of the cheefe Dukes and 10 of the lesser who have 600 servants which attend them in this hour: whose names are as followeth viz: **Abrasiel, Farmos, Nestorii, Manuel, Sagiel, Harmiel, Nastrus, Varmay, Tulmas,**

[137v]

---

32 See T2.6. T: "Genapherym"; S2, S1: "Genphorim."

33 S1, H: "Samiel."

34 T: "Nedabar."

35 S2, H: "Arnebiel, Charuch, Medusiel, Nathniel, Pemiel, Jamiel, Jenotriel, Sameon, Trasiel [H: Frasiel], Zamion, Nedaber, Permon, Brasiel, Camosiel, Enadar"; S1: "... Nathniel, Jamiel, Jenotriel, Sameon, Trasiel, Zamion, Nedaber, Permon, Brasiel, Comosiel, Enader."

36 See T2.7. S2, S1, H: "Hemarim."

37 H, S1: "Bargniel."

Crosiel, Pasriel, Venesiel, Evarym, Drufiel, Kathos.[38] They being sufficient for practice in this houre &c. Then make a seal here I giue you an Example Then lay on the Table as you was directed before & haveing all things in readines say the conjuration, &c.

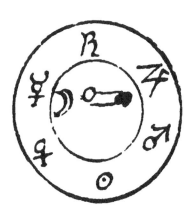

The 8th hour of every day is called **Jafanym,**[39] and the angell [that] governeth the same is called **Osmadiel,** who hath a 100 cheefe Dukes[40] and 100 lesser Dukes besides very many other servants whereof wee shall mention 5 of the cheefe Dukes and 10 of the lesser who have 1100 servants to attend them—They being sufficient for Practice: There names are as followeth viz[t]: **Sarfiel, Amalym, Chroel, Mesial, Lantrhots,**[41] **Demarot, Janofiel, Larfuty, Vemael, Thribiel, Mariel, Remasyn, Theoriel, Framion, Ermiel**[42] &c. Then make a seal for this 8th houre as is shewed by this seal which is made for an example—then lay it on the table: and say the conjuration following &c.

---

38   S2: "Abrasiel, Fermos, Nestori, Mamiel, Sagiel, Harmiel, Naustrus, Varmaÿ, Tusmas, Crosiel, Pastiel, Venesiel, Evarim, Dusiel, Kathos"; S1: "Abrasiel, Fermos, Nestori, Mamiel, Sagiel, Harmiel, Naustrus, Varmaÿ, Tusmas, Crosiel, Pastiel, Venesiel, Enarim, Dusiel, Kathos"; H: "Abrasul, Farmos, Nostori, Mamiel, Sagiel, Harmiel, Nastrus, Varmaÿ, Tusmas, Crosiel, Pastiel, Venesiel, Evarim, Dusiel, Kathos."

39   Cf. T2.8. S2: "Jasamin"; S1: "Jesamin"; H: "Jefamin."

40   T, H, S1, and S2.

41   T: "Lantrhotz."

42   S2, S1: "Serfiel, Amatim, Chroel, Mesiel, Lantrhes, Demaros, Janosiel, Larfuti, Vemael, Thribiel, Mariel, Remasin, Theoriel, Framion, Ermiel"; H: "Sarfiel, Amatim, Chroel, Mesiel, Lantrhos, Demaros, Janosiel, Larfuti, Vemael, Thribiel, Mariel, Remafin, Theor, Framion, Ermiel."

The 9th hour of every day is called **Karron**,[43] and the Angell rulling it is called **Quabriel**[44] who hath many Dukes, 66 of yᵉ greater and lesser order: besides many other servants: which are more Inferiour whereof 10 of the greater and 100 of the lesser Dukes have 192980 servants in 10 orders to obey and serve them whereof we shall mention the names of five great [greater] Dukes and 10 [of the] lesser Dukes who have 650 cheefe servants to attend on them in this houre they being sufficient for practice: These be their names: vizᵗ: **Astroniel, Charmy, Pamory, Damyel, Nadriel, Kranos, Menas, Brasiel, Nefarym, Zoymiel, Trubas, Xermiel, Lameson, Zasnor,**[45] **Janediel,**[46] and when you haue a desier to make an experiment in this house make a seal as you was tought before the forme of this is for an example and when it is made lay it on the Table as you was directed before Then say the Conjuration: &c.

---

43 See T2.9. S2, S1: "Carron."

44 H: "Vadriel."

45 T: "Zaznor."

46 S2: "Astroniel, Charnis, Pamorÿ, Damiel, Madriel, Kromos, Menos, Brasiel, Nesarin, Zoÿmiel, Trubas, Zarmiel, Lameson, Zasnoz, Janediel"; S1: "Astroniel, Charnis, Pamorÿ, Damiel, Madriel, Chromos, Menos, Brasiel, Nesarin, Zoÿmiel, Trubas, Zarmiel, Lameson, Zasnoz, Janediel"; H: "Astroniel, Charmis, Pamorÿ, Damiel, Nadriel, Kromos, Menos, Brasiel, Nefarin, Zoÿmiel, Trubas, Zarmiel, Lameson, Zasnoz, Janediel."

The 10th hour of every Day is called **Lamarhon**[47] and the angell rulling it is called **Oriel** who hath many Dukes and servants divided into 10 orders which contain 5600 spirits whereof wee shall mention 5 of the cheef Dukes & 10 of the next lesser Dukes who hath 1100 servants to attend on them. They being sufficient for practice. Their names are as followeth vizt **Armosy, Drabiel, Penaly, Mesriel, Choreb, Lemur, Ormas, Charny, Zazyor, Naveron, Xantros, Basilon, Nameron, Kranoti, Alfrael,**[48] and when you have a desier to practice in this houre make a seal sutable to the time: as this hear is made for the 10th hour on wednesday the 10th of march in the year 1641 it being for an examble [sic] and when it is made lay it on the Table of practice: and say the conjuration &c.

[138r]

The 11th hour in every day is called **Maneloym,**[49] and the angel governing that hour is called **Bariel,** who hath many Dukes and servants which are divided into 10 parts which contain y^e number of 5600 whereof wee shall mention 5 of the Dukes of the first order and 10 lesser Dukes of the second order, who have 1100 servants to attend them, They being sufficient for practice. Their names are as followeth vizt: **Almarizel, Prasiniel, Chadros, Turmiel, Lamiel, Menafiel, Demasor, Omary, Helmas, Zemoel, Almas, Perman, Comial, Temas, Lanifiel,**[50] and when you would practice make a seal sutable to ye time of the day: as I shew you here by an Example: and when it is made lay it on the Table of practice: and say the Conjuration &c.

---

47 See T2.10. S2, S1, and H: "Lamathon."

48 S1, S2: "Armasi, Darbiel, Penaly, Mefriel, Choreb, Lemur, Ormas [S1: Oymas], Charnÿ, Zazior, Naveron, Zantros, Busiton, Nameron, Krunoti, Alfrael"; H: "Armesi, Drabiel, Penaly, Mesriel, Choreb, Lemur, Ormas, Charnÿ, Zazior, Naveron, Zentros, Busiton, Nameron, Kruneli, Alfrael."

49 See T2.11. S2, S1, H: "Manelohim."

50 S2: "Almarizel, Prasiniel, Chadros, Turmiel, Lamiel, Menafiel, Demasor, Omary, Helmas, Zemoel, Almas, Perman, Comial, Temas, Lanifiel"; S1: "Almarizel, Parlimiel, Chadros, Turmiel, Lamiel, Menafiel, Demasor, Omary, Hehuas, Zemoel, Ahuas, Perman, Comial, Temas, Lanifiel"; H: "Almerizel, Pralimiel, Chadros, Turmiel, Lamiel, Menafiel, Demasar, Omarÿ, Hehuas, Zemoel, Ahuas, Perman, Lomiel, Temal, Lanifiel."

The 12th hour of every day is called **Nahalon**,[51] and the Angell governing that hour is called **Beratiel**,[52] who hath many Dukes and other servants which are divided into 12 degrees the which containe the number of 3700 spirits in all whereof wee shall mention 5 of the cheefe Dukes and 10 of the lesser Dukes: who have 1100 servants to attend them, they being sufficient for practice. Their names are as followeth: viz[t]: **Camaron, Astrofiel, Penatiel, Demarac, Famaras, Plamiel, Nerastiel, Fimarson,[53] Quirix, Sameron, Edriel, Choriel, Romiel, Fenosiel, Harmary [Hamary[54]]**, and when you have a desier to worke in this hour make a seal sutable to the time as I have here for the same hour But the 10th of march in y[e] year 1641. When you have thus made it lay it on the Table of practice and lay your hand on it. and say the conjuration &c.

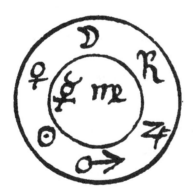

51 See T2.12. T reads, "Naybalon" in the chapter title, but "Nahalon" in the first paragraph.

52 H: "Beraliel."

53 T: "Nerostiel, Emarson."

54 T: "Hamary"; S2: "Camaron, Altrafrel, Penatiel, Demarec, Famaris, Pamiel, Nerostiel, Emarson, Vuirix, Sameron, Edriel, Choriol, Romiel, Tenostiel, Hamarÿ"; S1: "Camaron, Altrafrel, Penatiel, Demarec, Famaris, Pamiel, Nerostiel, Emarson, Uvirix, Sameron, Edriel, Chorion, Romiel, Tenostiel, Uamarÿ"; H: "Camaron, Astrafzel, Penaliel, Demarac, Farmaris, Plamiel, Nerostiel, Emarson, Uvirix, Sameron, Edriel, Choriel, Romiel, Fenosiel, Harmarÿ."

[Of the hours of the night.]

[138v]

The first hour of every night is called **Omalharien**,[55] and the Angell ruling it is called **Sabrathan**[56] who hath 1540 Dukes and other servants: which are divided into 10 orders or parts, whereof wee shall mention 5 of the cheefe Dukes and 10 of the lesser Dukes: which are next to the 5 first: They being sufficient for practice in this houre. Their names are as followeth viz: **Domaras [Domaros**[57]**], Amerany, Penoles, Mardiel, Nastul, Ramesiel, Omedriel, Franedac, Chrasiel, Dormason,**[58] **Hayzoym, Emalon, Turtiel, Quenol, Rymaliel.**[59] They have 2000 servants[60] to attend them and when you would worke in this houre make a seal sutable to the time as this is for an Example Then lay the seal on the Table of practice: and you cannot erre: saying the conjuration &c.

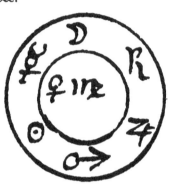

The 2ᵈ hour of ~~the~~ every night is called **Panezur**,[61] and the Angell rulling it is called **Tartys**,[62] who hath 101550 to attend him they being divided into 12 degrees or orders whereof wee shall mention 6 of the cheefe Dukes

---

55   See T2.13. S2: "Omalhauien"; S1: "Omalhavien"; H: "Omalhaveon."

56   S2, H: "Sabrachan"; S1: "Sabrachon."

57   T, S1, H.

58   T: "Dornason."

59   S2: "Domarof, Amerany, Penoles, Merdiel, Nastul, Ramasiel, Omedriel, Franedac, Charsiel, Dornason, Hayzoim, Emalon, Turtiel, Uvenel, Rimaliel"; S1: "Domaros, Amerany, Penoles, Merdiel, Nastul, Ramasiel, Omedriel, Frandedac, Charsiel, Darnason, Hayzoim, Enalon, Turtiel, Uvenel, Rimaliel"; H: "... whereof we shall mention five of the cheife Dukes, and ~~ten~~ ^ three of the lesser ... vizt. Domaros, Ameravy, Penoles, Hayͤzoim, Enalon, Furtiel, Uvenel, Rimaliel."

60   S1: "200."

61   See T2.14. S2, S1, H: "penazur."

62   S2, S1: "Taktis"; H: "Taklis."

of the first order & 12 of the next: They being sufficient for practice: Their names are as followeth viz **Almodar, Famoriel, Nedroz, Ormezyn, Chabriz, Praxiel, Permaz, Vameroz, Emaryel,**[63] **Fromezyn, Ramaziel, Granozyn, Gabrinoz,**[64] **Mercoph, Tameriel, Venomiel, Jenaziel, Xemyzin.**[65] These have 1320 servants to attend them in this hour to doe their will and when you will worke in this hour make a Seal sutable to [sic] for the time as I have here given an Example for the time aboue mentioned then lay it on yᵉ table: and say the conjuration, &c.

The 3ᵈ hour of the night is called **Quabrion,**[66] and the angel governing it is called **Serquanich**[67] who hath 101550 servient Dukes and servants to attend him: The which are divided into 12 Degrees of orders whereof wee shall mention 6 Dukes of the first order and 12 of the second: They being sufficient for practice. Whose names are as followeth viz **Menarym, Chrusiel, Penargos, Amriel, Demanoz, Nestoroz, Evanuel, Sarmozyn, Haylon, Quabriel, Thurmytz, Fronyzon, Vanosyr, Lemaron, Almonoyz, Janothyel, Melrotz, Xanthyozod.**[68] These have 1320 servants to attend them and when you will make any experiment in this houre make a Seal sutable to the time

63 H: "Ematyel."

64 T: "Gabrynoz."

65 S2: "Almodar, Famoriel, Nedros, Ormezin, Chabril, Praxiel, Permaz, Vameroz, Emariel, Fromezin, Romaziel, Granozyn, Gabrynoz, Mercoph, Tamariel, Venomiel, Janaziel, Zemizin"; S1: "Almodar, Famoriel, Nedros, Ormezin, Chabril, Praxiel, Parmaz, Vomeroz, Emariel, Fromezin, Ramaziel, Granozy, Gabrynoz, Mezcoph, Tamariel, Venomiel, janaziel, Zemizim"; H: "Almodar, Famoriel, Nedros, Ormezin, Chabril, Praxiel, Permaz, Vameroz, Emariel, Fromezin, Ramaziel, Granozÿn, Gabrinoz, Mezcoph, Famariel, Venomiel, Janaziel, Lemizim."

66 See T2.15. S1: "guabrion."

67 S2, S1, H: "Sarquamech."

68 T: "Xanthyoz"; S2: "Menarim, Chrusiel, Penergoz, Amriel, Deminoz, Nestozoz,

as I have here exemplifyed for the time aforesaid Then lay it on the Table
of practice and say the conjuration, &c.

[139r]   The 4th hour of the night is called **Ramersy**,[69] and the angell that governs it
is called **Jefischa**[70]—who hath 101550 Dukes and other servants,[71] which are
divided into 12 orders or degrees to attend him, whereof we shall mention 6
of the cheefe Dukes: and 12 of those that are of the second order, they being
sufficient for Practice: Their names are as followeth: vizt **Armosiel, Nedruan,
Maneyloz, Ormael, Phorsiel, Rimezyn, Rayziel, Gemezin, Fremiel, Hamayz,
Japuriel, Jasphiel, Lamediel, Adroziel, Zodiel, Bramiel, Coreziel, Enatriel.**[72]
Those have 7260 servants to attend them and if you haue a desier to operate
in this houre: make a seal sutable for the time you have one here for this howre

Evamiel, Sarmezyn, Haylon, Uvabriel, Thurmytzod, Fronizon, Vanoir, Lemaron,
Almonoyzod, Janoshyel, Melrotzod, Zanthyozod"; S1: "Menarim, Chrusiel, Penergoz,
Amriel, Deminoz, Neztozoz, Evamiel, Sarmezyrs, Haylon, Uvabriel, Thurmytzol,
Fromzon, Vanoir, Lemaron, Almonayzod, janoshyel, Melrotzod, Zanthyozod"; H:
"Menarim, Crusiel, Penargos, Amriel, Thurmytzod, Deminoz, Nestozoz, Evannel,
Sarmezÿn, Haylon, Uvabriel, ~~Thurmy~~, Fremzon, vanoie, Lemaron, Almonoyzod,
Janothyel, Melrotz, Zanthyozod."

69   See T2.16. T: "Ramerzy"; S2, H: "Ramerzi"; S1: "Ramersi."

70   H: "Jefisiel"; S1: "jdfischa" [sic].

71   H: "10550."

72   S2: "Armosiel, Nedruan, Maneÿlozor, Mael, Phersiel, Remezyn, Raisziel, Gemezin,
Fresmiel, Hamoyzod, Japuviel, Jasphiel, Lamediel, Adroziel, Zodiel, Bromiel, Coreziel,
Etnatriel"; S1: "Armosiel, Jvedruan, Maneÿ, Lozor, Mael, Phersiel, Remezyn, Raisiel,
Gemezin, Fresmiel, Haymoyzod, Japuviel, Jasphiel, Lamodiel, Adroziel, Zodrel,
Bromiel, Coreziel, Etnatriel"; H: "Armosiel, Nedrum, Maneyloz, Ormael, Phorsiel,
Rimesyn, Rayziel, Gemozin, Fremiel, Hamayzod, Japuviel, Jasphiel, Lamediel,
Adroziel, [Zodiel,] Bromiel, Coreziel, Enatriel."

for the time abouesaid it being for an Example Then lay the seal upon the Table of Practice and say the conjuration, &c.

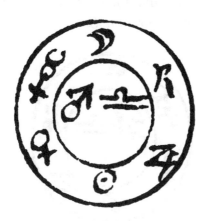

The 5th houre of the night is called **Sanayfar**,[73] and this [its] angel is called **Abasdarhon**.[74] He hath 101550 Dukes and other servants at his command: They being divided into 12 degrees of orders whereof wee shall mention 12 of the Dukes belonging to the first order and as many of the second order, They being sufficient for practice for this hour: There names are as followeth vizt: **Meniel, Charaby, Appiniel, Deinatz, Nechorym, Hameriel, Vulcaniel, Samelon, Gemary, Vanescor, Sameryn**,[75] **Xantropy, Herphatz, Chrymas, Patrozyn, Nameton, Barmas, Platiel, Neszomy, Quesdor, Caremaz, Umariel, Kralym, Habalon**,[76] who have 3200 servants[77] to attend them and if you

---

73   See T2.17. S2, H: "Sanayfor"; S1: "Sanaysor."

74   H: "Abasdarho."

75   S2, S1, H: "Samerin."

76   S2: "Meniel, Charaby, Appinel, Dematron, Nechorin, Hameriel, Vulcaniel, Semelon, Gemary, Venescar, Samerin, Zantropis, Herphatzal, Chrymos, Patrozin, Nameton, Barmas, Phatiel, Neszomy, Uvesolor, Caremaz, Umariel, Kralim, Habalon"; S1: "Meniel, Charaby, Appinel, Dematron, Necorin, Hameriel, Vulcamiel, Semelon, Clemary, Venescar, Samerin, Zantropis, Herphatzal, Chrymos, Patrozin, Nameton, Baymasos, Phaytiel, Neszomy, Uvesolor, Carmax, Vmariel, Kralim, Habalon"; H: "Meniel, Charby, Appiniel, Dematron, Nechoxin, Hameriel, Vntramiel, Semelon, Gemari, Vanesior, Samerin, Zantropÿ, Herphtzal, Chrymos, Patrozin, Namelon, Barmas, Phaliel, Neszomi, Uvesolor, Caremax, Amariel, Kralim, Hubalom."

77   S3 alone agrees with Trithemius, who reads, "Habemus deputatos ministeriales 3200 quibus per vices in diuersis operationibus magicis vtuntur." S2, S1, and H all read "2400."

make any Experiment In this hour, make a seal sutable to the time as this seal is suted for the time aforesaid being yᵉ 10ᵗʰ of March 1641 it being for an example. Then lay it on the Table of practice and doe as you where directed before & say the conjuration, &c.

[139v]   The 6ᵗʰ houre of every night is called **Thaazaron**,[78] and the angell governing it is called **Zaazenach**, who hath 101550 Dukes and other servants at his command to attend him, they being divided in 12 parts and [or] orders; whereof wee shall mention 12 of the cheefest Dukes in the first order and 6 of the second order they being sufficient for practice in this hour. Their names are as followeth: vizᵗ: **Amonazÿ, Menoriel, Prenostix, Namedor, Cherasiel, Dramaz, Tuberiel, Humaziel, Lanoziel, Lamerotzod,[79] Xerphiel, Zeziel, Pammon, Dracon, Gematzod,[80] Enariel, Rudefor, Sarmon,[81]** who have 2400 servants to attend on them & if you make any experiment in this hour make a seal fitt for the time as this is for The Time before spoken of Then lay it on the Table and say the conjuration, &c.

---

78   See T2.18. S2, H: "Thaazoron"; S1: "Thaasoron."

79   T: "Lamerotz."

80   T: "Gematz."

81   S2: "Amonzy, Menorik, Prenostix, Namendor, Cheraliel, dramaz, Tuberiel, Humaziel, Lenaziel Lamerotzod, Xerphiel, Zeziel, Pammon, Dracon, Gemotzol, Enariel, Rudozor, Satmon"; S1: "Amonzy, Menoyik, Prenostix, Ivamendor, Cherahel, Dramazed, Tuberiel, Humaziel, Lenaziel Lamerotzod, Xerphiel, Zeziel, Pammon, Dracon, Gemotzol, Gnaviel, Rudozor, Satmon"; H: "Amonzy, Menorike, Prenostix, Namedor, Cherahel, Dramazed, [Tuberiel, Humaziel, Lenaziel Lamerotzod, Xerphiel,] Zeziel, Pammon, Dracon, Gemtzod, Enariel, Rudefor Satmon." H does not seem to notice the omission of five names, since it also numbers them twelve and six.

The 7th houre of every [the] night is called **Venaydor**,[82] and its angell is called **Mendrion**, who hath 101550 dukes & other servants to attend him. They being divided into 12 orders, whereof we shall mention 12 of the first cheefe dukes and 6 of yᵉ next lesser sort They being sufficient for practice—Their names are as followeth: vizᵗ: **Ammiel, Choriel, Genarytz, Pandroz, Menesiel, Sameriel, Ventariel, Zachariel, Dubraz, Marchiel, Jonadriel, Pemoniel, Rayziel, Tarmytz, Anapion, Jmonyel, Framoth, Machmag**,[83] who have 1860 servants to attend them & when you make any Experiment make a seal sutable to the time as you have hear an Example. Then lay it on yᵉ Table: and say the conjuration, &c.

---

82   See T2.19. S2, S1, H: "Venador."

83   S2: "Mumiel, Choriel, Genaritzos, Pondroz, Memesiel, Semeriel, Ventariel, Zachariel, Dubraz, Marchiel, Jonadriel, Pemoniel, Rayziel, Tarmitzod, Anapion, Imonyel, Framoch, Machmag"; S1: "Mumiel, Choriel, Genaritzos, Poudroz, Memesiel, Someriel, Ventariel, Zachariel, Dubraz, Marchiel, Jonadriel, Pemoniel, Rayziel, Tarmitzod, Amapion, Imonyel, Framoch, Machmag"; H: "Ammiel, Choriel, Genaritzod, Pendroz, Memesiel, Semeriel, Ventariel, Zachariel, Dubraz, Marchiel, Jonadriel, Pemoniel, Rayziel, Tarmitzod, Anapion, Imoniel, Framoch, Machmag."

Nota I suppose this seal to be wrong and that it must be as the following seal of the 8th houre[84]:

The 8th hour of every night is called **Xymalim**,[85] and the angell rulling it is called **Narcoriel**,[86] who hath 101550 Dukes & other servient spirits to attend him, they being divided into 12 degrees or orders, whereof we shall mention 12 of the first order and 6 of the next order, They being sufficient to practice in this hour. Their names are as followeth viz[t] **Cambiel, Nedarym, Astrocon, Marifiel, Dramozyn, Lustifion, Amelson [Amelzon[87]], Lemozar, Xernifiel, Kanorsiel, Bufanotz, Jamedroz, Xanoriz,[88] Jastrion, Themaz, Hobrazym,[89] Zymeloz, Gamsiel,[90]** who have 30200 servants to attend them and when you make any Experiment in this houre make a seal sutable to the time as you have here in Example for the time aforesaid. Then lay it on the Table and say the conjuration, &c.

---

84 This note is only found in S3. In S2, Venus is replaced with the Sun at the bottom of the seal. In S1 and H, the symbols on the border are: Moon, Saturn, Mars, Sun, Venus, and Mercury, as in the eighth seal.

85 See T2.20. S2, S1, H: "Ximalim."

86 S2, S1: "Narcriel."

87 T: "Amelzon"; S2, S1, H: "Amelzom."

88 T: "Xanoryz."

89 S2, S1, H: "Hobrazim."

90 S2: "Cambiel, Nedarim, Astrocon, Marifiel, Dramozin, Lustision, Amelzom, Lemozar, Xernisiel, Kanorfiel, Bufanotzod, Jamearoz, Xanoriz, Jastrion, Themax, Hobrazim, Zimeloz, Gramsiel"; S1: "Cambiel, Nedarim, Astrocon, Marifiel, Dramozin, Lustision, Amelzom, Lemozar, Xernisiel, Kanorfiel, Bufanotzod, Jamodroz, Xanoriz, Pastrion, Themax, Hobrazim, Zimeloz, Gramsiel"; H: "Cambiel, Nedarim, Astrocon, Marifiel, Dremozin, Lustifion, Amelzom, Lemozor, Xernifiel, Hanorfiel, Bufanotzod, Jamedroz, Hanoriz, Jastrion, Themax, Hobrazim, Zimeloz, Gamsiel."

The 9th hour of the night is called **Zeschar**[91] and the angell rulling it is called **Pamyel** [Pamiel].[92] He hath 101550 dukes & other servants to at-tend him who are divided into 12 parts or orders, whereof wee shall men-tion 18 of the cheefe Dukes whose names are as followeth: vizt **Demaor, Nameal, Adrapon,**[93] **Chermel, Fenadros,**[94] **Vemasiel, Comary, Matiel, Zenoroz, Brandiel, Evandiel, Tameriel, Befranzy, Jachoroz, Xanthir, Armapy, Druchas, Sardiel.**[95] Who have 1320 servants to Attend them and when you make any Experiment in this hour make a seal sutable to the time as you have hear and [sic] example for the time aforesaid. Then lay it on the table and lay your hands on it: and say the conjuration, &c.

The 10th hour of the night is called **Malcho,**[96] and the angell governing it is called **Iassuarim** [Jasguarim],[97] who hath a 100 cheefe dukes and a 100 lesser dukes besides many other servants, whereof wee shall mention 6 that is three of the first order and 3 of the second order who have 1620 servants. There names are as followeth: vizt **Lapheriel, Emarziel, Nameroyz,**

---

91   See T2.21.

92   T, S2, S1, H.

93   S1: "Adyapon."

94   T: "Fenadroz."

95   S2: "Demaor, Nameal, Adrapan, Chermel, Fenadros, Vemasiel, Cmary, Matiel, Xenoroz, Brandiel, Evandiel, Jamriel, Befranzij, Jachoroz, Xanthir, Armapi, Drucas, Saraiel"; S1: "Demnnameals, Adyapon, Chermel, Fenadross, Vemasiel, Cmary, Matiel, Xenoroz, Brandiel, Evandiel, Jamriel, Befranzij, Jachoroz, Xanthir, Armapi, Orucas, Saraiel"; H: "Demannor, Nameal, Adrapon, Chermes, Fenadros, Vemasiel, Comarÿ, Maliel, Xenoroz, Brandiel, Evandiel, Jamiriel, Befranzÿ, [Jachoroz,] Xanthir, Armapi, Drachas, Sarajel." Again, H does not seem aware of the missing name.

96   See T2.22.

97   T: "Iasguarim"; S2, S1, H: "Jasgnarim."

Chameray, Hazaniel, Uraniel.[98] And when you operate in this houre make a seal sutable to the time as this is for time in the month of March 1641. Then lay it on the Table And say the conjuration, &c.

The 11th hour of yᵉ night is called **Aalacho**,[99] and the angell governing it is called **Dardariel**, who hath many servants and dukes whereof we shall mention 14 of the cheefe dukes and 7 of yᵉ lesser Dukes who have 420 servants to attend them: They are all good and obey gods lawes. Their names are as followeth: vizt **Cardiel, Permon, Armiel, Nastoriel, Casmiroz, Dameriel, Furamiel, Mafriel [Masriel[100]], Hariaz, Damar, Alachuc, Emeriel, Naveroz Alaphar, Nermas, Druchas, Carman, Elamyz, Jatroziel, Lamersy, Hamarytzod.**[101] And when you haue a desere to make an Experiment: make a Seal sutable for the time as this is for the time in the month of March 1641. Then lay it on the Table and say the conjuration, &c.

98 S2: "Lapheriel, Emerziel, Nameroizod, Chameray, Hazaniel, Uraniel"; S1: "Laphoriel Emerziel, Nameroizod, Chameray, Hazaniel, Vraniel"; H: "Lapheriel, Emarziel Nameroizod, Chameray, Hazaniel, Vraniel."

99 See T2.23. S2, S1: "Alacho"; H: "Aulacho."

100 T: "Masriel."

101 T: "Hamarytz"; S2, S1: "Cardiel, Permon, Armiel, Nastoriel, Casmiros, Dameriel, Fumarel Masriel, Hariaz, Damer, Alachus, Emeriel, Mavezoz, Alaphar, Hemas, Druchas, Carman Elamiz, Jatrziul, Lamersy, Hamerytzod"; H: "Cardiel, Permon, Armiel, Nastoriel, Casmiros Dameriel, Fumarel, Masriel, Hariaz, Dumar, Alachus, Emeriel, Mavezoz, Alaphar, Hermas Druchas, Charmas, Elamis, Jatroziul, Lamersy, Hamerytzod."

The 12th hour of the night is called **Xephan**,[102] and the angell governing it is called **Sarandiel**, who hath many dukes and servants whereof wee shall mention 14 of ye cheefe and good Dukes of the first order and 7 of those of ye second order: who have 420 servants to attend on them. Their names are as followeth: vizt **Adoniel, Damasiel, Ambriel, Meriel, Denaryz, Emarion, Kabriel, Marachy, Chabrion, Nestoriel, Zachriel, Naveriel, Damery, Namael, Hardiel, Nefrias, Irmanotzod,**[103] **Gerthiel, Dromiel, Ladrotzod,**[104] **Melanas,**[105] and when you haue a desier to make any Experiment in this hour make a sigill sutable to the time as this is hear for the same hour for the 10th of March in the year 1641 and when it is so made lay it on the Table of practice and lay your hand on it and say this conjuration following:

[140v]

The Conjuration as followeth:

O thou mighty great and potent Angell Samael who ruleth in the first hour of ye day—I the servant of the most high god: doe conjure and entreat thee in the name of ye most omnipotent and Immortall Lord god of hosts: **Jehovah * Tetragrammaton,** and by the name of that god that you are obedient to and by ye head of ye[106] hierarchy and by the

---

102 See T2.24. S2, S1: "Xphan."

103 T: "Irmanotz."

104 T: "Ladrotz."

105 S2: "Adoniel, Damasiel, Ambriel, Meriel, Denaryzod, Etharion, Kbriel, Marachy, Chabrion, Nestorel, Zackriel, Naveriel, Damery, Namael, Hardiel, Nefrias, Irmanotzod, Gerthiel, Dromiel, Ladrotzod, Melanas"; S1: "Adomel, Damasiel, Ambriel, Meriel, Denaryzod, Etharion, Kbriel, Marachy, Chabrion, Nestorel, Zachriel, Naveriel, Damery, Namael, Hardiel, Nefrias, Irmanotzod, Gerthiel, Dromiel, Ladrotzod, Melanas"; H: "Adoniel, Damasiel, Ambriel, Meriel, Denaryzod, Emarion, Kabriel, Marachy, Chabrion, Nestoriel, Zachriel, Naveriel, Damery, Namael, Hardiel, Nefryas, Irmanotzod, Gerthiel, Dromiel, Ladrotzod, Melanas."

106 S1: "your."

seal or marke that you are known in power by and by the 7 Angels
that stand before the Throne of god and by the 7 planetts and their
seals and characters and by the angel that rulleth The signe of ye 12th
house wch now ascends in this ~~last~~ ^first hour that you would be graciously pleased to gird up and gather ~~thy~~ ^your selfe together & by
devine permission to move and come from all parts of the world, wheresoever you be and shew ~~thy~~ ^your 107 selfe visibly and plainly in this
Cristall stone to the sight of my Eyes speaking with a voice Intelligible and to my understanding and that you would be favorably pleased
That I may have familliar frindship [friendship] and constant socity
[society] both now and at all times when I shall call thee forth to
visible appearance to Informe and direct me in all things that I shall
seem good and lawful unto the Creator and Thee: o thou great and
powerfull angele Samael. I invocate, adjure, command & most powerfully call you forth from your orders and place of Residence to visible
appirition [appearance] in and through these great and mighty Incomprehensible signals and divine names of the great god who was
and is and ever shall be **Adonay, Zebaoth, Adonay Amioram, Hagios,
Agla, On,**108 **Tetragrammaton** and by and in the name **Primeumaton,**
which commandeth the whole host of heaven whose power and vertue
is most Effectual for the calling you forth [and ordering of the cre-
ation] and commandeth you to Transmitt your Rayes vissible and perfectly into [unto] my sight: and your voice to my Ears, in and threw
this Cristall stone: That I may plainly see you and perfectly hear you
speak unto me. Therefore move yee, o Thou mighty and blessed angell
Samael: and in this potent name of the great god **Jehovah**: and by the
Imperiall dignity Thereof descend and shew your self vissible and perfectly in a pleasant and comely form before me in this Cristall stone:
to the sight of my Eyes speaking with a voyce Intelligible and to my
apprehension: shewing, declaring & accomplishing all my desires that
I shall aske or Request of you both herein and in whatsoever Truths or
things else that is Just and lawfull before the presence of Almighty
god: the giver of all good gifts: unto whome I begg that he would be
graciously plased [pleased] to bestow upon me: O thou servant of mercy
Samael, be thou therefore unto me friendly: and doe for me as for the
servant of the highest [most high] god: so farr as god hath given you
power in office to performe: whereunto I move you in Power and presence to appear that I may sing with his holy angells **Omappa-la-man,
Hallelujah,** Amen.

[141r]

But before you call any of the princes or the Dukes: you are to Invocate his cheefe governing Angell that governeth the hour of the day or of the night, as follows:

The Invocation as followeth:

> O Thou mighty and potent angell Samael, who is by the decree of the most high king of glory Ruler and governour of the first hour of the day I the servant of the highest doe desier and entreat you by these 3 great and mighty names of god: **Agla**, [On[109]], **Tetragrammaton** and by the power and vertue Thereof to assist and help me in my affairs: and by your power and authority, to send and cause to come and appear to me all or any of these angells that I shall call by name: that are residing under your government, to Instruct, help, aid and assist me, in all such matters and Things according to their office, as I shall desier and request of them (or him) and that they may doe for me as for the servant of ye highest creator.[110]

Then Beginn to Invocate them as followeth:

> O thou mighty and potent angel **Ameniel**, who rulleth by divine permission under The great and potent angell **Samael**, who is the great and potent angel rulling this first hour of the day: I the servant of the most high god doe conjure and entreat thee In the name of the most omnipotent and Immortall lord god of hosts **Jehovah** *

Note[111] from this sign *: to continue the contents of ye above written conjuration, &c. and when any spirit is come bidd him wellcome: Then aske your desier, and when you have done, dismiss him according to your orders of dissmission. &c.

& so endeth the first part of the Art Pauline, &c

---

109 S2, H. S1: "Aglaon."

110 S2, S1, H: "... of the highest Amen."

111 In S1, this paragraph reads, "So on as before at this Mark * in the Conjuration of Samael."

The second part of the Art Pauline.

Which containeth the Mysticall names of the Angells of yᵉ signes in general, and allso the names of the Angells of every degree and yᵉ signes in general who are called the angells of men: because in some one of those signs and degrees, every man is born under. Therefore he that knoweth the moment of his Birth he may know the angel that governeth him [by the following art]: and thereby he may obtaine to all arts and sciences, yea to all yᵉ wisdome and knowledge that any mortall man can desier in this world:

[The Ancient philosophers[112] haue taught how a man may know the nature of a Genius whether good or bad from the Influx and aspects of the starrs in his Geniture. Porphyrius seekes after it from the star that was Lord or Lady of the Geniture. Chaldeans finde it out from the Sun or the Moon in his Nativity located. Others finde it out from the sixth house in the Geniture, and call the Genius a good or bad genius or Dæmon.

A threefold Dæmon attends every man one is his proper keeper, One indeed is holy, the other belongs to his geniture or Nativity. The holy Dæmon proceeds not from the starrs but from a supreeme power, even from God who himselfe is the president of Dæmons, and descends to the Rational Soul being assigned thereto, and is universall above Natures consception.

But the Dæmon of the Birth or Geniture which is also called the Genius, this Genius doth descend to the Birth from the disposition of the stars their Circuits round the world, who are Conversant in the generation.

The Dæmon of the profession or Calling of the Native is given from the starrs to which such a profession or calling is subject to which any man professes, and the Soul shall make choice of. But this Dæmon is changed as any man changes his Calling from a meane one to a more sublime accordingly more worthy and sublime. Dæmons are present with us according as we dayly ascend from one vertue to another And these Dæmons do successfully take care & defend us.]

But note this: Those angells that are attributed to the fire have more knowledge therin than any other: So those that belong to the Aire have more knowledge therin [in aerial matters] than any other [order of spirit]: and those of yᵉ water have more knowledge therin then any other: and allso those of the Earth have more knowledge therein then any other: and to know wᶜʰ belong to the

---

112   This section is only found in H. It is abstracted from Agrippa, *De Occulta Philosophia* (Leiden: E. J. Brill, 1992), pp. 462–464, Book III, chaps. 21-22. It is followed by a fourteen-page narrative about a "Gentleman by Descent from the lines of the Plantagenets" and his conversation with Dr. Rudd.

fire, ayre, Earth, or water: observe the nature of the signes and you cannot erre: for those that are attributed to ♈: are of the same nature, [firey,] and so the like in the rest. But if any Planett is in that degree that ascends: Then that angell is of the nature of the signe and Planett both, &c. Observe this following method and you cannot but obtaine your desiere &c.

[Here followeth a table of the signs & Planets & their natures[113]]

Table 1.   The Planets, Their Signs, and Their Natures.[114]

The Planets	The signes	The Nature of the signes	The Angels
♂	♈	Fire	Aiel
♀	♉	Earth	Tual
☿	♊	Ayer	Giel
☽	♋	wayter	Cael
☉	♌	Fire	Ol
☿	♍	Earth	voil
♀	♎	Ayer	Jael
♂	♏	wayter	Josel [Sosol]
♃	♐	Fire	Suiajasel
♄	♑	Earth	Casujojah [Casuijah]
♄	♒	Ayer	Ausiul [Ansuil]
♃	♓	wayter	Pasil [Pasiel]

These 12 names are attributed by 12 signes of the Zodiac: Because of these [those] that doe not know the very [i.e. exact] decree [degree] of their nativity: so that they may make use of these if he know but the signe that ascends, &c. The names of the other angells which are attributed to Every degree are as followeth:

---

113 S1, S2, H.

114 S1 lists the Angels as follows: "Aiel, Tual, Giel, Cael, Ol, Violl, Jael, So Sol, Suiaiaseh, Casuiasah, Ausim, Pasel."

[142r]

Table 2. The Planets, Their Signs, and Their Geniis Names.[115]

Signs:	1st Degree	2nd Degree	3rd Degree	4th Degree	5th Degree
♈ ♂	Biael	Gesiel	Hael	Vaniel	Zaciel
♉ ♀	Latiel	Hujael	Sachiel	Gneliel	Panae1
♊ ☿	Latiel	Nagael	Sachael	Gnaliel	Paniel
♋ ☽	Sachiel	Metiel	Asel	Sachiel	Mihel
♌ ☉	Mechie1	Satiel	Ajel	Mechiel	Sahel
♍ ☿	Celiel	Senael	Nasael	Sangiel	Gnaphiel
♎ ♀	Ibajah	Chaiel	Sahael	Naviel	Saziel
♏ ♂	Teliel	Jeniel	Cesiel	Lengael	Naphael
♐ ♃	Taliel	Janiel	Casiel	Langael	Naphael
♑ ♄	Chushel	Temael	Jaajah	Cashiel	Lamajah
♒ ♄	Chamiel	Tesael	Jaajeh	Camiel	Lashiel
♓ ♃	Lachiel	Neliel	Sanael	Gnasiel	Pangael

Signs:	6th Degree	7th Degree	8th Degree	9th Degree	10th Degree
♈ ♂	Cegnel	Japhael	Itael	Cakiel	Lariel
♉ ♀	Jezisiel	Kingael	Raphiel	Tezael	Gnakiel
♊ ☿	Tzisiel	Kingael	Raphiel	Gnetiel	Bakiel
♋ ☽	Aniel	Sasael	Magnael	Aphiel	Sersael
♌ ☉	Aniel	Masiel	Sengael	Aphiel	Metziel
♍ ☿	Parziel	Tzakiel	Kriel	Rathiel	Tangiel
♎ ♀	Gnachiel	Patiel	Trajael	Kachiel	Baliel
♏ ♂	Satziel	Gnakiel	Periel	Tzethiel	Rengliel
♐ ♃	Satziel	Gnakiel	Periel	Tzangiel	Jebiel
♑ ♄	Naajah	Sasajah	Gnamiel	Paajah	Izashiel
♒ ♄	Naajah	Samiel	Gnashiel	Paajah	Izamiel
♓ ♃	Tzapheal	Kphiel	Ratziel	Tarajah	Gnathiel

115 S2, S1: "The table of Geniis Names followeth / (vizt)."

Table 2. The Planets, Their Signs, and Their Geniis Names (cont.).

Signs:	11th Degree	12th Degree	13th Degree	14th Degree	15th Degree
♈ ♂	Natheel	Sagnel	Gabiel	Pegiel	Gadiel
♉ ♀	Beriel	Gethiel	Dagnel	Vabiel	Zegiel
♊ ☿	Geriel	Dathiel	Hegnel	Vabiel	Zagiel
♋ ☽	Makael	Ariel	Sethiel	Magnael	Abiel
♌ ☉	Sekiel	Ariel	Gnethiel	Sagiel	Abiel
♍ ☿	Gnasiel	Bagiel	Gediel	Dahiel	Hevael
♎ ♀	Tamael	Gnamiel	Bangiel	Gepheel	Datziel
♏ ♂	Rebiel	Tagiel	Gnadiel	Bevael	Geziel
♐ ♃	Regael	Tediel	Gnaheel	Bevael	Geziel
♑ ♄	Kmiel	Riajah	Tashiel	Gnamiel	Baajah
♒ ♄	Kshiel	Raajah	Tamiel	Gnashiel	Baajah
♓ ♃	Bengiel	Gebiel	Dagiel	Hadiel	Vahajah

Signs:	16th Degree	17th Degree	18th Degree	19th Degree	20th Degree
♈ ♂	Kheel	Leviel	Hezael	Geciel	Betiel
♉ ♀	Chadiel	Tahiel	Javiel	Chazael	Bachiel
♊ ☿	Chadiel	Tahiel	Javiel	Chazael	Bachiel
♋ ☽	Sagel	Madiel	Athiel	Savael	Maziel
♌ ☉	Magiel	Sadiel	Athiel	Muviel	Saviel
♍ ☿	Vaziel	Zachiel	Chetiel	Tiiel	Jechiel
♎ ♀	Hekiel	Variel	Zethiel	Chengiel	Tibiel
♏ ♂	Dachiel	Hephiel	Vagael	Zackiel	Chabiel
♐ ♃	Dachiel	Hephiel	Vagael	Zackiel	Chabiel
♑ ♄	Gashiel	Dashiel	Haajah	Vashiel	Zamiel
♒ ♄	Gashiel	Dashiel	Haajah	Vashiel	Zamiel
♓ ♃	Zavael	Chazael	Tachael	Jatael	Cajaiel

Table 2. The Planets, Their Signs, and Their Geniis Names.

Signs:	21st Degree	22nd Degree	23rd Degree	24th Degree	25th Degree
♈ ♂	Giel	Dachael	Habiel	Vagel	Zadiel
♉ ♀	Getiel	Dajiel	Hachael	Vabiel	Zagiel
♊ ☿	Getiel	Dajiel	Hachael	Vabiel	Zagiel
♋ ☽	Achiel	Setiel	Maiel	Achael	Sabiel
♌ ☉	Achiel	Metiel	Siel	Achael	Mabiel
♍ ☿	Cabiel	Bagiel	Gediel	Dahiel	Hoviel
♎ ♀	Jagiel	Cediel	Behel	Gevael	Daziel
♏ ♂	Tagiel	Jadiel	Cahael	Baviel	Gezael
♐ ♃	Tagiel	Jadiel	Cahael	Baviel	Gezael
♑ ♄	Chael	Tashiel	Jashiel	Ciajah	Beshael
♒ ♄	Chael	Tashiel	Jashiel	Ciajah	Beshael
♓ ♃	Bachiel	Gabiel	Dagiel	Hediel	Vahejah

Signs:	26th Degree	27th Degree	28th Degree	29th Degree	30th Degree
♈ ♂	Chahel	Tavael	Jezel	Cechiel	Hetiel
♉ ♀	Chadiel	Gehiel	Javael	Chasiel	Sachael
♊ ☿	Chadiel	Tahiel	Daviel	Heziel	Vachael
♋ ☽	Magiel	Adiel	Sahiel	Meviel	Aziel
♌ ☉	Sagiel	Adiel	Mahiel	Savael	Aziel
♍ ☿	Vaziel	Zachiel	Chetivel	Tajael	Jachiel
♎ ♀	Heckiel	Vatiel	Zajel	Chechiel	Tehiel
♏ ♂	Dachael	Hatiel	Vajael	Zachiel	Chasiel
♐ ♃	Dachael	Hatiel	Vajael	Zachiel	Chasiel
♑ ♄	Gamael	Daael	Heshael	Vamiel	Zaajah
♒ ♄	Gamael	Daael	Heshael	Vamiel	Zaajah
♓ ♃	Zavael	Chazael	Tachiel	Jatael	Cajael

These are the 12 Seales wch are attributed
*to the Signes & Angells aforegoeing.*116

Make this seal of ♂ℨss ☉ ℨii [P adds: ☽ℨi] ♀ ℨss and melt them together
when the ☉ entereth the first Degree of ♈. Then on ♂, the ☽ being in 9 or
10 degrees of ♈, and make it and finish it &c.

116 Note that the following formulae are given in apothacary symbols that have the
   following meaning:

    ℨ = 1 ounce = 28.35 grams   ♀ = copper
    ℨ = 1 dram = 3.54 grams = 1/8 oz   ♂ = iron
    ☉ = gold   ♄ = lead
    ♃ = tin   ☿ = mercury
    ☽ = silver

   "Roman numerals (lower case) are always used following a symbol to designate the
   number of units read, but if the abbreviation is used, Arabic numerals are used and
   preceed the abbreviation; for example ℨiv or 4dr. For less that one unit, 1/2 may be
   designated by 'ss' following the symbol, but other fractions must be designated by
   Arabic numeral fractions." [*Merck Index, and Encyclopedia of Chemicals and Drugs,*
   (New Jersey: Merck & Co. 10th Edition, 1983), p. MISC-71.]

Make this seal of ♀ ℨi ♃ ℨi ♂ ℨss ☉ ℨii [P reads ☉ ℨii] and melt them together in the very point the ☉ entereth ♉, and so finish itt &c.

Ⅱ

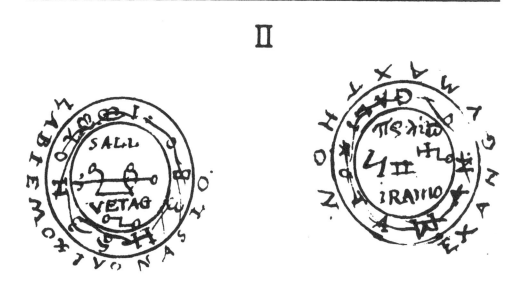

Make this seal of ☉ ℨi ☽ ℨi and melt them together when the ☉ entereth Ⅱ, and make a lamin thereof when ☽ is in ♌ or ♓ &c.

[143r]

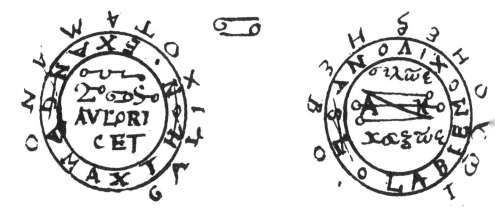

Make this seal of ☽ when the sun entereth ♋ in the hour of ☽ [Monday at 6, 13, or 20 hours,] she [the Moon] encreasing and in a good aspect &c.

Make this seal of ☉ when he [the Sun] entereth ♌, then after when ♃ is in ♓ engrave the first figure, and the other side, when the ☽ is in ♓, it must not come into the fire any more, but once, that is, when it is melted &c.

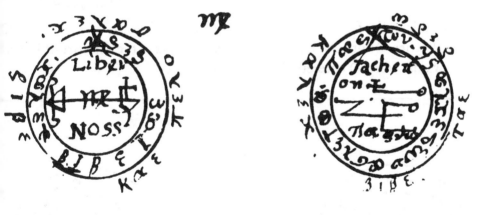

Make this seal of ♀ ʒi ☉ ʒss ☽ ʒii ♃ ʒss and melt them on ☉ day when the ☉ entereth ♍, then afterwards, when is well aspected, on his day [Wednesday] engrave the words and Characters as you see in the figure &c.

[143v]

Make this seal of ♀ melted powered [poured] & made when ⊙ entreth ♎.

Make this seal of ♂ and in this day and hour [Tuesday at 6, 13, or 20 hours], when ⊙ entereth ♏, and in that hour engrave the forepart of it, and afterwards, when ⊙ entereth ♈, engrave the other.

Make this seal of pure ♃ in the hour that ☉ entereth ♐, and engrave it in the hour of ♃ [Thursday at 6, 13, or 20 hours]. This seal is to be hung in a silver Ring.

Make this seal of ☉, and a Ring of ♀ to hang it in, and when ☉ entereth ♑, and engrave it when ♄ is well aspected and in his day and houre [Saturday at 6, 13, 20 hours.]

Make this seal of ☉ ℥ss ♄ ʒii ♂ ʒi and melt them when ☉ entereth ♒, and engrave them as you see in the figure when ♄ is in yᵉ 9th house &c.

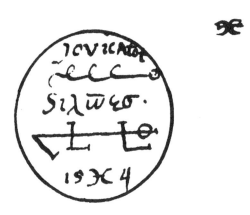

Make this seal when ☉ entereth ♓, of ☉ ♂ ♀ ☽ of each ℨii, of ♃ ℨss, and let them be melted and engraven both in that hour of his increase, &c.

[144v]   *S*o when you know the Angell that governeth the sign, & degree of your nativity, and haveing the seal redy prepared that is suetable to the sign and dgree [degree] as is shewed before, then you are next to understand what order he is of and under what prince as is shewed hereafter in the ffollowing part.

First those genii that are attibruted [attributed] to ♈, ♌, & ♐ are of the Fiery region, and are governed by **Michael**, The great Angell who is one of the great messengers of god, which is towards the South; therefore those geniis are to be observed in the first hour on a Sunday and at the eighth, allso at three and ten at night directing yourselfe towards that quarter. They appear in Royal Robes holding scepters in their hands, oft Ryding on a Lion or a Cock. their robes are of a red and saffron collor and most commonly the [they] assume the sheap of a crowned queen, very beautifull to behold &c.

Secondly those geniis [sic] that are attributed to ♉, ♍, & ♑, are of the Earthy [terrestrial] Region and governed by **Uriel**, who hath three princes to attend him viz, **Cassiel, Sachiel, & Assaiel.**[117] Therefore the geniis that are attributed

---

117   S2, S1: "Asaiel, Sochiel, & Cassiel"; H: "Asaiel, Sachiel, and Cassiel."

to him and those signs are to be observed in the West, They appear like Kings having green and silver Robes, or like little children or women delighting in hunting &c. [They are to be observed on] Saturdays. At the first and eighth hours of the day and at night at the third and tenth hours, You are with privacy to obtaine your desiers, directing yourselfe towards the West &c.

Thirdly those geniis that are attributed to ♊, ♎, & ♒, are of the aeiry [aerial] region, whose sovereign prince is called **Raphael**; who hath under him 2 princes, wch are called **Miel & Seraphiel**. Therefore those genii wch are attributed to him and those signs are to be observed towards the east, on a wednesday, the first and eighth hours of the day and at night the third & tenth houre. they appear like kings or beautiful young men cloathed in Robes of divers collours, But most commonly like women Transcendently handsome; by reason of their admirable whiteness and Beauty &c.

Fourthly & lastly Those genii that are attributed to ♋, ♏, & ♓ are of the watry [watery] region, and are governed by **Gabriel**, who hath under him 3 mighty princes, vizt **Samael, Madiel, & Mael**. Therefore those genii which are attributed to these signes that are governed by gabriel, and are to be observed on a munday towards the north at the first & 8th houres of the day, and at night at the 3d & 10th houres; they appear like kings haveing green and silver Robes or like little Children or women delighting in hunting &c.

So in the next place wee are to ~~consider~~ ^observe the season of the year according to the constellations of the celestial Bodies, otherwise wee shall lose all our labour, for if the genius be of Jyneal [Igneal[118]] Hierarchy, its in vaine to observe him in any other season but when the sun entereth those signs which are of his nature, that is ♈, ♌, & ♐:

So if it be a geniis [genius] of the Earth he is to be observed when ☉ entereth ♉, ♍, and ♑, and so the like in the rest.   [145r]

Or otherwise thus [Another rule that may be observed instead is this]: those geniis that are of the order of the fire, are to be observed in ye summer quarter & those of the earthy in Autume [autumn], and those of the ayr [air] in the spring, and those of ye water in the winter quarter—&c.

---

118 S2, S1, H.

Their offices are to all things that are Just and not against the laws of the great god **Jehovah** But what is for our good and what shall concerne the protection of our life, our beinge & well being & doeing good to & oblidging [obliging] our neighbours, &c.

Now he that desireth to see his genius, ought to prepare himselfe accordingly. Now if his genius be of the fire his demands must be the ~~consecration~~ ^conservation of his Body or person that he receives no hurt ffrom or by any fire armes guns or the like and haveing a seal sutable, ready prepared, he is to weare it when he hath a desier to see his genius, That he may conferme it to him & for the time to come he may not fail of his assistance and protection at any time or occasion &c.

But if his genius be ayeriall [aerial] he reconcileth mens natures Increaseth love and affection between them causeth the deserved favour of kings and princes & secretly promoteth marriages: & Therefore he that hath such a genius before he observeth him should prepare a seal suitable to his order that he may have it confermed by him in the day and hour of observation, where of he shall see wonderfull & strange Effects and so the like of yᵉ other 2 hierarchies:

And when the time is come that you would see yʳ genius Turne yʳ face towards that quarter the signe is, and that with prayers to god: they being composed to your fancy, but sutable to yᵉ matter in hand and there thou shalt find him; and haveing found him and sincerely acknowledged him doe your duty. Then will he, as being Benigne & sociable Illuminate your minde, takeing away all that is obscure & darke in the memory and make thee knowing in all sciences sacred & divine in an instant &c—

[Here followeth] a form of prayer wᶜʰ ought to be said upon that cos. [coast] or quarter where the genius is several times, it being an Exorcisme to call the genius into the christall [crystal] stone that is to stand upon the Table of practice before shewed, it being covered with a white linnen [linen] cloth.[119] Note this prayer may be altered to the mind of the worker, for it is here set for [to serve as] an Example &c.

[The Conjuration of the Holy Guardian Angel[120]]

O thou great and blessed N. my angell guardian vouchsafe to descend from thy holy mansion which is Celestial, with thy holy Influence and presence, into this cristall stone, that I may behold thy glory; and enjoy

---

119 S1 omits, "that is to stand … cloth."
120 S1, S2, H: "The Prayer."

thy society, aide and assistance, both now and for ever hereafter. O thou who art higer [higher] than the <u>fortly</u> [fourth] heaven, and knoweth the secrets of **Elanel**. Thou that rideth upon the wings of yᵉ winds and art mighty and potent in thy Celestial and superlunary motion, do thou descend and be present I pray thee; and I humbly desiere and entreat thee. That if ever I have merited Thy socity [society] or if any of my actions and Intentions be real and pure & sanctified before thee bring thy external presence hither, and converse with me one of thy submissive pupils, By and in yᵉ name of [the] great god **Jehovah**, whereunto the whole quire [choir] of heaven singeth continualy: O Mappa la man Hallelujah. Amen.

When you have said this over several times you will at last see strange sights and pasages [passages] in the stone and at last you will see your genius: Then give him a kind entertainement as you was [were] before directed declaring to him your minde and what you would have him doe,[121] &c.

So Endeth the second Part of the
Art Pauline

---

[121] S1: "you would have done."

Here beginneth the fourth part of this Booke which is called

Salomon's
Almadel Art

[Ars Almadel Salomonis]

By this Rule [art[1]] Salomon obtained great wisdom from the cheefe Angells that governe the 4 Altitudes of the world for you must observe [that] there be 4 Altitudes, representing the 4 corners of the world, East, West, North and South. The which are divided into 12 parts, that is, every part or Altitude into 3, and the Angells of every of these altitudes[2] have their particulars vertues and powers, as shall be shewed in this following matter &c.

[The Making of the Almadel]

Make the Almadel of pure white wax, but [the others must be[3]] colloured sutable to the altitude [as will be shown]; it is to be four squares [square], and six Inches [over] every way;[4] and in every corner a hole and write betwixt every hole with a new pen, These words or names of god, following, but this is to be done in the day and hour of Sol. Write upon the first part towards the East, **Adonai, Helomi, Pine,** and upon the second towards the south, **Helion, Heloi, Heli,** and upon the west part: **Jod, Hod, Agla:** and upon the fourth part which is the north write these names: **Tetragrammaton, Shadai, Jah,** and betwixt the first and the other quarters

---

1   S1.

2   S1: "parts."

3   S1.

4   S2, S1: "it is to be 4 inches square & 6 inches ouer euery way"; H: "four square and six Inches."

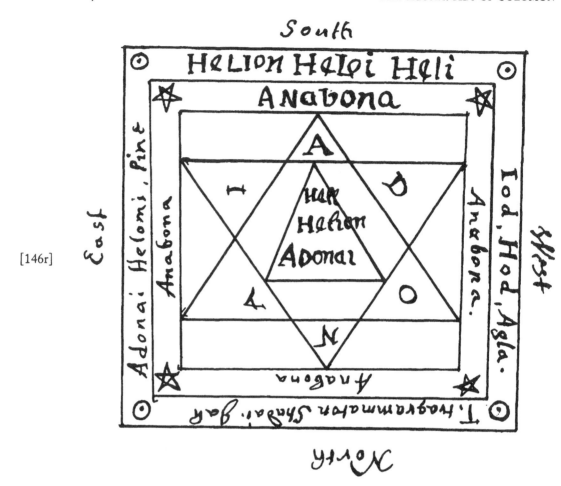

Figure 10.   The Almadel.

make The Pentacle of Salomon thus ✮, and betwixt the first and [the] other quarters write this word, **Anabona** and in the middle of the Almadel make a six angled figure and in the middest off it a Triangle wherin must be written these names of god, **Hel**,[5] **Helion**, **Adoni** [Adonai], And this last name round in the 6 Angled figure, [as well,] as you may see in this figure, here made it being ffor an example &c.

And of the same wax there must be made four Candles, and they must be of the same collour as the Almadel is of. You must divide the wax into three parts, one part for to make the Almadel of, and the other 2 parts for to make the candles of, and let there come forth from every one of them a foot made of yᵉ same wax, for to suporte yᵉ Almadel with; This being done: in the next place you are to make a seal of pure gold or silver, but Gold is

---

5   S1: "Hell."

best wherein must be engraven these three names: **Helion, Hellujon, Adonai;** &c.

Nota The first Altitude is called Chora Orientis or the East Altitude and to make any experiment in this Chora, it is to be done in the day and houre of the Sun: and the power and office of those Angells is to make all things fruitfull & encrease, both Animals & vegetables, in creation & generation; advancing the Birth of [the] children & makeing barren women fruitfull, &c. Their names are those. vizt, **Alimiel, Gabriel, Borachiel,**[6] **Lebes & Hellison;**[7]

Note: you must not pray for any Angells but those that belong to the same Altitude, you have a desier to call forth. And when you operate, set the four candles upon 4 candle sticks, but be carefull you doe not light them before you begin to operate, then lay the Almadel between the four candles upon the waxen feet that cometh from the candles and lay the golden seal upon the Almadel, and and [sic] [Then] haveing the Invocation redy written on virgins Parchment: Light the Candles and read the Invocation as is set down at the latter end of this part &c.

And when he appeareth, he appeareth in the form of an Angell carrying in his hand a fan or flagg, having the picture of a white cross upon it, his body is wrapped round about with a fair cloud, and his face very fair and bright, and a Crown of Rose flowers [is] upon his head: he descends first upon the superscription of ye Almadel as if it were a Mist or Fogg. Then must the exorcist have in readyness a vessell of Earth of ye same collour of [that] the Almadel is of, and the other of his furniture, it being in the form of a Basin, and put therein a few hot ashes or coales but not too much lest it should melt the wax of ye Almadel, & put therein[8] 3 little grains of Masticke in powder, so that it fumeth and the smell may goe upwards threw the holes of the Almadel when it is under it, and as soon as the angell smells it he beginneth to speake with a low voice asking what your desier is and why you have called the princes and governers of his Altitude. then you must Answer him, saying,

I desire that all my requests may be granted, and what I pray for may be accomplished, for your office maketh appeare and declareth that such is to be fullfild by you if it pleases god, &c,

---

6   S2, S1: "Barachiel."
7   S1: "Helison."
8   In S3, the words "a few hot ashes or coales but not too much lest it should ... put therein" are in the margin, sec. man.

adding further the particulars of your Requests praying with humility† for what is lawfull and Just and that you shall indeed obtain from him:

But if he doth not appear presently, you must then take the golden seal, And make with it three or four marks upon the candles, by which means the angell will presently appeare as aforesaide: and when the Angell departeth he will fill the whole place with a sweet and pleasant smell which will be smelt a long time.

Nota. The golden seal will serve and is to be used in the operation of all the Altitudes. The Collour of the Almadel belonging to the first Chora is lilly [lily] white. To the second Chora a Perfect red Rose Collour; The 3d Chora is to be a green mixt with [a] white silver collour. The Fourth Chora is to be a black mixt with a little green of a sadd collour &c.

Of the second Chora or Altitude:

[146v]

Note: all the other three Altitudes with their signes and princes have power over goods and riches, and can make any man Rich or poor, and as the first Chora giveth Encrease and maketh fruitfull, so these giveth decrease and Barrenness, &c.

And if any have a desire to operate in any of the other 3 Choras or Altitudes, they must doe it on Sundays in the manner as above is shewed; But doe not pray for anything that is contrary to the nature of their office, or against god and his laws, but what God giveth according to the course of nature, that you may desier and obtaine, and all the furniture that is to be used is to be of the same collour as the Almadel is of, and the princes of this second Chora are named as Followeth Vizt: **Alphariza,**9 **Genon, Geron, Armon, Gereinon** [Gereimon10] &c.

And when you operate kneel before the Almadel with cloathes of ye same collour in a closet hung with the same collours allso, for the holy apparation will be of the same collour: and when he is appeared, put the earthen Bason under the Almadel with fire and hott ashes and 3 graines of Mastic in poweder to fume as above written, and when the Angell smelleth the perfume, he turneth his face towards you, asking the Exorcist with a low voyace why he called the princes of this Chora or Altitude, then you must answer as before; saying: I desire that my Request

---

†   Original had "sincerity" corrected to "humility."

9   S1: "Aphiriza."

10   S2, S1, H: "Gereimon."

may be granted, and the contents thereof may be accomplished, for your offices maketh appear and declareth that such is to be done by you if it pleases god, &c: you must not be fearfull but speak humbly saying &c: I recomend my my [sic] selfe wholy into your office, and I pray unto your princes of this Altitude that I may enjoy [and obtain all things according to] my wishes and desiers, &c: you may further express your mind in all particulars in your prayer &c. doe the like in the 2 other Choras that follow &.c.

The Angell[11] of this second Altitude appears in the form of a young childe with clothes of sattin and of a Red Rose collour, haveing a crown of Red gilly flowers upon his head, his face looking upwards to heaven, and is of a Red Collour and is compassed round about with a Bright splendour, as the Beams of the Sunn; and before he departeth he speaks to the Exorcist, saying *I am your friend and brother*, and [he] Illuminateth the ayre round above with splendour, and [he leaveth a] pleasant smell, which lasteth a long time,[12] &c.

Of the Third Chora or Altitude:

In this Chora you are to doe in all things as you are before directed in the other Two. The Angells of this Altitude are named as foll: vizt **Eliphamasai** [Eliphaniasai[13]], **Gelomiros, Gedobonai, Saranana, & Elomnia;**[14] They appeare in the form of children or little women drest in green and silver collours, very delightfull to behold, and a crown of Bay leaves, beset with Flowers of white and green collours upon their heads and they seeme to look a little downwards with their faces, &c. They speak as the others doe to the Exorcist and leave a mighty, sweet perfume behind them, &c.

Of the fourth Chora or Altitude:

In this Chora you must doe as in the other [others], and the Angells of this Chora are called **Barchiel, Gediel, Gabiel,**[15] **Deliel, & Captiel**. &c. These

[147r]

---

11 S1: "Angels."

12 S1 adds, "upon there heads."

13 S2, S1, H.

14 S2, S1: "Saranava & Elomina"; H: "... Gedobenai, Saranava and Elomnia."

15 In S3, "Gabiel" is written *supra linea*. S2 and S1 omit, "Gabiel"; H reads, "Gobiel."

appeare in the forme of little men or Boys with cloathes of a Black collour, mixt with a darke green and in their hands they hold a Bird which is naked & their heads are Beare, only it is compassed round & Besett with Ivy [and] Berries. The [They] are all very beautifull and comely and are compassed round with a Bright shineing of diveres [divers] colours. They leave a sweet smell behinde them allso; but [it] differeth from the others something [somewhat] &c.

[Of the proper times for invoking these angels]

Nota: There are 12 princes rulling besides those in the 4 Altitudes, and they distribute their offices amongst themselves, every one rulling 30 dayes [or thereabouts,] every yeare, now it will be in vain to call any of those Angells unless it be those that then governeth, For every Chora or Altitude, hath its limited time according to the 12 signs of the Zodiack and in that [what] signe the Sunn is in. That Angell or those angells that belong to that signe have the government: as for Example; suppose I would call the 2 first of those 5 that belong to the first Chora, Then chuse the first Sunday on March: that is after the Sun is entred ♈, and then I make my Experiment; and so doe the like if you will the next Sunday after againe; But if you will call the 2 second that belong to yᵉ first Chora, Then you must take the Sundays that are in Aprill, after the ☉ is entered ♉. But if you call the last of the 5th [five] Then you must take those Sundays that are in May after the ☉ is entered ♊; to make your Experiment in; doe the like in the other Altitudes, for they have all one way of working: But the Altitudes have a Name formed severally in the substance of heaven even as a Character, for when the Angells hear the names of god that are attributed to them they hear it by the vertue of that carecter [character]. Therefore it is in vain to call any angell or spirit unless you knew [know] what names of god to call them by; Therefore observe the forme of this Following conjuration, or Invocation &c.

The Invocation

O thou great mighty[16] and blessed angell of god, N, who ruleth as the cheefe & first governing angell in the first Chora or Altitude in the

---

16 S1 jumbles this somewhat: "O thou great blessed & Glorious Angel of God (N) who rulest and is the cheif governing Angel in the first Chora or Altitude in / [sic] I the

East, under the great prince of the East whom you obey, and [who] is sett over you as king by the divine power of god, **Adonai, Helomi, Pine**; who is the distributter & disposer of all things, holly in heaven and Earth and hell; I the servant of that god **Adonai, Helomi, Pine**; which you obey, doe Invocate, Conjure & entreat thee N. that thou forthwith appeareth, & by the vertue & power of the same god, [Adonai, Helomi, Pine], I doe command thee forth [by him whom you do obey and who is set over you as king by the divine power of God, that you forthwith descend] ffrom thy order or please [place] of abode to come into me, and shew thy selfe plainly and visibly here before me in this Cristall stone, in thy owne [and] proper shape and glory speaking with a voice intelligible and to [unto] my understanding: O thou mighty and blessed angell N, who art by the power of god ordained to governe all vegetables and Animalls, and causeth them, and all other creatures of god to spring, encrease, and bring forth according to their kinds and natures; I the servant of the same your god I doe entreat and humbly beseech thee to come and shew unto me all things that I shall desiere of you, so farr as in office you can, or be capable to perform, if god permitt to the same; O thou servant of mercy N, I entreat thee, and humbly beseech thee, in and by these 3 names of your true god, **Adonai, Helomi, Pine**, And doe constraine you in and by this [powerful] name **Anabona**, That thou forthwith appeareth vissibly and plainely in thy own proper shape and glory in and throwgh this Cristall stone; That I may visibly see Thee, and audibly hear you speake unto me, That I may have thy blessed and Glorious angellicall assistance; familiar, friendship, and constant society, communication and Instruction, both now and at all other times, to Informe and rightly Instruct me in my Ignorant and depraved Intellect Judgement and understanding; and to assist me both herein, and in all other truths, else what the Almighty **Adonai**, the King of Kings, The giver of all good gifts, shall in his Bountifull, and Fatherly Mercy be graceously pleased to bestow upon me; Therefore O thou blessed angell N. be friendly unto me, and doe for me, so farr as god hath given you power in office to performe, whereunto I move you in power and presence to appeare That I may sing with his holy Angells, O Mappa-laman! Hallelujah amen.

[147v]

---

servant of the highest the same your god Adonai Helomi & Pine whom you do obey & is the distributer & disposer of / all things both in Heaven earth & Hell do Invocate conjure & intreat yee (N) that thou forthwith appear in the virtue / & power of the same God Adonai Helomi & Pine & I do command thee by him whom you do obey & is set over you as King by / the divine power of God that you forthwith descend from thy orders or place of abode to come unto me & shew thy self / ..."

[Note this invocation is to be altered according to the Altitude and angell you wish to call forth.[17]]

When he is appeared, give him or them a kind entertainement, and then Aske what is Just and lawfull; and that which is proper and suetable to his office, and you shall Obtaine it.

So endeth the Booke Almadel of Salomon. &c.

[Finis[18]]

---

17   H.

18   S2, S1. S1 omits the 5th book, *Ars Notoria*, but instead inserts three folios (30–32), starting with a list of names, some with corrupt Hebrew lettering. I have included these in Appendix 1.

Ars Notoria :

THE
NOTORY ART
OF
SOLOMON,

Shewing the

CABALISTICAL KEY

of $\left\{\begin{array}{l}\text{Magical Operations,}\\ \text{The liberal Sciences,}\\ \text{Divine Revelation, and}\\ \text{The Art of Memory.}\end{array}\right.$

Whereunto is added

An Aſtrological Catechiſm,

fully demonſtrating the Art of

JUDICIAL ASTROLOGY.

Together with a rare Natural ſecret, neceſſary to be learn'd by all perſons; eſpecially Sea-men, Merchants, and Travellers.

An excellent Invention, done by the Magnetick Vertue of the Load-ſtone.

Written originally in Latine, and now Engliſhed by ROBERT TURNER Φιλομαθής.

London, Printed by *J. Cottrel*, and are to be ſold by *Martha Hariſon*, at the Lamb at the Eaſt-end of Pauls, 1657.

The Epistle Dedicatory.

To his Ingenious and respected friend Mr. William Ryves, of St. Saviours Southwark, Student in Physick and Astrology.

Sir.

T He deep inspection and *dove-like* piercing Eye of your apprehension into the deepest Cabinets of Natures *Arcana's*, allures me (if I had no other attractive Magnetick engagements,) to set this Optick before your sight: not that it will make any addition to your knowledge; but by the fortitude of your judgment, be walled against the art-condemning and virtue-despising *Calumniators*. I know the candor of your Ingenuity will plead my excuse, and save me from that labour; resting to be

Little Brittain, die ♀. in ☉. in ♎   Your real affectionate Friend,
6.49.16,6.

ROBERT TURNER.

To the Ingenious Readers.

Amongst the rest of the labours of my long Winter hours, be pleased to accept of this as a flower of the Sun; which I have transplanted from the copious Roman banks into the English soyle; where I hope it will fruitfully spread its branches, and prove not a perishing gourd, but a continual green Laurel, which Authors say is the plant of the good Angel, and defends all persons neer its shade from the Penetrating blasts of Thunder and Lightening; so will this be a flower fit for every man's Garden; its virtues will soon be known, if practised, and the blasts of vice dispersed: its subject is too sublime to be exprest. Let not the carping Momi, nor envious black-jaw'd Zoili rayl; let not the ignorant bark at that which they know not; here they learn no such lesson: and against their Calumnies, the book I thus vindicate: *quod potest per fidem intelligi, & non aliter, & per fidem in eo operare potes.* Διὰ πίστεως κατήγω ἰσχιτο Βασιλείας, εἰργάσαντο δικαιοσύνης, ἐπί τυχον ἐπαγξελιῶν, ἔφραξαν ςὁματα λεόντων. Βαβεσαν δυναμιν πυρός, &c. Heb. 11. &c. and my own intention I thus demonstrate; *Dico coram omnipotenti Deo, & coram Jesu Christo unigento Filio ejus, qui judicaturus est vivos & mortuous; quod omnia & singula quæ in hoc opere dixi, omnesque hujus Scientiæ vel artis proprietates, & universa quæ ad ejus speculationem pertinent, vel in hoc Volumine continenter, veris & naturalibus principiis innituntur, fuintque cum Deo & bona Conscientia, sine injuria Christianæ fidei, cum integritate; sine superstitione vel Idololatria quacunque, &*

non dedeceant virum sapientem Christianum bonum atque fidelem; Nam & ego
Christianus sum, baptizatus in nomine Patris, &c. quam fidem cum Dei auxilio
quam diu vixero firmiter inviolatam tenebo; Procul ergo absit a me, discere aut
scribere aliquid Christianæ fidei & puritati contrarium, sanctis moribus noxium,
aut quomodolibet adversum. Deum timeo & in ejus cultum Juravi, a quo nec
vivus nec (ut confido) mortuus separabor: This small treatise I therefore com-
mend to all the lovers of art and learning, in which I hope they will attain
their desires, quantum a Deo concessi erit; so that I hope I have not cast a
Pearle before the swine, but set a glasse before the grateful doves.

12 March 1656.
ROBERT TURNER

[INTRODUCTION[1]:

It is called the Notory Art because in certain breif notes it teacheth and comprehendeth the knowledge of all arts. This fifth part is a book of orations and prayers that wise Solomon used upon the altar in the temple, called Ars Nova, & was revealed to Solomon by the holy angel of God called Michael and he also received many breif notes written by the finger of god which was delivered to him by the said angel with thunder claps, without which notes King Solomon had never obtained his great knowledge from those notes it is called the notary art.

This is a flower of the sun (as Dr. Rudd calls it) fit for every mans garden; its vertues will soon be knowne if practised, and the blasts of vice dispersed. Its subject is too sublime to be expresed *quod portess per fidem intelligi et non aliter et perfidem in es sporare potes.*

And Dr. Rudd saith in vindication of this book and himselfe - Dico coram . . . separabor (see p. 159).]

---

1   From H.

The Notory Art of Solomon.

The Notory Art revealed by the Most High Creator to Solomon.

In the Name of the holy and undivided Trinity, beginneth this most holy Art of Knowledge, Revealed to SOLOMON, which the Most High Creator by his holy Angel ministred to SOLOMON upon the Altar of the Temple; that thereby in a short time he knew all Arts and Sciences, both Liberal and Mechanick, with all the Faculties and Properties thereof: He had suddenly infused into him, and also was filled with all wisdom, to utter the sacred mysteries of most holy words.

Alpha and Omega! Oh Almighty God, the beginning of all things, without beginning, and without end: Graciously this day hear my prayers; neither do thou render unto me according to my sins, nor after mine iniquities, O Lord my God, but according to thy mercy, which is greater then all things visible and invisible. Have mercy upon me, O Christ, the Wisdom of the Father, the Light of Angels, the Glory of Saints, the Hope, Refuge, and Support of Sinners, the Creator of all things, the Redeemer of all humane Frailties, who holdest the Heaven, Earth, and Sea, and all the whole World, in the palm of thy Hand: I humbly implore and beseech, That thow wilt mercifully with the Father, illustrate my Minde with the beams of thy holy Spirit, that I may be able to come and attain to the perfection of this most holy Art, and that I may be able to gain the knowledge of every Science, Art, and Wisdom; and of every Faculty of Memory, Intelligences, Understanding, and Intellect, by the Vertue and Power of thy most holy Spirit, and in thy Name. And thou, O God my God, who in the beginning hast created the Heaven and the Earth, and all things out of nothing; who reformest, and makest all things by thy own Spirit; compleat, fulfil, restore, and implant a sound Understanding in me, that I may glorifie thee and all thy Works, in all my Thoughts, Words, and Deeds. O God the Father, confirm and grant this my Prayer, and increase my Understanding and Memory, and strengthen the same, to know and receive the Science, Memory, Eloquence, and Perseverance in all manner of Learning, who livest and reignest World without end. *Amen.*

Here beginneth the first Treatise of this Art, which Master Apollonius calleth, The golden Flowers, being the generall Introduction to all Natural Sciences; and this is Confirmed, Composed, and Approved by the Authority of Solomon, Manichæus, and Euduchæus.

I *Apollonius* Master of Arts, duly called, to whom the Nature of Liberal Arts hath been granted, am intended to treat of the Knowledge of Liberal Arts, and of the Knowledge of Astronomy; and with what Experiments and Documents, a Compendious and Competent Knowledge of Arts may be attained unto; and how the highest and lowest Mysteries of Nature may be competently divided, and fitted and applied to the Natures of Times; and what proper dayes and hours are to be elected for the Deeds and Actions of men, to be begun and ended; what Qualifications a man ought to have, to attain the Efficacy of this Art; and how he ought to dispose of the actions of his life, and to behold and study the Course of the Moon. In the first place therefore, we shall declare certain precepts of the Spiritual Sciences; that all things which we intend to speak of, may be attained to in order. Wonder not therefore, at what you shall hear and see in this subsequent Treatise, and that you shall finde an Example of such inestimable Learning.

Some things which follow, which we will deliver to thee as Essayes of wonderful Effects, and have extracted them out of the most ancient Books of the Hebrews; which, where thou seest them, (although they are forgotten, and worn out of any humane Language) nevertheless esteem them as Miracles: For I do truly admire the great Power and Efficacy of Words in the Works of Nature.

Of what efficacy words are.

T here is so great Vertue, Power and Efficacy in certain Names and Words of God, that when you reade those very Words, it shall imme-

diately increase and help your Eloquence, so that you shall be made eloquent of speech by them, and at length attain to the Effects of the powerful
Sacred Names of God: but from whence the power hereof doth proceed,
shall be fully demonstrated to you in the following Chapters of Prayers:
and those which follow next to our hand, we shall lay open.

An explanation of the Notary Art.

T his art is divided into two parts: The first containeth general Rules,
the second special Rules.[2] We come first to the special Rules; that is,
First, to a threefold, and then to a fourfold Division: And in the third place
we come to speak of Theology; which Sciences thou shalt attain to, by the
Operation of these Orations, if thou pronounce them as it is written: Therefore there are certain Notes of the Notary Art, which are manifest to us;
the Vertue whereof Human Reason cannot comprehend. The first Note
hath his signification taken from the Hebrew; which though the expression
thereof be comprehended in a very few words; nevertheless, in the expression of the Mystery, they do not lose their Vertue: That may be called their
Vertue, which doth happen and proceed from their pronunciation, which
ought to be greatly admired at.

[General Rules[3]*]*

The first precept.

H *ely Scemath, Amazaz, Hemel; Sathusteon, hheli Tamazam,* &c.[4] which
Solomon entituled, *His first Revelation*; and that to be without any
Interpretation: It being a Science of so Transcendent a purity, that it hath
its Original out of the depth and profundity of the *Chaldee, Hebrew,* and
Grecian Languages; and therefore cannot possible [sic] by any means be
explicated fully in the poor Thread-bare Scheme of our Language. And of
what nature the Efficacy of the aforesaid words are, *Solomon* himself doth

---

2   The special rules are for obtaining mastery of the seven liberal arts. The general rules
are prerequisite skills such as memory and eloquence. See Claire Fanger, *Conjuring
Spirits, Texts and Traditions of Medieval Ritual Magic* (University Park, PA: Pennsylvania State University Press, 1998), pp. 219-220, for an analysis of the structure of
the text.

3   This heading does not occur in the texts, but is supplied here for clarity.

4   This oration occurs in full at the end.

describe in his Eleventh Book, *Helisoe,* of the Mighty Glory of the Creator: but the Friend and Successor of *Solomon,* that is, *Apollonius,* with some few others, to whom that Science hath been manifested, have explained the same, and defined it to be most Holy, Divine, Deep, and Profound Mysteries; and not to be disclosed nor pronounced, without great Faith and Reverence.

A Spiritual Mandate of the precedent Oration.

Before any one begin to reade or pronounce any Orations of this Art, to bring them to effect, let them alwayes first reverently and devoutly rehearse this Prayer in the beginning.

If any one will search the Scriptures, or would understand, or eloquently pronounce any part of Scripture, let him pronounce the words of the following Figure, to wit, *Hely scemath,* in the morning betimes of that day, wherein thou wilt begin any work. And in the Name of the Lord our God, let him diligently pronounce the Scripture proposed, with this Prayer which follows, which is, *Theos Megale;* And is mystically distorted, and miraculously and properly framed out of the *Hebrew, Greek ,* and *Chaldean* Tongues: and it extendeth itself briefly into every Language, in what beginning soever they are declared. The second part of the Oration of the second Chapter, is taken out of the *Hebrew, Greek,* and *Chaldee;* and the following Exposition thereof, ought to be pronounced first, which is a Latine Oration: The third Oration of the three Chapters, always in the beginning of every Faculty, is first to be rehearsed.

The Oration is, *Theos Megale, in tu ymas Eurel, &c.*

This sheweth, how the foregoing Prayer is expounded: But although this is a particular and brief Exposition of this Oration; yet do not think, that all words are thus expounded.

The Exposition of this Oration.

Oh God, the Light of the World, Father of Immense Eternity, Giver of all Wisdom and Knowledge, and of all Spiritual Grace; most Holy and Inestimable Dispenser, knowing all things before they are made; who makest Light and Darkness: Stretch forth thy Hand, and touch my Mouth, and make my Tongue as a sharp sword; to shew forth these words with Eloquence; Make my Tongue as an Arrow elected to declare thy Wonders, and to pronounce them memorably: Send forth thy holy Spirit, O Lord, into my Heart and Soul, to understand and retain them, and to meditate on them in my Conscience: By the Oath of thy Heart, that is, By the Right-hand of thy holy Knowledge, and mercifully inspire thy Grace into me; Teach and instruct me; Establish the coming in and going out of my Senses, and let thy Precepts teach and correct me until the end; and let the Councel of the most High assist me, through thy infinite Wisdom and Mercy. *Amen.*

The words of these Orations cannot be wholly Expounded.

Neither think, that all words of the preceding Oration can be trans-lated into the Latin Tongue: For some words of that Oration contain in themselves a greater Sense of Mystical Profundity, of the Authority of *Solomon*; and having reference to his Writings, we acknowledge, That these Orations cannot be expounded nor understood by humane sense: For it is necessary, That all Orations, and distinct particulars of Astronomy, Astrology, and the Notary Art, be spoken and pronounced in their due time and season; and the Operations of them to be made according to the disposition of the Times.

Of the Triumphal Figures, how sparingly they are to be pronounced, and honestly and devoutly spoken.

There are also certain Figures or Orations, which *Solomon* in *Chaldeack, calleth Hely*; that is, Triumphal Orations of the Liberal Arts, and sudden excellent Efficacies of Vertues; and they are the Intro-duction to the Notary Art. Wherefore *Solomon* made a special begin-ning of them, that they are to be pronounced at certain determinate times of the Moon; and not to be undertaken, without consideration of the end. Which also *Magister Apollonius* hath fully and perfectly taught, saying, Whosoever will pronounce these words let him do it in a deter-minate appointed time, and set aside all other occasions, and he shall profit in all Sciences in one Moneth, and attain to them in an extraor-dinary wonderful manner.

The Expositions of the Lunations of the Notary Art.

These are the Expositions of the Lunation, and Introduction of the Notary Art, to wit, in the fourth and the eighth day of the Moon; and in the twelfth, sixteenth, four and twentieth, eight and twentieth, and thir-tieth they ought to be put in operation. From whence *Solomon* saith, That to those times, we give the expositive times of the Moon; of the fourth day of the Moon which are written by the four Angels; and in the fourth day of the Moon is manifested to us; and are four times repeated and explained by the Angel, the Messenger of these Orations; and are also revealed and delivered to us that require them from the Angel, four times of the year, to shew the Eloquence and Fulness of the four Languages, *Greek, Hebrew, Chaldee* and *Latine*; and God hath determined the Power of the Faculties of Humane Understanding, to the four Parts of the Earth; and also the four Vertues of Humanities, Understanding, Memory, Eloquence, and the Faculty of Ruling those three. And these things are to be used as we have before spoken.

He sheweth how the precedent Oration is the Beginning and Foundation of the whole Art.

That is the first Figure of the Notary Art, which is manifestly sited upon a Quadrangle Note: And this is Angelical Wisdom, understood of few in Astronomy; but in the Glass of Astrology, it is called, The Ring of Philosophy; and in the Notary Art it is written, To be the Foundation of the whole Science. But it is to be rehearsed four times a day, beginning in the morning once, about the third hour once, once in the ninth hour, and once in the evening.

The precedent Oration ought to be spoken secretly; and let him that speaks it be alone, and pronounce it with a low voyce, so that he scarcely hear himself. And this is the condition hereof, that if necessity urge one to do any great works, he shall say it twice in the morning, and about the ninth hour twice; and let him fast the first day wherein he rehearseth it, and let him live chastly and devoutly. And this is the oration which he shall say:

This is the Oration of the four Tongues, *Chaldee, Greek, Hebrew* and *Latine*, evidently expounded, which is called, "the Splendor or *Speculum* of Wisdom." In all holy Lunations, these Orations ought to be read, once in the morning, once about the third hour, once about the ninth hour, and once in the evening.

The Oration.

Azzaylemath, Assay, Lemeth, Azzabue.

The second part of the precedent Orations, which is to be said only once.

Azzaylemath, Lemath, Azacgessenio.

The third part of the precedent Oration, which is to be spoken together with the other.

Lemath, Sebanche, Ellithy, Aygezo.

This Oration hath no Exposition in the Latine.

This is a holy Prayer, without danger of any sin, which *Solomon* saith, is inexplicable by humane sense. And he addeth, and saith, That the Explication thereof is more prolixious, than can be considered of or apprehended by man; excepting also those secrets, which is not lawful, neither is it given to man to utter: Therefore he leaveth this Oration without any Exposition, because no man could attain to the perfection thereof: and it was left so Spiritual, because the Angel that declared it to *Solomon*, laid an inexcusable prohibition upon it, saying, See that thou do not presume to give to any other, nor to expound any thing out of this Oration, neither thou thy self, nor any one by thee, nor any one after thee: For it is a holy and Sacramental Mystery, that by expressing the words thereof, God heareth thy Prayer, and increaseth thy Memory, Understanding, Eloquence, and establisheth them all in thee. Let it be read in appointed times of the Lunation; as, in the fourth day of the Moon, the eighth and twelfth, as it is written and commanded: say that Oration very diligently four times in those dayes; verily believing, That thereby thy study shall suddenly be increased, and made clear, without any ambiguity, beyond the apprehension of humane Reason.

Of the Efficacy of that Oration which is inexplicable to humane sense.

This is that onely which *Solomon* calls The happiness of Wit, and *M. Apollonius* termeth it, The Light of the Soul, and the *Speculum* of Wisdom: And, I suppose, the said Oration may be called, The Image of Eternal Life: the Vertue and Efficacy whereof is so great, that it is understood or apprehended of very few or none.

Therefore having essayed some Petitions, Signs and Precepts, we give them as an entrance to those things whereof we intend to speak; of which they are part, that we have spoken of before. Nevertheless, before we come to speak of them, some things are necessary to be declared, whereby we may more clearly and plainly set forth our intended History: For, as we have said before, there are certain Exceptions of the Notary Art; some whereof are dark and obscure, and others plain and manifest.

For the Notary Art hath a Book in Astronomy, whereof it is the Beginning and mistris; and the Vertue thereof is such, that all Arts are taught and derived from her. And we are further to know, That the Notary Art doth in a wonderful manner contain and comprehend within it self, all Arts, and the Knowledge of all Learning, as *Solomon* witnesseth: Therefore it is called, *The Notary Art*, because in certain brief Notes, it teacheth and comprehendeth the knowledge of all Arts: for so *Solomon* also saith in his Treatise *Lemegeton*, that is, in his Treatise of Spiritual and Secret Experiments.

Here he sheweth, in what manner those Notes differ in Art, and the reason thereof; for a Note is a certain knowledge, by the Oration and Figure before set down.

But of the Orations and Figures, mention shall be made in their due place, and how the Notes are called in the Notary Art. Now he maketh mention of that Oration, which is called, The Queen of Tongues: for amongst these Orations, there is one more excellent than the rest, which King *Solomon* would therefore have be called, The Queen of Tongues, because it takes away, as it were, with a certain Secret covering the Impediments of the Tongue, and giveth it a marvellous Faculty of Eloquence. Wherefore before we proceed further, take a little Essay of that Oration: For this is an Oration which in the Scriptures we are taught to have alwayes in our mouthes; but it is taken out of the *Chaldean* Language: which, although it be short, is of a wonderful Vertue; that when you reade that Scripture, with the Oration before-mentioned, you cannot keep silent those things, which the Tongue and Understanding suggest, and administer to thee.

The Oration which follows, is a certain Invocation of the Angels of God, and it provoketh Eloquence, and ought to be said in the beginning of the Scripture, and in the beginning of the Moneth.

The Oration

> *Lameth, Leynach, Semach, Belmay,* (these Orations have not proper Lunations, as the Commentator saith upon the Gloss, *Azzailement, Gesegon, Lothamasim, Ozetogomaglial, Zeziphier, Josanum, Solatar, Bozefama, Defarciamar, Zemait, Lemaio, Pheralon, Anuc, Philosophi, Gregoon, Letos, Anum, Anum, Anum.*)

How this Oration is to be said in the beginning of every Moneth, chastly, and with a pure minde.

In the beginning of the Scriptures, are to be taught, how the precedent Oration ought to be spoken most secretly, and nothing ought to be retained, which thy Minde and Understanding suggests and prompts to thee in the reading thereof: Then also follow certain words, which are Precepts thereof, which ought alwayes to be begun in the beginning of the Moneth, and also in other dayes. I would also note this, That it is to be pronounced wisely, and with the greatest reverence; and that fasting, before you have taken either Meat or Drink.

Here followeth the Prayer we spake of before, to obtain a good Memory.

O Most Mighty God, Invisible God, *Theos Patir Heminas*; by thy Archangels, *Eliphamasay, Gelonucoa, Gebeche Banai, Gerabcai, Elomnit*; and by thy glorious Angels, whose Names are so Consecrated, that they cannot be uttered by us; which are these, *Do. Hel. X. P. A. Li. O. F.* &c. which cannot be Comprehended by Humane Sense.

Here following is the Prologue of the precedent Oration, which provoketh and procureth Memory, and is continued with the precedent Note.

This Oration ought to be said next to the precedent Oration; to wit, *Lameth:* and with this, I beseech thee to day, *O Theos*, to be said always as one continued Oration. If it be for the Memory, let it be said in the morning; if for any other effect, in the evening. And thus let it be said in the hour of the evening, and in the morning: And being thus pronounced, with the precedent Oration, it increaseth the Memory, and helpeth the Imperfections of the Tongue.

Here beginneth the Prologue of this Oration.

I Beseech thee, O my Lord, to illuminate the Light of my Conscience with the Splendor of thy Light: Illustrate and confirm my Understanding, with the sweet odour of thy Spirit. Adorn my Soul, that hearing I may hear and what I hear, I may retain in my Memory. O Lord, reform my heart, restore my senses, and strengthen them; qualifie my Memory with thy Gifts: Mercifully open the dulness of my Soul. O most merciful

God, temper the frame of my Tongue, by thy most glorious and unspeakable Name: Thou who are the Fountain of all Goodness; the Original and Spring of Piety, have patience with me, give a good Memory unto me, and bestow upon me what I pray of thee in this holy Oration. O thou who dost not forthwith Judge a sinner, but mercifully waitest, expecting his Repentance; I (though unworthy) beseech thee to take away the guilt of my sins, and wash away my wickedness and offences, and grant me these my Petitions, by the verture of thy holy Angels, thou who art one God in Trinity. *Amen.*

Here he sheweth some other Vertue of the precedent Oration.

If thou doubt of any great Vision, what it may foreshew; or if thou wouldst see any great Vision, of any danger present or to come; or if thou wouldst be certified of any one that is absent, say this Oration three times in the evening with great reverence and devotion, and thou shalt have and see that which thou desirest.

Here followeth an Oration of great Vertue, to attain the knowledge of the Physical Art, having also many other Vertues and Efficacy.

If you would have the perfect knowledge of any Disease, whether the same tend to death or life: if the sick party lie languishing, stand before him, & say this Oration three times with great reverence.

The Oration of the Physical Art.

I *Hesus fili Dominus Incomprehensibilis: Ancor, Anacor, Anylos, Zohorna, Theodonos, hely otes Phagor, Norizane, Corichito, Anosae, Helse Tonope, Phagora.*

Another part of the same Oration.

Elleminator, Candones helosi, Tephagain, Tecendum, Thaones, Behelos, Belhoros, Hocho Phagan, Corphandonos, Humanæ natus & vos Eloytus Phugora: Be present ye holy Angels, advertise and teach me, whether such a one shall recover, or dye of this Infirmity.

This being done, then ask the sick person, Friend, how dost thou feel thy self? And if he answer thee. I feel my self at good ease, I begin to mend, or the like; then judge without doubt, The sick person shall recover: but if he answer, I am very grievously ill, or worse and worse; then doubtless conclude, He will dye on the morrow: But if he answer, I know not how my state and condition is, whether better or worse; then you may know likewise, That he will either dye, or his disease will change and alter for the worse. If it be a Childe, that is not of years capable to make an answer; or that the sick languish so grievously, that he knoweth not how, or will not answer, say this Oration three times; and what you finde first revealed in your minde, that judge to come to pass of him.

Furthermore if any one dissemble and seek to hide or cover his infirmity; say the same Oration, and the Angelical Vertue shall suggest the truth to thee. If the diseased person be farre off; when you hear his Name, say likewise this Oration for him, and your minde shall reveal to you whether he shall live or dye.

If you touch the Pulse of any one that is sick, saying this Oration, the effect of his Infirmity shall be revealed to you.

Or if you touch the Pulse of any Woman with Childe, saying the same Oration, it shall be revealed, whether she shall bring forth a Male or Female.

But know, that this Miracle proceeds not from your own Nature, but from the Nature and Vertue of the holy Angels; it being a part of their Office, wonderfully to reveal these things to you. If you doubt of the Virginity of any one, say this Oration in your minde, and it shall be revealed to you, whether she be a Virgin, or Corrupt.

Here follows an efficacious Preface of an Oration, shewing what Verture and Efficacy you may thereby prove every day.

Of this Oration *Solomon* saith, That by it a new knowledge of Physick is to be received from God: Upon which, he hath laid this command, and calleth it, The Miraculous and Efficacious Foundation of the Physical Science; and that it containeth in it the quantity and quality of the whole Physical Art and Science: wherein there is contained, rather a miraculous and specious, then fearful or terrible Miracle, which as often-soever as thou readest the same, regard not the paucity of words, but praise the Vertue of so great a Mystery: For, *Solomon* himself speaking of the subtility of the Notory Art, wonderfully extolls the Divine Help; to wit, Because we have proposed a great thing, that is to say so many and so great Mysteries of Nature, contained under so specious brevity, that I suppose them to be as a general Problem to be proposed in the ordination of so subtile and excellent a work;

that the minde of the Reader or Hearer may be the more confirmed and fixed hereupon.

Here he sheweth how every Note of every Art, ought to exercise his own office; and that the Notes of one Art profit not to the knowledge of another Art; and we are to know, That all Figures have their proper Orations.

We come now, according to our strength, to divide the families of the Notory Art; and leaving that part which is natural, we come to the greater parts of the Art: for *Solomon*, a great Composer, and the greatest Master of the Notory Art, comprehendeth divers Arts under the Notion thereof. Therefore he calleth this a Notory Art, because it should be the Art of Arts, and Science of Sciences; which comprehendeth in it self all Arts and Sciences, Liberal and Mechanick: And those things which in other Arts are full of long and tedious locutions, filling up great prolixious Volumes of Books, wearying out the Student, through the length of time to attain to them: In this Art are comprehended very briefly in a few words or writings, so that it discovereth those things which are hard and difficult, making the ingenious learned in a very short time, by the wonderful and unheard-of Vertue of the words.

Therefore we, to whom such a faculty of the knowledge of the Scripture of Sciences is granted, have wholly received this great gift, and inestimable benefit, from the overflowing grace of the most high Creator. And whereas all Arts have their several Notes properly disposed to them, and signified by their Figures; and the Note of every Art, hath not any office of transcending to another Art, neither do the Notes of one Art profit or assist to the knowledge of another Art: Therefore this may seem a little difficult, as this small Treatise, which may be called a *Preludium* to the Body of the Art: we will explain the Notes severally; and that which is more necessary, we shall by the Divine Providence diligently search out the several Sciences of the Scripture.

A certain special Precept.

This is necessary for us, and necessarily we suppose will be profitable to posterity, that we know how to comprehend the great prolixious Volumes of writings, in brief and compendious Treatises; which, that it may easily be done, we are diligently to enquire out the way of attaining to it out of the three most ancient Books which were composed by *Solomon*; the first and chiefest thing to be understood therein, is, That the Oration before the second Chapter, is to be used long before every speech, the beginning whereof is *Assay:* and the words of the Oration are to be said in a competent space of time; but the subsequent part of the Oration is then chiefly to be said, when you desire the knowledge of the Volumes of writings, and looking into the Notes thereof. The same Oration is also to be said, when you would clearly and plainly understand and expound any Science or great Mystery, that is on a sudden proposed to you, which you never heard of before: say also the same Oration at such time, when any thing of great consequence is importuned of you, which at present you have not the faculty of expounding. This is a wonderful Oration, whereof we have spoken; the first part whereof is expounded in the Volume of the Magnitude of the quality of Art.

The Oration.

Lamed, Rogum, Ragia, Ragium, Ragiomal, Agaled, Eradioch, Anchovionos, Lochen, Saza, Ya, Manichel, Mamacuo, Lephoa, Bozaco, Cogemal, Salayel, Ytsunanu, Azaroch, Beyestar, Amak.

To the operation of the Magnitude of Art, this Oration containeth in the second place, a general Treatise of the first Note of all Scripture, part of the Exposition whereof, we have fully explained in the Magnitude of the quality of the same Art. But the Reader hath hardly heard of the admirable Mystery of the Sacramental Intellect of the same: Let him know this for a certain, and doubt not of the Greek words of the Oration aforesaid, but that the beginning of them is expounded in Latine.

The beginning of the Oration.

Oh Eternal and Unreprehensible Memory! Oh Uncontradictible Wisdom! Oh Unchangeable Power! Let thy right-hand encompass my heart, and the holy Angels of thy Eternal Counsel; compleat and fill up my Conscience with thy Memory, and the odour of thy Ointments; and let the sweetness of thy Grace strengthen and fortifie my Understanding, through the pure splendor and brightness of thy holy Spirit; by vertue whereof, the holy Angels always behold and admire the brightness of thy face, and all thy holy and heavenly Vertues; Wisdom, wherewith thou hast made all things; Understanding, by which thou hast reformed all things; Perseverance unto blessedness, whereby thou hast restored and confirmed the Angels; Love, whereby thou hast restored lost Mankinde, and raised him after his Fall to Heaven; Learning, whereby thou wer't pleased to teach *Adam* the knowledge of every Science: Inform, repleat, instruct, restore, correct, and refine me, that I may be made new in the understanding [of] thy Precepts, and in receiving the Sciences which are profitable for my Soul and Body, and for all faithful believers in thy Name which is blessed for ever, world without end.

Here is also a particular Exposition of the fore-going Oration, which he hath left unexpounded, to be read by every one that is learned in this Art; and know, that no humane power nor faculty in man is sufficient to finde out the Exposition thereof.

This Oration is also called by *Solomon*, The Gemme and Crown of the Lord: for he saith, It helpeth against danger of Fire, or of wilde Beasts of the Earth, being said with a believing faith: for it is affirmed to have been reported from one of the four Angels, to whom was given power to hurt the Earth, the Sea, and the Trees. There is an example of this Oration, in the Book called, *The Flower of heavenly Learning*; for herein *Solomon* glorifieth God, because by this he inspired into him the knowledge of Theologie, and dignified him with the Divine Mysteries of his Omnipotent Power and Greatness: which *Solomon* beholding in his night-Sacrifice, bestowed upon him by the Lord his God, he conveniently gathered the greater Mysteries together in this Notory Art, which were holy, and worthy, and reverend Mysteries. These things and Mysteries of Theologie the erring Gentiles have not all lost, which *Solomon* calleth The Signe of the holy Mystery of God revealed by his Angel before and that which is contained in them, is the fulness of our dignity and humane Salvation.

The first of these Orations which we call Spiritual, the vertue whereof teacheth Divinity, and preserveth the memory thereof.

These are Orations also, which are of great virtue and efficacy to our Salvation: The first whereof is Spiritual, and teacheth Divinity; and also Perseverance in the Memory thereof: Therefore *Solomon* commandeth it to be called, The Signe of the Grace of God: for, as *Ecclesiastes* saith, This is the Spiritual Grace of God, that hath given me knowledge to treat of all Plants, from the Cedar of Lebanon, to the Hyssop that groweth on the wall.

The election of time, in what Lunation these Orations ought to be said.

The first Oration ought to be said once in the first Lunation; in the third, three times; in the sixth, six times; in the ninth, nine times; in the twelfth. twelve times; in the seventeenth, seventeen times; and in the eighteenth, as many times; in the twenty sixth, as many; in the twenty ninth, as many; and so many in the thirty ninth: for this Oration is of so great vertue and efficacy, that in the very day thou shalt say the same, as if it were determined by the Father, it shall increase thy knowledge in the Science of Divinity.

But if otherwise that thou art ignorant, and it hath been seen by thy Companions, thy Superiours or Inferiours, though unto others thou shalt seem to have knowledge; enter into the study of Divinity, and hear the Lectures by the space of some moneths, casting off all doubt from thee, of them who shall see thee, to know such things: and in that day wherein thou wouldst say it, live chastly, and say it in the Morning.

Solomon testifieth, That an Angel delivered the following Oration in Thunder, who standeth alwayes in the Presence of the Lord, to whom he is not dreadful. The Mystery hereof is holy, and of great efficacy: neither ought this Oration to be said above once, because it moveth the heavenly Spirits to perform any great work.

Of this Oration he saith, That so great is the Mystery thereof, that it moveth the Celestial Spirits to perform any great work which the Divine Power permitteth. It also giveth the vertue of its Mystery, that it exalteth the tongue and body of him that speaketh it, with so great inspiration, as if some new and great Mystery were suddenly revealed to his understanding.

Here followeth the beginning of this Oration, wherein is so great vertue and efficacy, as we have said, it being said with great devotion.

Achacham, Yhel, Chelychem, Agzyraztor, Yegor, &c.

This is the beginning of the Oration, the parts whereof are four: But there is something to be said of the beginning by itself, and of the four parts severally; and then between the beginning and these Orations, which are four, we shall make this competent division.

For this is that which is to be spoken of the beginning severally: And this Oration is to be divided into four parts; and the first part thereof is to be said, that is, the beginning, before any other part of the Oration is to be compleated. These Greek Names following are to be pronounced. This is the division of these Orations, *Hielma, Helma, Hemna,* &c.

> Oh God the Father, God the Son, God the Holy Spirit, Confirm this Oration, and my Understanding and Memory, to receive, understand, and retain the knowledge of all good Scriptures; and give me perseverance of minde therein.

This is the beginning of that Oration, which, as we have said before, ought to be said according to the Prolations and Constitutions thereof; and ought to be repeated, because of the forgetfulness of our Memory, and according to the exercise of our wit, and according to the sanctity of our life; there being contained in it so great a Mystery, and such efficacious Vertue.

There followeth another subtile Oration, wherein is contained a Sacramental Mystery, and wherein every perfect Science is wonderfully compleated: For hereby God would have us to know, what things are Celestial, and what are Terrene; and what heavenly things the Celestial effecteth, and what earthly things the Terrene: because the Lord hath said, My eyes have seen the imperfect, and in thy book every day shall be formed and written, and no man in them, &c. So it is in the Precepts of God: for we are not able to write all things, how the Sun hath the same course as at first, that our order may be confirmed: for all writing whatsoever, which is not from God, is not to be read; for God himself would have all things to be divided: & this is how these are to be used, before the second part, which containeth so glorious and excellent Consecrations of Orations, & defineth the Consecrated part to have power in the Heavens, and in no wise can be defined by humane tongues.

This is the beginning of the second part of that Oration spoken of before, which is of so great vertue.

Aglaros, Theomiros, Thomitos, &c.

This is the second part of the precedent Oration, of which some singular thing is to be spoken. Wherefore if thou sayest this Oration, commemorating the first part thereof, say the Oration following, and thou shalt perceive the precepts which are therein.

> Oh God of all things, who art my God, who in the beginning hast created all things out of nothing, and hast reformed all things by the Holy

Spirit; compleat and restore my conscience, and heal my understanding, that I may glorify thee in all my works, thoughts and words. And after thou hast said this Oration, make a little respite the space of half an hour, and then say the third part of the Oration, which follows: *Megal, Legal, Chariotos,* &c. having said this third part of the Oration, then meditate with thy self about the Scriptures thou desirest to know; and then say this Oration:

Oh thou that art the Truth, Light, and Way, of all Creatures: Oh just God, vivify me, and confirm my understanding, and restore my knowledge and conscience unto me, as thou didst unto King *Solomon, Amen.*

Commemorating the parts according to that which is laid down, add the Oration following: the other Orations being said, say the fourth part of the Oration, which is this: *Amasiel, Danyi, hayr,* &c.

Then the parts being commemorated as is directed, add also the following Oration.

I speak these things in thy presence, Oh Lord my God, before whose face all things are naked and open, that I being washed from the error of infidelity, thy all-quicking [sic] Spirit may assist me, and take away all incredulity from me.

How the Latine Orations are not expounded by the words of the Orations.

We are therefore to know, that the whole Oration remaineth unexpounded; because the words thereof are of so great subtilty, adorned with the Hebrew and Chaldean Tongue, with the subtile and wonderful elocution of God: that the office of the free exposition thereof, cannot possibly be transferred upon me. The Latine words which are subjoyned to the parts of the Oration aforesaid, are such words as have been translated out of the Chaldean Tongue: for they are not the whole Oration; but as certain heads of every Oration pertaining thereunto.

Here he speaketh of the efficacy of all these.

For this Oration is such a mystery, as King *Solomon* himself witnesseth, that a Servant of his House having found this book by chance, and being too much overcome with Wine in the Company of a Woman, he presumptuously read it; but before he had finished a part thereof, he was stricken dumb, blind and lame, and his Memory taken from him; so he continued to the day of his death: and in the hour of his death, he spoke and said, that four Angels which he had offended in presumptuous [sic] reading so sacred a mystery, were the daily keepers and afflicters, one of his Memory, another of his speech, a third of his sight, and the fourth of his hearing.

By which Testimony this Oration is so much commended by the same King *Solomon*, and great is the mystery thereof: we do greatly require and charge every one, that will say or read it, that he do it not presumptuously; for in presumption is sin; wherefore let this Oration be said, according as is directed.

We therefore hold it convenient and necessary, to speak something of the general precepts of art, and of the knowledge of all arts; and of the several precepts of every singular art: but because we have touched somthing of the course of the Moon, it is necessary that we shew what her course signifies. The Moon passeth through 12 signs in one Moneth; and the Sun through 12 signs in a year; and in the same term and time, the Spirit inspireth, fructifieth and illustrateth them; whence it is said, that the Sun and the Moon run their course: it is understood the course which first they had. But because this is wanting in the Hebrew, we thought good to omit it in the Latine, having spoken sufficiently of the preceding Oration, and the three parts thereof.

In this Chapter he sheweth the efficacy of the subsequent Oration, it being special to obtain Eloquence.

This Holy Oration which followeth, is a certain special Oration, to obtain eloquence; whereas all others have virtue and efficacy in other things, this containeth this certain special mystery in it self: And whereas one of the generals is shewing in it self, certain general precepts, common to all arts for so God instituted the soul in the body, saying, This I give unto you, that ye may keep and observe the Law of the Lord; And these are they that stand in the presence of God alwayes, and see their Saviour face to face night and day. So of this Oration, I say, This is that most glorious, mystical and intelligible Oration, containing such mysteries in it, which the mind, conscience and tongue succeedeth. This is such a mystery, that a man shall keep it according to his will, who foreseeth all things in his sight that are made; for the mystery of this Oration is glorious and sacramental: let no man presume to say any of this Oration after too much drinking or Luxury; nor fasting, without great reverence and discretion. Whence *Solomon* saith, Let no man presume to treat any thing of this Oration, but in certain determinate and appointed times, unless he make mention of this Oration before some great President, for some weighty business; for which this Oration is of wonderful excellent virtue.

The goodness of this Oration, and the attaining to the effects thereof, it is read in that Psalm wherein it is said, Follow me, and I will make you fishers of men, as he said and did.

We know that it is not of our power, that this Oration is of so great Virtue, and such a mystery, as sometimes also the Lord said to his disciples, This we are not able to know: for this Oration is such a mystery, that it containeth in it the great Name of God; which many have lyed in saying they knew it; for *Jesus* himself performed many Miracles in the Temple by it: But many have lyed about what he did, and have hid and absconded the truth thereof; so that none have declared the same before it came to passe: but we suppose have spoken somthing about or concerning it.

In this chapter he setteth down the time and manner how this Oration is to be pronounced.

For this Oration is one of the generals, and the first of particulars, containing both in it self; having a special virtue and faculty, to gain Eloquence in it self: therefore it is necessary to be understood what time, ordination, and what dayes it is to be said and published.

It may alwayes be rehearsed in every 14 Lunary as above said; but the ordination of the time for every day, wherein it is to be said, is especially in the morning betimes, before a man is defiled; and then all Orations are chiefly to be said. And this Oration must be then pronounced totally together, without any division. And although there are divisions therein, the Oration is not divided in it self; but only the Divine and Glorious Names are written severally, and are divided into parts, according to the terminations of every great and Glorious Name; and it is to be said together as a most excellent Name, but not as one Word, because of the fragility of our nature; Neither is it needful to know the Elements of sillables, posited in this Oration; they are not to be known; neither let any one presumptuously speak them; neither let him do any thing by way of temptation, concerning this Oration, which ought not to be done: *Elmot, Sehel, Hemech, Zaba,* &c.

No Man that is impedited[5] or corrupted with any crime, ought to presume to say this Oration.

This is a thing agreed unto amongst the wise men of this World, that these things, as we have said before, be pronounced with great reverence and

---

5   That is, "has an impediment."

industry: it may be said every day, wherein thou art not hindred by some criminal sin; and in that day wherein thou art impedited by some criminal sin, thou maist remember it in thy heart; and if thou dost desire to be made Eloquent, repeat it three times. And if any evil thing trouble thee, or thou art ermerged [sic] and involved into any great business, repeat this Oration once, and Eloquence shall be added to thee, as much as is needful; and if thou repeat it over twice, great Eloquence shall be given to thee: so great a Sacrament is this Oration.

The third thing to be considered in this Oration, is; This Oration ought so to be pronounced, that confession of the Heart and Mouth ought to precede it: let it be pronounced in the morning early, and after that Oration say the Latine Oration following.

This is a Prologue or Exposition of the precedent Oration, which ought to be said together.

> Oh omnipotent and eternal God, and merciful Father, blessed before all Worlds; who art a God eternal, incomprehensible, and unchangeable, and hast granted this blessed gift of Salvation unto us; according to the omnipotency of thy Majesty, hast granted unto us the faculty of speaking and learning, which thou hast denied to all other animals; and hast disposed of all things by thy infallible providence: thou art God, whose nature is eternal and consubstantial, exalted above the Heavens; in whom the whole Deity corporally dwells: I implore thy Majesty, and Glorify thy omnipotency, with an intentive imploration, adoring the mighty Virtue, Power and Magnificence of thy eternity. I beseech thee, Oh my God, to grant me the inestimable Wisdome of the Life of thy holy Angels. Oh God the Holy Spirit, incomprehensible, in whose presence stand the Holy quires of Angels; I pray and beseech thee, by thy Holy and Glorious Name, and by the sight of thy Angels, and the Heavenly Principalities, to give thy grace unto me, to be present with mee, and give unto me power to persevere in the Memory of thy Wisdome, who livest and reignest eternally one eternal God, through all worlds of worlds; in whose sight are all celestial virtues, now and alwayes, and everywhere, *Amen*.

This Oration being thus finished, there must of necessity some Mystery be added; so that you are to be silent a while after the Latine Oration is ended: and after a little taciturnity, that is, a little space of silence, begin to say this Oration following seriously: *Semet, Lamen*, &c.

This (saith *Solomon*) is the Oration of Orations, and a special experiment, whereby all things, whether generals or particulars, are known fully, efficaciously and perfectly, and are kept in the Memory. But when thou hast by this Oration attained the Eloquence thou desirest, be sparing thereof, and do not rashly declare those things which thy Tongue suggests and administers to thee; for this is the end of all general precepts, which are given to obtain Memory, Eloquence, and understanding. All those things which are before delivered, of general precepts, are given as signs how the faculty of attaining to the understanding of the general precepts may be had, which also *Solomon* calleth Spirituals; and those singular arts have singular virtues and powers.

Having now given a sufficient definition of general precepts; and the Orations are laid down, and the Authority of the Orations unto what they are designed; it is now necessary to set down what is to be done, concerning the singular Orations; because we are now to treat of the several and particular arts, that we may follow the example which our builder and Master hath laid before us; for *Solomon* saith, before we proceed to the singular notes and Orations of arts before noted, there ought to be said a *Præludium*, which is a beginning or Prologue.

[*Special Rules*6]

How every several art hath its proper note.

Before we proceed to the singular precepts of several Arts, it is necessary to discover how every several Art hath a several Note.

Of the liberal Sciences and other things, which may be had by that Art.

The liberal Arts are seaven, and seaven exceptives, and seaven Mechanicks. The seaven exceptives are comprehended under the seaven liberal: It is manifest what the seaven liberal Arts are, of which we shall first treat. The Mechanicks are these, which are adulteratedly called *Hydromancy, Pyromancy, Nigromancy, Chiromancy, Geomancy, Geonegia,* which is comprehended under *Astronomy,* and *Neogia.*

Hydromancy, is a science of divining by the Water; whereby the Masters thereof judged by the standing or running of the Water. *Pyromancy,* is an experiment of divining by the flaming of the fire; which the ancient Philosophers esteemed of great efficacy. *Nigromancy,* is a Sacrifice of dead Animals, whereby the Ancients supposed to know many great Experiments

---

6   This heading does not occur in the texts, but is supplied here for clarity.

without sin, and to attain to great knowledge: from whence *Solomon* commandeth that they might read seaven Books of that Art without sin; and that two he accompted [judged] Sacriledge, and that they could nor [not] read two Books of that Art without sin. But having spoken enough hereof, we proceed to the rest.

Of the liberal Sciences and other things which may be had thereby.

There are seaven liberal Arts, which every one may learn and read without sin. For Philosophy is great, containing profound Mysteries in it self: These Arts are wonderfully known.

He declareth what notes the three first liberal Arts have.

For *Grammar* hath three notes only, *Dialects* two, and *Rhetorick* four, and every one with open and distinct Orations. But wherefore *Grammar* hath three, *Dialects* two, and *Rhetorick* four; that we know King *Solomon* himself testifieth and affirmeth; for he saith, And as I was admiring and revolving in my heart and mind, which way, from whom and from whence was this science, An Angel brought one book, wherein was written the Figures and Orations, and delivered unto me the Notes and Orations of all Arts, plainly and openly, and told me of them all as much as was necessary: And he explained unto me, as to a Child are taught by certain Elements, some tedious Arts in a great space of time, how that I should have these Arts in a short space of time: Saying unto me, So shalt thou be promoted to every science by the increase of these virtues. And when I asked him, Lord, whence and how cometh this? The Angel answered, This is a great Sacrament of the Lord, and of his will: this writing is by the power of the Holy Ghost, which inspireth, fructifieth and increaseth all knowledge; And again the Angel said, Look upon these Notes and Orations, at the appointed and determinate times, and observe the times as appointed of God, and no otherwise. When he had thus said he shewed to King *Solomon* a book wherein was written, at what times all these things were to be pronounced and published, and plainly demonstrated it according to the Vision of God: Which things I having heard and seen, did operate in them all, according to the Word of the Lord by the Angel: And so *Solomon* declareth, it came to passe unto him: But we that come after him, ought to imitate his Authority, and as much as we are able observe those things he hath left unto us.

Here Solomon sheweth, how the Angel told him distinctly, wherefore the Grammar hath three Figures.

Behold wherefore the Grammatical Art hath only three Notes in the Book of *Solomon Gemeliath*, that is, in The Book of the Art of God, which we read is the Art of all other sciences, and of all other Arts; For *Solomon* saith, When I did inquire every thing singularly of the Angel of God, with fear, saying, Lord, from whence shall this come to passe to me, that I may fully and perfectly know this Art? Why do so many Notes appertain to such an Art, and so many to such an Art, and are ascribed to several determinate Orations, to have the efficacy thereof? The Angel is thus said to answer: The Grammatical Art is called a liberal Art, And hath three things necessary thereunto: Ordination of words and times; and in them, of Adjuncts or Figures; Simple, compound and various; and a various declination of the parts to the parts, or a relation from the parts, and a Congruent and ordinate division. This is the reason, why there is three Notes in the Art of *Grammar*. And so it pleased the Divine Wisdome, that as there should be a full knowledge of declining by one; by another, there should be had a convenient Ordination of all the parts; by the third, there should be had a continual and convenient Division of all the parts, simple and compound.

The Reason why the Dialectical Art hath two Figures onely.

Dialect, which is called the form of Arts, and a Doctrinal speech, hath two things necessary thereunto, to wit, Eloquence of Arguing, and Prudence to answer; Therefore the greatness of the Divine Providence and Piety, hath appointed two Notes to it; that by the first, we may have Eloquence to Argue and Dispute; and by the second, industry to answer without ambiguity: Wherefore there are ascribed to *Grammar* three Notes, and to *Dialect* two Notes.

The Reason why Rhetorick hath four Figures.

Let us see wherefore *Rhetorick* hath four Notes. For there are four things necessary therein; as the Angel of the Lord said unto *Solomon*; to wit, a continual and flourishing adornment of locution, an ordinate, competent and discreet judgement, a Testimony of Causes or Offices, of Chances & Losses, a composed disposition of buying and selling; An Eloquence of the matters of that Art, with a demonstrative understanding. Therefore the greatness of God hath appointed to the Art of *Rhetorick* four Notes, with their Holy and Glorious Orations; as they were reverently sent by the Hand of God; that every Note in this Art aforesaid, might have a several faculty, That the first Note in that Art, might give a continual locution, a competent and flourishing adornment thereof: The second, to discern Judgements, just and unjust, ordinate and inordinate, true and false: The third, competently to discover offices and causes: and the fourth giveth understanding and eloquence in all the operations of this Art, without prolixity. See therefore how in *Grammar, Logick,* and *Rhetorick,* the several Notes are disposed in the several Arts.

But of the other Arts and their Notes, we shall speak in their due place and time, as we find them disposed in the book of the same *Solomon*.

At what times and hours the Notes of these three liberal Arts are to be looked into.

Now we proceed to shew at what time, and how the Notes of these Arts are to be looked into, and the Orations to be said, to attain to these Arts. If thou art altogether ignorant of the Grammatical Art, and wouldst have the knowledge thereof: if it be appointed thee of God to do this work of works, and have a firm understanding in this Art of Arts: Then know that thou maist not presume to do otherwise than this book commandeth thee; for this book of his shall be thy Master, And this Art of his thy Mistress.

How the Grammatical Notes are to be looked into in the first Moon.

For in this manner, the Grammaticall Notes are to be looked into, and the Orations to be said.

In the dayes when the Moon is in her prime, the first Note is to be looked into 12 times, and the Orations thereof repeated 24 times with Holy reverence; making a little space between, let the Orations be twice repeated at the inspection of every Note, and chiefly abstain from sins: do this from the first day of the Moon to the 14, and from the 14 to the 17. The first and second Notes are to be looked into 20 times, and the Orations to be repeated 30 times, on the 15 and 17 dayes, using some interval between them, All the three Notes are then every day to be looked into 12 times, and the Orations to be repeated 20 times: and thus of the Notes of the Art of *Grammar.* But if thou hast read any books of this Art, and desirest perfection therein, do as is commanded; using the general Orations to increase

Memory, Eloquence, understanding and perseverance therein, repeating these above in the due time and hours appointed; lest that going beyond thy precept, thou committest sin: but when thou dost this, see that it be secret to thy self, and that thou have no looker on but God. Now we come to the Notes.

Here followeth the knowledge of the Notes.

In the beginning of the inspection of all Notes, fast the first day till the evening, if you can; if thou canst not, then take another hour. This is the Grammatical precept.

Of the logical notes.

The Dialectical Notes may be used every day, except only in those dayes before told of: The Rhetorical every day, except only three dayes of the Moneth, to wit, ☽. 11, 17, and 19. And they are forbidden on these dayes, as *Solomon* testifyes, the Notes of all Arts, except the Notes of this Art are offered. These precepts are generally to be observed.

How the Logical Notes are to be inspected, and the Orations thereof said.

Know, that the Dialectical Notes are four times to be looked into, and the Orations thereof in that day are 20 times to be repeated, making some respite, and having the books of that Art before your Eyes; and so likewise the books of Rhetorick, when the Notes thereof are inspected, as it is appointed. This sufficeth for the knowledge of the 3 Arts.

How we must beware of offences.

Before we proceed to begin the first Note of the Art of *Grammar*, somthing is to be tryed before, that we may have the knowledge of the 1, 2, and 3 Notes. And you ought first to know, in what the Notes of the Grammatical, Logical, or Rhetorical Art are to be inspected, it being necessary that your greatest intentions be to keep from all offences.

How the Notes ought to be inspected, at certain elected times.

This is a special and manifest knowledge, wherewith the Notes of the Grammatical Art are known: how they are to be published, at what times, and with what distinction, is duly and competently manifest; it is spoken already of the publishing and inspection of the Notes and Orations: now we shall digresse a little to speak somthing of the times, it being in part done already.

How divers Months are to be sought out in the inspection of the Notes.

We have spoken already of the tearms of this Art, wherein the Orations are to be read, and the Notes to be looked into: it remaineth to declare, how the Lunations of these Orations are to be inspected and found out. But see that you mistake not: yet I have already noted the Lunations, wherein the Notes ought to be looked into, and the Orations rehearsed: But there are some Months, wherein the Lunation is more profitable than others: if thou wouldst operate in Theology or Astronomy, do it in a fiery sign; if Grammar or Logick, in Gemini or Virgo; if Musick or Physick, in Taurus or Libra; if Rhetorick, Philosophy, Arithmetick or Geometry, in Gemini or Cancer; for Mathematicks, in Taurus or Gemini: so they are well placed, and free from evil; for all the Heavenly Potestates and Chorus of Angels do rejoyce in their Lunations, and determinate dayes.

Here is made mention of the Notes of all Arts.

I *Apollonius* following the power of *Solomon*, have disposed my self to keep his works and observations, as it is spoken of the three Notes of Grammar so will I observe the times as they are to be observed: But the Orations thereof are not written, but are more fully demonstrated in the following work; for what is written of those three Notes, are not Orations, but Definitions of those Notes, written by the Greek, Hebrew, and Chaldean, and other things which are apprehended by us: For those writings which are not understood in Latine, ought not to be pronounced, but on those dayes which are appointed by King *Solomon*, and in those dayes wherein the Notes are inspected, but on those dayes those Holy writings are alwayes to be repeated: and the Latine, on those dayes wherein the Notes are not inspected. The Notes of the Logical Art are two: and at what times they are to be published is already shewn in part: more shall hereafter be said of them: now we come to the rest. The Latine writings may be published according to the Antiquity of the Hebrews, except on those dayes we have spoken of: for *Solomon* saith, See that thou perform all those precepts as they are given: But of the rest which follow, it is to be done otherwise: for when thou seest the first Note of Logick, repeat in thy heart the sign in the first Note, and so in the Notes of all Arts except those whereof a definition shall be given.

Definitions of several Arts, and the Notes thereof.

We will give also Definitions of several Arts, as it is in the Book of *Solomon*; Geometry hath one Note, Arithmetick a Note and a half; Philosophy, with the Arts and Sciences contained therein, hath 7 Species; Theology and Astronomy, with the Sciences in them contained, hath 7 Notes, but they are great and dangerous; not great in the pronunciation, but have great efficacy: Musick hath one Note, and Physick one Note; but they are all to be published and rehearsed in their appointed dayes: But know, that in every day wherein you beholdest the Notes of Theology, Philosophy, or of any Arts contained in them, that thou neither laugh nor play, nor sport, because King *Solomon*, when he saw the forms of these Notes, having over-drunk himself, God was angry with him, and spoke unto him by his Angel, saying, *Because thou hast despised my Sacrament, and Polluted and derided my Holy things; I will take away part of thy Kingdome, and I will shorten the dayes of thy Children.* And the Angel added, *The Lord hath forbid thee to enter into the Temple 80 days, that thou maist repent of thy sin.* And when *Solomon* wept and besought mercy of the Lord, the Angel answered, *Thy dayes shall be prolonged; nevertheless many evills and iniquities shall come upon thy Children, and they shall be destroyed of the iniquities that shall come upon them.*

At the beginning of a Note, having seen the generals; let the specials be looked into. The word of *Solomon* is to seek unto God for his promises, before the Notes of the three Arts.

The first Oration at the beginning of the Note.

[1] The Light, Truth, Life, Way, Judge, Mercy, Fortitude and Patience, preserve, help me, and have Mercy upon me, *Amen.*

This Oration, with the preceding, ought to be said in the beginning of the first Note of Grammar.

[2] Oh Lord, Holy Father, Almighty, eternal God, in whose sight are all the foundations of all Creatures, and invisible beings, whose Eyes behold my imperfections, of the sweetness of whose love the Earth and Heavens are filled; who sawest all things before they were made, in whose book every day is formed, and all mankind are written therein: behold me thy

Servant this day prostrate before thee, with my whole Heart and Soul, by thy Holy Spirit confirm me, blesse me, protect all my Actions in this inspection or repetition, and illuminate me with the constancy of thy visitation.

The 3 Oration. This Oration ought to be said before the second Note of Grammar.

[3] Behold, O Lord, merciful Father of all things; eternal dispensor of all virtues, and consider my operations this day; Thou art the Beholder and Discerner of all the Actions of Men and Angels: Let the wonderful grace of thy promises condescend to fulfil this sudden virtue in me, and infuse such efficacy into me, operating in thy Holy and great Name, thou who infusest thy praise into the mouths of them that love thee, *Amen.*

The 4 Oration. Let this Oration be rehearsed before the third Grammatical Note:

[4] O *Adonay*, Creator of all visible Creatures! Oh most Holy Father, who dwellest incompassed about with eternal light, disposing and by thy power governing all things before all beginnings; I most humbly beseech thy eternity and thy incomprehensible goodness may come to perfection in me, by the operation of thy most Holy Angels; And be confirmed in my Memory, and establish these thy Holy works in me, *Amen.*

A little space after this Oration, say the following: the first Oration ought to be said before the first Note of Logick.

[5] Oh Holy God, great good, and the eternal Maker of all things, thy Attributes not to be exprest, who hast Created the Heaven and the Earth, the Sea and all things in them, and the bottomless pit, according to thy pleasure; in whose sight are the Words and Actions of all men: Grant unto me, by these Sacramental Mysteries of thy Holy Angels, the precious knowledge of this art, which I desire by the Ministry of thy Holy Angels, it being without any Malignant or Malitious intent, *Amen.*

Pronounce this Oration in the beginning of the first Figure of the Logick art; and after this Oration rehearse incontinently with some interval, the Orations written between the first Figure.

The 6 Oration ought to be said before the first Note of the Dialect.

[6] Helay: Most Merciful Creator, Inspirer, Reformer, and Approver of all Divine wills, Ordeyner of all things, Mercifully give ear to my Prayer, gloriously intend unto the desires of my heart, that what I humbly desire, according to thy promises, thou wilt Mercifully grant, *Amen*.

This Oration following, ought to be pronounced before the first Note of the Rhetorical Art.

[7] Omnipotent and merciful Father, Ordeyner and Creator of all Creatures: Oh most Holy Judge, eternal King of Kings, and Lord of Lords; who wonderfully condescendest to give wisdome and understanding to thy Saints, who judgest and discernest all things: I beseech thee to illuminate my heart this day with the Splendor of thy Beauty, that I may understand and know what I desire, and what things are considerable to be known in this Art, *Amen*.

This Oration with the following *Hanazay*, &c. ought to be pronounced before the first Figure of Rhetorick: and although the Oration is divided into two parts, yet it is one and the same: And they are divided only for this cause, that there might be some mean interval used in the pronouncing of them; and they ought to be pronounced before the other Orations written in the Figure.

Hanazay, Sazhaon, Hubi, Sene, Hay, Ginbar, Ronail, Selmora, Hyramay, Lohal, Yzazamael, Amathomatois, Yaboageyors, Sozomcrat, Ampho, Delmedos, Geroch, Agalos, Meihatagiel, Secamai, Saheleton, Mechogrisces, Lerirencrhon.

The 8 Oration, let it be pronounced before the second Note of the Rhetorical Art:

[8] Oh great eternal and wonderful Lord God, who of thy eternal counsel hast disposed of all virtues, and art Ordeyner of all goodness; Adorn and Beautify my understanding, and give unto me Reason to know and learn the Mysteries of thy Holy Angels: And grant unto me all knowledge and learning thou hast promised to thy Servants by the vertue of thy holy Angels, *Amen*.

This Oration, with the other two following, ought to be pronounced, *(viz. Vision*, &c.) *Azelechias*, &c. in the beginning of the second Figure of Rhetorick, and before the other Orations; and there ought to be some interval between them.

Let this Oration following be said, before the second Note of Rhetorick.

[9] *Vision*; beholding with thy eternal conspiration all Powers, Kingdomes and Judges, Administring all manner of Languages to all, and of whose power there is no end; restore I beseech thee and increase my Memory, my heart and understanding, to know, understand, and judge all things which thy Divine authority commendeth necessary in this art, perfectly fulfill them in me, *Amen.*

Let this Oration following, with the Precedent, be rehearsed before the second Note of Rhetorick.

[10] *Azelechias, Velozeos, Inoanzama, Samelo, Hotens, Sagnath, Adonay, Soma, Jezochos, Hicon, Jezomethon, Sadaot.* And thou Oh God propitiously confirm thy promises in me, as thou hast confirmed them by the same words to King *Solomon*; send unto me, Oh Lord, thy virtue from Heaven, that may illuminate my mind and understanding: strengthen, Oh God, my understanding, renew my Soul within me, and wash me with the Waters which are above the Heavens; pour out thy Spirit upon my flesh, and fill my bowels with thy Judgements, with humility and charity: thou who hast created the Heaven and the Earth, and made man according to thy own Image; pour out the light of thy love into my understanding, that being radicated [rooted] and established in thy love and thy mercy, I may love thy Name, and know, and worship thee, and understand all thy Scriptures, And all the Mysteries which thou hast declared by thy Holy Angels, I may receive and understand in my heart, and use this Art to thy Honor and Glory, through thy mighty Counsel, *Amen.*

The 11 Oration ought to be said before the pronounciation of the third Note of Rhetorick.

[11] I know, that I love thy Glory, and my delight is in thy wonderful works, and that thou wilt give unto me wisdome, according to thy goodness and thy power, which is incomprehensible: *Theon, Haltanagon, Haramalon, Zamoyma, Chamasal, Jeconamril, Harionatar, Jechomagol, Gela Magos, Kemolihot, Kamanatar, Hariomolatar, Hanaces, Velonionathar, Azoroy, Jezabali;* by these most Holy and Glorious profound Mysteries, precious Offices, virtue and knowledge of God, compleat and perfect my beginnings, and reform my beginnings, *Zembar, Henoranat, Grenatayl, Samzatam, Jecornazay:* Oh thou great Fountain of all goodness, knowledge and virtue, give unto thy Servant power to eschew all evill, and cleave unto goodness and knowledge, and to follow the same with an Holy intention, that

with my whole heart I may understand & learn thy Laws and Decrees; especially these Holy Mysteries; wherein that I may profit, I beseech thee, *Amen.*

This Oration ought to be said before the ninth Rhetorical Note:

[12] Oh most reverend Almighty Lord, ruling all Creatures both Angels and Arch-Angels, and all Celestial, terrestrial, and infernal Creatures; of whose greatness comes all plenty, who hast made man after thy own Image; Grant unto me the knowledge of this Art, and strengthen all Sciences in me, *Amen.*

Pronounce this before the first Figure of Arithmetick:

[13] Oh God who numbrest, weighest, and measurest all things, given the day his order, and called the Sun by his Name; Grant the knowledge of this Art unto my understanding, that I may love thee, and acknowledge the gift of thy goodness, *Amen.*

Say this before the semi-note of Arithmetick:

[14] Oh God, the Operator of all things, from whom proceeds every good and perfect gift; sow the Seeds of thy Word in my Heart, that I may understand the excellent Mysteries of this Art, *Amen.*

Say this before the second Figure of Arithmetick:

[15] Oh God the perfect Judge of all good works, who makest known thy saving goodness amongst all Nations; open my Eyes and my Heart, with the beams of thy mercy, that I may understand and persevere in these thy Heavenly Mysteries, *Amen.*

This Oration before the second Note of Geometry:

[16] Oh God the giver of all wisdome and knowledge to them that are without sin, Instructor and Master of all Spiritual Learning, by thy Angels and Arch-Angels, by Thrones, Potestates, Principates and Powers, by Cherubim and Seraphim, and by the 24 Elders, by the 4 Animals, and all the host of Heaven, I adore, invocate, worship and glorify thy Name, and exalt thee: most terrible and most merciful, I do humbly beseech thee this day to illuminate and fill my Heart with the grace of thy Holy Spirit, thou who art three in one, *Amen.*

Say this Oration before the second Note of Theology.

> [17] I adore thee, Oh King of Kings, my light, my substance, my life, my King, and my God, my Memory, and my strength; who in a Moment gavest sundry Tongues, and threwest down a Mighty Tower, And gavest by thy Holy Spirit the knowledge of Tongues to thy Apostles, infusing thy knowledge into them in a Moment, giving them the understanding of all Languages: inspire my Heart, and pour the dew of thy grace and Holy Spirit into me, that I may understand the Exposition of Tongues and Languages, *Amen.*

Three Chapters to be published, before any of the Notes.

What we have spoken of the three first Chap. are generally and specially to be pronounced, so that you say them, and the Orations on the dayes appointed, and work by the Notes as it is demonstrated to you. These Orations ought to be said always before noon, every day of the Moneth; and before the Notes say the proper Orations: and in all reading, observe the precepts commanded.

How the Proper Notes are to be inspected.

If you would learn anything of any one Art, look into the proper Notes thereof in their due time. Enough is said already of the three liberal Arts.

What dayes are to be observed in the inspection of the Notes of the four Arts.

In the four other Arts, only the four first dayes are to be observed: The Philosophical Notes, with all Sciences contained therein, the 7 and 17 dayes of the Moon are to be inspected, 7 times aday, with their several Orations. The Note is to be looked into, with fear, silence and trembling.

   Of the Notes of the liberal Arts, it is spoken already; but only know this, that when you would use them, live chaste and soberly; for the Note hath in it self 24 Angels, is fully and perfectly to be pronounced, as you have heard: but when you look into them, repeat all the Theological Orations, and the rest in their due time.

Of the inspection of general Notes.

Say the general Notes 10 times a day, when you have occasion to use any common Arts, having the books of those Arts before you, using some interval or space of time between them, as you have been taught already.

How the three first Chapters are to be pronounced before Orations.

To have perfection herein, know, that in the general pronunciation of Orations, the Notes of the three heads are to be rehearsed; whether the Orations be pronounced or not.

How the fifth Oration of Theology ought to be rehearsed upon these Orations.

There is also somthing else to be said of the four other liberal Arts; if you would have the perfect knowledge of them, make the first Oration of Theology before you say the Orations of the other Notes. These are sufficiently declared, that you may understand and know them; And let the capitular Orations be pronounced before the several Notes of every Art, and kept as is determined, &c. These are the Augmentations of the Orations, which belong to all Arts liberal and exceptive, except *Mechanick*, and are especially ascribed to the Notes of Theology. And they are thus to be pronounced, that whensoever you would look into any one Note of any Art, and would profit therein, say these Orations following.

> 1. *Ezomamos, Hazalat, Ezityne, Hezemechel, Czemomechel, Zamay, Zaton, Ziamy Nayzaton, Hyzemogoy, Jeccomantha, Jaraphy, Phalezeton, Sacramphal, Sagamazaim, Secranale, Sacramathan; Jezennalaton Hacheriatos, Jetelemathon, Zaymazay, Zamaihay, Gigutheio Geurlagon, Garyos, Megalon Hera Cruhic, Crarihuc, Amen.*

Let this Oration with the following be pronounced before the first Note of Philosophy:

> Oh Lord God, holy Father, almighty and incomprehensible; hear my Prayers, thou that art invisible, immortal and intelligible, whose face the Angels and Arch-angels, and all the powers of Heaven, do so much desire to see; whose Majesty I desire eternally to adore, and honour the only one God for ever and ever, *Amen.*

2. Say this before the second Note of Philosophy:

> Oh Lord God, Holy and Almighty Father, hear my Prayers this day, and incline thy ears to my Orations; *Gezomelion Samach, Semath, Cemon,*

Gezagam, Gezatrhin, Zheamoth, Zeze Hator Sezeator Samay Sarnanda, Gezyel, Iezel, Gaziety, Hel, Gazayethyhel, Amen.

Say this following with the former:

Oh God eternal, the way, the truth, and the life; give thy light and the flower of thy Holy Spirit into my mind and understanding, and grant that the gift of thy grace may shine forth in my heart, and into my Soul, now and for ever, *Amen.*

Pronounce the Oration following before the third Note of Philosophy;

Lemogethom, Hegemochom, Hazachay Hazatha, Azamachar, Azacham, Cohathay. Geomothay Logomothay, Zathana, Lachanma, Legomezon, Legornozon, Lembdemachon, Zegomaday, Hathanayos, Hatamam, Helesymom, Vagedaren, Vadeyabar, Lamnanath, Lamadai, Gomongchor, Gemecher, Ellemay, Gecromal, Gecrohahi, Colomanos, Colomaythos, Amen.

Say this following with the precedent Oration:

Oh God the life of all visible Creatures, eternal brightness, and virtue of all things; who art the original of all piety, who knewest all things before they were; who judgest all things, and discernest all things by thy unspeakeable knowledge: glorify thy Holy and unspeakable Name this day in my heart, and strengthen my intellectual understanding; increase my Memory, and confirm my eloquence; make my Tongue ready, quick, and perfect in thy Sciences and Scriptures, that by thy power given unto me, and thy wisdome taught in my heart, I may praise thee, and know and understand thy Holy Name for ever World without end, *Amen.*

Say this Oration following before the fourth Note of Philosophy.

Oh King of Kings, the Giver and Dispenser of infinite Majesty, and of infinite mercy, the founder of all foundations; lay the foundation of all thy virtues in me, remove all foolishness from my heart, that my senses may be established in the love of thy charity, and my Spirit informed by thee, according to the recreation and invocation of thy will, who livest and reignest God throughout all Worlds of Worlds, *Amen.*

How these Orations are to be said every day once before the general Notes, and the Notes of the liberal Arts.

These 4 Orations are necessary for liberal Arts, but chiefly do appertain to Theology, which are to be said everyday before the general Notes, or the Notes of the liberal Arts; but to Theology say every one of these 7 times to every Note; but if you would learn or teach any thing of dictating, versifying, singing or Musick, or any of these Sciences, first teach him these Orations, that thou would'st teach, how he should read them: but if he be a Child of mean understanding, read them before him, and let him say after thee word for word; but if he be of a good understanding, let him read them 7 times a day for 7 dayes: or if it be a general Note, pronounce these Orations, and the Virtue thereof shall profit you much, and you shall therein find great virtue.

Solomon saith of these Orations, let no man presume to make use of them unless for the proper office they are instituted for.

Oh Father, incomprehensible, from whom proceedeth every thing that is good; whose greatness is incomprehensible: Hear this day my Prayers, which I make in thy sight, and grant to me the Joy of thy saving health, that I may teach unto the wicked the Wayes and Paths of thy Sciences, and convert the Rebellious and incredulous unto thee, that whatsoever I commemorate and repeat in my heart and mouth, may take root and foundation in me; that I may be made powerful and efficacious in thy works, *Amen.*

Say this Oration before the 6 Note of Philosophy:

Gezemothon, Oromathian, Hayatha, Aygyay, Lethasihel, Lechizliel, Gegohay, Gerhonay, Samasatel, Samasathel, Gessiomo, Hatel, Segomasay, Azomathon, Helomathon, Gerochor, Hejazay, Samin, Heliel, Sanihelyel, Siloth, Silerech, Garamathal, Gesemathal, Gecoromay, Gecorenay, Samyel, Samihahel, Hesemyhel, Sedolamax, Secothamay, Samya, Rabiathos, Avinosch, Annas, Amen.

Then say this following:

Oh eternal King! O God, the Judge and discerner of all things, knower of all good Sciences; instruct me this day for thy Holy Names sake, and by these Holy Sacraments; and purify my understanding, that thy knowledge may enter into my inward parts, as water flowing from Heaven, and as Oil into my bones, by thee, Oh God Saviour of all things, who art the Fountain of goodness, and original of piety; instruct me this day in those Sciences which I desire, thou who art one God for ever, *Amen*. Oh God Father, incomprehensible, from whom proceedeth all good, the greatness of whose mercy is fathomless, hear my Prayers, which I make this day before thee, and render unto me the joy of thy Salvation, that I may teach the unjust the knowledge of thy wayes, and convert the unbelieving and Rebellious unto thee; and may have power to perform thy works, *Amen*.

The 7 Oration, which is the end of the Orations, belonging to the ineffable Note, the last of Theology, having 24 Angels.

Oh God of all piety, Author and Foundation of all things, the eternal Health and Redemption of thy people; Inspirer and great Giver of all graces, Sciences and Arts, from whose gift it cometh: Inspire into me thy servant, an increase of those Sciences: who hast granted life to me miserable sinner, defend my Soul, and deliver my Heart from the wicked cogitations of this World; extinguish and quench in me the flames of all lust and fornication, that I may the more attentively delight in thy Sciences and Arts; and give unto me the desire of my Heart, that I being confirmed and exalted in thy glory, may love thee: and increase in me the power of thy Holy Spirit, by thy Salvation and reward of the faithful, to the Salvation of my Soul and Body, *Amen*.

Then say this following:

Oh God most mighty Father, from whom proceedeth all good, the greatness of whose mercy is incomprehensible; hear my Prayers, which I make in thy sight.

Special precepts of the Notes of Theology, chiefly of the 1. 2. and 3.

These 7 Orations are an augmentation of the rest, and ought to be said before all the Notes of Theology, but especially before the ineffable Note; these are the precepts to make thee sufficient, which we command thee to observe by the authority of *Solomon*: diligently inquire them out, and do as we have proposed, and perfectly pronounce the Orations, and look into the Notes of the other Arts.

How Solomon received that ineffable Note from the Angel.

Because thou desirest the Mystery of the Notes, take this of the ineffable Note, the expression whereof is given in the Angels by the Figures of Swords, birds, trees, Flowers, Candles, and Serpents; For *Solomon* received this from the Lord in the night of Pacification, ingraven in a book of Gold; and heard this from the Lord: Doubt not, neither be affraid; for this Sacrament is greater than all the rest; And the Lord joyned it unto him, When thou look'st into this Note, and read'st the Orations thereof, observe the precepts before, and diligently look into them; And beware that thou prudently conceal and keep whatsoever thou read'st in this Note of God, and whatsoever shall be revealed to thee in the vision. And when the Angel of the Lord appeareth to thee, keep and conceal the words and writings he revealeth to thee; and observe them to practice and operate in them, observing all things with great reverence, and pronounce them at the appointed dayes and hours, as before is directed: and afterwards say: *Sapienter die illo; Age, & caste vivas.* But if thou dost anything uncertain, there is danger; as then wilt have experience from the other Notes and the Orations of them; but consider that which is most wonderful in those Orations; for these words are ineffable Names, and are spiritually to be pronounced before the ineffable Note, *Hosel, Jesel, Anchiator, Aratol, Hasiatol, Gemor, Gesameor.* Those are the Orations which ought to be pronounced after the inspection of all Arts, and after the Note of Theology.

This is the fulfilling of the whole work; but what is necessary for an experiment of the work, we will more plainly declare. In the beginning of the knowledge of all Art, there is given almost the perfect doctrine of operating: I say almost, because some flourishing institutions hereof remain, whereof this is the first beginning.

How the precepts are to be observed in the operation of all Arts.

Observe the 4 ☽ in every operation of Theology. Exhibit that operation with efficacy every 4 ☽ *quartam lunam*; and diligently look into the books and writings of those Arts; if thou doubt of any of the Chapters, they are to be pronounced, as is taught of the superiour Chapters; but know this, that these Holy Words of Orations, we appoint to be said before the bed of the sick, for an experiment of life or death. And this thou maist do often, if thou wilt operate nothing else in the whole body of Art: And know this, that if thou hast not the books in thy hands, or the faculty of looking into them is not given to thee; the effect of this work will not be the lesse therefore: but the Orations are twice then to be pronounced, where they were to be but once: And as to the knowledge of a vision, and the other virtues which these holy Orations have; thou maist prove and try them, when and how thou wilt.

These precepts are specially to be observed.

But when thou would'st operate in Theology, observe only those dayes which are appointed; but all times are convenient for those Notes and Operations, for which there is a competent time given; but in the pronounciation of the three liberal Arts, or in the inspection of their Notes, perhaps thou maist pretermit [omit] some day appointed, if thou observe the rest; or if thou transgress two dayes, leave not off the work, for it loseth not its effect for this, for the Moon is more to be observed in the greater numbers than the dayes or hours. For *Solomon* saith, if thou miss a day or two, fear not, but operate on the general Chapters. This is enough to say of them: but by no means forget any of the words which are to be said in the beginning of the reading to attain to Arts; for there is great virtue in them. And thou maist frequently use the Holy Words of the visions: but if thou wouldst operate in the whole body of the Physical Art, the first Chapters are first to be repeated as before are defined. And in Theology, thou must operate only by thy self: Often repeat the Orations, and look into the Notes of Theology: this produceth great effects. It is necessary that thou have the Note of the 24 Angels alwayes in Memory; and faithfully keep those things, which the Angel reveales to thee in the vision.

[*Ars Nova*[7]]

The Experiment of the precedent work, is the beginning of the following Orations, which Solomon calleth Artem Novam.

These Orations may be said before all Arts generally, and before all Notes specially; And they may be pronounced without any other Chapters, if thou wouldst operate in any of the aforesaid Arts, saying these Orations in due time and order; thou maist have great efficacy in any Art. And in saying these Orations, neither the time, day, nor ☽, are to be observed: but take

---

7   This heading does not occur in the texts, but is supplied here for clarity.

heed, that on these dayes you abstain from all sin, as drunkenness, gluttony, especially swearing, before you proceed thereunto, that your knowledge therein may be the more cleer and perfect.

Wherefore *Solomon* saith, When I was to pronounce these Orations, I feared lest I should offend God; and I appointed unto my self a time wherein to begin them; that living chastly, I might appear the more innocent.

These are the Prœmiums [preliminaries]of these Orations, that I might lay down in order every thing whereof thou maist doubt, without any other definition. And before thou begin to try any of these subtile works, it is good to fast two or three dayes; that it may be divinely revealed, whether thy desires be good or evil.

These are the precepts appointed before every operation; but if thou doubt of any beginning, either of the three first Chapters, or of the four subsequent Arts, that thou maist have the effect of perfect knowledge; if thou consider and pronounce the Orations, as they are above described, although thou overpass somthing ignorantly; thou maist be reconciled by the spiritual virtue of the subsequent Orations.

The Angel said of these Orations to *Solomon*: See the holiness of these Orations; and if thou hast transgrest any therein presumptuously or ignorantly, say reverently and wisely these Orations, of which the great Angel saith: This is a great sacrament of God, which the Lord sendeth to thee by my hand; at the veneration of which sacrament, when King *Solomon* offered with great patience before the Lord upon the Altar, he saw the book covered with fine linen, and in this book were written 10 Orations, and upon every Oration the sign of golden Seal: and he heard in his Spirit, These are they which the Lord hath figured, and are far excluded from the hearts of the unfaithful.

Therefore *Solomon* trembled lest he should offend the Lord, and kept them, saying it was wickedness to reveal them to unbelievers: but he that would learn any great or spiritual thing in any Art or necessary Science, if he cannot have a higher work, he may say these Orations at what time soever he will; the three first, for the three first liberal Arts; a several Oration for every several Art, or generally all the three for the three Arts are to be said; and in like manner the four subsequent Orations, for four other liberal Arts. And if thou wouldst have the whole body of Art, without any definition of time, thou maist pronounce these Orations before the several Arts, and before the Orations and Notes of these Arts, as often as thou wilt, fully, manifestly and secretly; but beware that thou live chastly and soberly in the pronounciation thereof.

This is the first Oration of the 10, which may be pronounced by its self, without any precedent work to acquire Memory, Eloquence and understanding, and stableness of these three and singularly to be rehearsed before the first figure of Theology:

Omnipotent, Incomprehensible, invisible and indissolvable Lord God; I adore this day thy Holy Name; I an unworthy and miserable sinner, do lift up my Prayer, understanding and reason towards thy Holy and Heavenly Temple, declaring thee, Oh Lord God, to be my Creator and Saviour: and I a rational Creature do this day invocate thy most glorious clemency, that thy Holy Spirit may vivify my infirmity: And thou, Oh my God, who didst confer the Elements of letters, and efficacious Doctrine of thy Tongue to thy Servants *Moses* and *Aaron*, confer the same grace of thy sweetness upon me, which thou hast investigated [invested] into thy Servants and Prophets: as thou hast given them learning in a moment, confer the same learning upon me, and cleanse my Conscience from dead works; direct my Heart into the right way, and open the same to understand, and drop the truth into my understanding. And thou, Oh Lord God, who didst condescend to create me after thy own image, hear me in thy Justice, and teach me in thy truth, and fill up my soul with thy knowledge according to thy great mercy, that in the multitude of thy mercies, thou maist love me the more, and the greater in thy works, and that I may delight in the administration of thy Commandments; that I being helped and restored by the work of thy grace, and purified in Heart and Conscience to trust in thee, I may feast in thy sight, and exalt thy name, for it is good, before thy Saints, Sanctifie me this day, that I may live in faith, perfect in hope, and constant in charity, and may learn and obtain the knowledge I desire; and being illuminated, strengthened, and exalted by the Science obtained, I may know thee, and love thee, and love the knowledge and wisdome of thy Scriptures; and that I may understand and firmly retain, that which thou hast permitted man to know: Oh Lord Jesus Christ, eternal only begotten Son of God, into whose hands the Father gave all things before all Worlds, give unto me this day, for thy Holy and glorious Name, the unspeakable nutriment of Soul and Body, a fit, fluent, free and perfect Tongue; and that whatsoever I shall ask in thy mercy, will and truth, I may obtain; and confirm all my Prayers and actions, according to thy good pleasure. Oh Lord my God, the Father of Life, open the Fountain of Sciences, which I desire; open to me, Oh Lord, the Fountain which thou openedst to *Adam*, and to thy Servants *Abraham*, and *Isaac*, and *Jacob*, to understand, learn and judge; receive Oh Lord my Prayers, through all thy Heavenly virtues, *Amen.*

The next Oration is the second of ten, and giveth Eloquence, which ought to be said after the other; a little interval between, and before the first Figure of Theology.

> I adore thee, thou King of Kings, and Lords, eternal and unchangeable King: Hearken this day to the cry and sighing of my Heart and Spirit, that thou maist change my understanding, and give to me a heart of flesh, for my heart of stone, that I may breath before my Lord and Saviour; and wash Oh Lord with thy new Spirit the inward parts of my heart, and wash away the evil of my flesh: infuse into me a good understanding, that I may become a new man; reform me in thy love, and let thy salvation give me increase of knowledge: hear my Prayers, O Lord, wherewith I cry unto thee, and open the Eyes of my flesh, and understanding, to understand the wonderful things of thy Law; that being vivified by thy Justification, I may prevail against the Devil, the adversary of the faithful; hear me Oh Lord my God, and be merciful unto me, and shew me thy mercy; and reach to me the vessel of Salvation, that I may drink and be satisfied of the Fountain of thy grace, that I may obtain the knowledge and understanding; and let the grace of thy Holy Spirit come, and rest upon me, *Amen.*

For Eloquence and stability of mind.

This is the third Oration of the ten, and is to be said before the first Figure of Astronomy.

> I confesse my self guilty this day before thee Oh God, Father of Heaven and Earth, Maker of all things, visible and invisible, of all Creatures, Dispenser and Giver of all grace and virtue; who hidest wisdome and knowledge from the proud and wicked, and givest it to the faithful and humble; illuminate my Heart, and establish my Conscience and understanding: set the light of thy countenance upon me, that I may love thee, and be established in the knowledge of my understanding, that I being cleansed from evil works, may attain to the knowledge of those Sciences, which thou hast reserved for believers. Oh merciful and omnipotent God, cleanse my Heart and reins [sic], strengthen my Soul and Senses with the grace of thy Holy Spirit, and establish me with the fire of the same grace: illuminate me; gird up my loyns, and give the staffe of thy Consolation into my right hand, direct me in thy Doctrine, root out of me all vices and sin, and comfort me in the love of thy mercies: Breath into me Oh Lord the breath of Life, and increase my reason and understanding; send thy Holy Spirit into me, that I may be perfect in all knowledge: behold Oh Lord, and consider

the dolour of my mind, that my will may be comforted in thee; send into me from Heaven thy Holy Spirit, that I may understand those things I desire. Give unto me invention, Oh Lord, thou Fountain of perfect reason and riches of knowledge, that I may obtain wisdom by thy Divine assistance, *Amen*.

To Comfort the outward and inward Senses.

Oh Holy God, mercyful and omnipotent Father, Giver of all things; strengthen me by thy power, and help me by thy presence, as thou wert mercyful to *Adam*, and suddenly gavest him the knowledge of all Arts through thy great mercy; grant unto me power to obtain the same knowledge by the same mercy: be present with me Oh Lord, and instruct me: Oh most mercyful Lord Jesus Christ Son of God, breath thy Holy Spirit into me, proceeding from thee and the Father; strengthen my work this day, and teach me, that I may walk in thy knowledge, and glorify the abundance of thy grace: Let the flames of thy Holy Spirit rejoyce the City of my Heart, by breathing into me thy Divine Scriptures; replenish my Heart with all Eloquence, and vivify me with thy Holy visitation; blot out of me the spots of all vices, I beseech thee, Oh Lord God incomprehensible; let thy grace alwayes rest upon me, and be increased in me; heal my Soul by thy inestimable goodness, and comfort my heart all my life, that what I hear I may understand, and what I understand I may keep, and retain in my Memory; give me a teachable Heart and Tongue; through thy inexhaustible grace and goodness; and the grace of the Father, Son, and Holy Ghost, *Amen*.

This following is for the Memory.

O Holy Father, merciful Son, and Holy Ghost, inestimable King; I adore, invocate, and beseech thy Holy Name, that of thy overflowing goodness, thou wilt forget all my sins: be mercyful to me a sinner, presuming to go about this office of knowledge, and occult learning; and grant, Oh Lord, it may be efficatious in me; open Oh Lord my ears , that I may hear; and take away the scales from my Eyes, that I may see: strengthen my hands, that I may work; open my face, that I may understand thy will; to the glory of thy Name, which is blessed for ever, *Amen*.

This following strengtheneth the interiour and exteriour Sences.

Lift up the senses of my Heart and Soul unto thee, Oh Lord my God, and elevate my heart this day unto thee; that my words and works may please thee in the sight of all people; let thy mercy and omnipotency shine in my bowels; let my understanding be enlarged, and let thy Holy Eloquence be sweet in my mouth, that what I read or hear I may understand and repeat: as *Adam* understood, and as *Abraham* kept, so let me keep understanding; and as *Jacob* was founded and rooted in thy wisedome, so let me be: let the foundation of thy mercy be confirmed in me, that I may delight in the works of thy hands, and persevere in Justice, and peace of Soul and Body; the grace of thy Holy Spirit working in me, that I may rejoyce in the overthrow of all my adversaryes, *Amen*.

This following giveth Eloquence, Memory and Stability.

Disposer of all Kingdomes , and of all visible and invisible gifts: Oh God, the Ordeyner and Ruler of all wills, by the Counsel of thy Spirit dispose and vivify the weakness of my understanding, that I may burn in the accesse of thy Holy will to good: do good to me in thy good pleasure, not looking upon my sins; grant me my desire, though unworthy; confirm my Memory and reason to know, understand, and retain, and give good effect to my senses through thy grace, and justify me with the justification of thy Holy Spirit, that what spots soever of sin are contracted in my flesh, thy Divine power may blot out; thou who hast been pleased in the beginning, to create the Heaven and Earth, of thy Mercy restore the same, who art pleased to restore lost man to thy most Holy Kingdome; Oh Lord of wisdome, restore Eloquence into all my senses, that I, though an unworthy sinner, may be confirmed in thy knowledge, and in all thy works, by the grace of the Father, Son, and Holy Ghost, who livest and reignest three in one, *Amen*.

An Oration to recover lost wisdome.

Oh God of living, Lord of all Creatures visible and invisible, Administrator and Dispenser of all things, enlighten my Heart this day by the grace of thy Holy Spirit, strengthen my inward man, and pour into me the dew of thy grace, whereby thou instructest the Angels; inform me with the plenty of thy knowledge, wherewith from the beginning thou hast taught thy faithful; let thy grace work in me, and the flouds [floods] of thy grace and Spirit, cleanse and correct the filth of my Conscience. Thou who comest from Heaven upon the Waters of thy Majesty, confirm this wonderful Sacrament in me.

To obtain the grace of the Holy Spirit.

Oh Lord my God, Father of all things, who revealest thy celestial and terrestrial secrets to thy Servants, I humbly beseech and implore thy Majesty, as thou art the King and Prince of all knowledge, hear my Prayers; and direct my works, and let my Actions prevail in Heavenly virtues, by thy Holy Spirit: I cry unto thee, Oh God, hear my Clamor, I sigh to thee, hear the sighings of my heart, and always preserve my Spirit, Soul, and Body, under the Safeguard of thy Holy Spirit; O God thou Holy Spirit, perpetual and Heavenly charity, whereof the Heaven and Earth is full, breath upon my operation; and what I require to thy honour and praise, grant unto me; let thy Holy Spirit come upon me, rule and reign in me, *Amen.*

To recover intellectual wisdome.

Oh Lord, I thy Servant confesse my self unto thee, before the Majesty of thy glory, in whose Spirit is all Magnificence and Sanctimony: I beseech thee according to thy unspeakeable Name, extend thy merciful Ears and Eyes to the office of my operation; and opening thy hand, I may be filled with the grace I desire, and satiated with charity and goodness; whereby thou hast founded Heaven and Earth, who livest, &c.

Say these Orations from the first day of the month, to the fourth day: in the fourth day Alpha and Omega, and that following it, *viz.* *Helischemat azatan* ; **As it is in the beginning: afterwards say,**

Theos Megale patyr, ymas heth heldya, hebeath heleotezygel, Salatyel, Salus, Telli, Samel, Zadaziel, Zadan, Sadiz Leogio, Yemegas, Mengas, Omchon Myeroym, Ezel, Ezely, Yegrogamal, Sameldach, Somelta, Sanay, Geltonama, Hanns, Simon Salte, Patyr, Osyon, Hate, Haylos, Amen.
    Oh light of the World immense God, &c.

Hereby is increased so much Eloquence, that nothing is above it.

Thezay lemach ossanlomach azabath azach azare gessemon relaame azathabelial biliarsonor tintingote amussiton sebamay halbuchyre gemaybe redayl hermayl textossepha pamphilos Cytrogoomon bapada lampdayochim yochyle tahencior yastamor Sadomegol gyeleiton zomagon Somasgei baltea achetom gegerametos halyphala semean utangelsemon barya therica getraman sechalmata balnat hariynos haylos halos genegat gemnegal saneyalaix samartaix camael satabmal simalena gaycyah salmancha sabanon salmalsay silimacroton zegasme bacherietas zemethim theameabal gezorabal craton henna glungh hariagil parimegos zamariel leozomach rex maleosia mission zebmay aliaox gemois sazayl neomagil Xe Xe Sepha caphamal azeton gezain holhanhihala semeanay gehosynon caryacta gemyazan zeamphalachin zegelaman hathanatos, semach gerorabat syrnosyel, halaboem hebalor halebech ruos sabor ydelmasan falior sabor megiozgoz neyather pharamshe forantes saza mogh schampeton sadomthe nepotz minaba zanon suafnezenon inhancon maninas gereuran gethamayh passamoth theon beth sathamac hamolnera galsemariach nechomnan regnali phaga messyym demogempta teremegarz salmachaon alpibanon balon septzurz sapremo sapiazte baryon aria usyon sameszion sepha athmiti sobonan Armissiton tintingit telo ylon usyon, Amen.

Azay lemach azae gessemon thelamech azabhaihal sezyon traheo emagal gyeotheon samegon pamphilos sitragramon limpda jachim alna hasios genonagal samalayp camiel secal hanagogan heselemach getal sam sademon sebmassan traphon oriaglpan thonagas tyngen amissus coysodaman assonnap senaly sodan alup theonantriatos copha anaphial Azathon azaza hamel hyala saraman gelyor synon banadacha gennam sassetal maga halgozaman setraphangon zegelune Athanathay senach zere zabal somayel leosamach githacal halebriatos Jaboy del masan negbare phacamech schon nehooz cherisemach gethazayhy amilya semem ames gemay passaynach tagayl agamal fragal mesi themegemach samalacha nabolem zopmon usyon felam semessi theon, Amen.

The third part, the sign Lemach.

Lemach sabrice elchyan gezagan tomaspin hegety gemial exyophyam soratum salathahom bezapha saphatez Calmichan samolich lena zotha phete him hapnies sengengeon lethis, Amen.

For the memory.

Oh great invisible God, *Theos patyr behominas Cadagamias imas* by thy Holy Angels, who are *Michael* the Medicine of God; *Raphael* the Fortitude of God, *Gabriel ardens holy per Amassan, Cherubin, Gelommeios, Sezaphim gedabanan, tochrosi gade anathon, zatraman zamanary gebrienam:* Oh fulness, Holy Cherubins, by all thy Angels, and by all thy glorious Arch-angels, whose Names are consecrated by God, which ought not to be spoken by us, which are these, *dichal, dehel depymon exluse exmegon pharconas Nanagon hossyelozogon gathena ramon garbona vramani Mogon hamas;* Which humane sence cannot apprehend: I beseech thee, Oh Lord illuminate my Conscience with the Splender of thy light, and illustrate and confirm my understanding with the sweet odor of thy Spirit; adorne my Soul, reform my heart, that hearing I may understand, and retain what I hear in my Memory. Oh merciful God, appease my bowels, strengthen my Memory, open my mouth mercifully; temperate my Tongue by thy glorious and unspeakable Name: thou who art the Fountain of all goodness, have patience with me, and give a good Memory unto me, &c.

Say these Orations in the fourth ☽, *viz. Hely-schemath, Alpha and Omega, Theos megale.*

Oh light of the World *Azalemach*, great God I beseech thee:

These ought to be said in the 8, 12, 10, 20, 24, 28, 30. and in all these Lunations rehearse them four times; in the morning once, the third hour once, the ninth once, and once in the evening; and in the other dayes rehearse none, but them of the first day, which are Alpha and Omega *Helyschemat,*

> Almighty, incomprehensible, I adore thee; I confesse my self guilty: O *Theos hazamagiel:* Oh mercyful Lord God, raise up the sences of my flesh: Oh God of all living, and of all Kingdomes, I confesse Oh Lord this day, that I am thy servant.

Rehearse these Orations also in the other dayes four times, once in the morning, once in the evening, once about the third hour, and once on the ninth; And thou shalt acquire Memory, Eloquence and stability fully, *Amen*

The Conclusion of the whole work, and Confirmation of the Science obtained.

> Oh God, Maker of all things; who hast created all things out of nothing; who hast wonderfully created the Heaven and Earth, and all things by degrees in order, in the beginning, with thy Son, by whom all things are made, and into whom all things shall at last return: Who art Alpha and Omega: I beseech thee though a sinner, & unworthy, that I may attain to my desired end in this Holy Art, speedily, and not lose the same by my sins; but do good unto me, according to thy unspeakable mercy: who doth not to us after our sins, nor rewardeth us after our iniquities, *Amen.*

Say this in the end devoutly:

> Oh wisdome of God the Father incomprehensible, Oh most mercyful Son , give unto me of thy ineffable mercy, great knowledge and wisdome, as thou didst wonderfully bestow all Science to King *Solomon*, not looking upon his sins or wickedness, but thy own mercies: wherefore I im-

plore thy mercy, although I am a most vile and unworthy sinner, give such an end to my desires in this art, whereby the hands of thy bounty may be enlarged towards me, and that I may the more devoutly walk by thy light in thy wayes, and be a good example to others; by which all that see mee, and hear me, may restrain themselves from their vices, and praise thy holyness through all Worlds, *Amen*.

Blessed be the Name of the Lord, &c. rehearse these two Orations alwayes in the end, to confirm thy knowledge gained.

The Benediction of the place.

Blesse Oh Lord this place, that there may be in it Holy Sanctity, chastity, meekness, victory, holiness, humility, goodness, plenty, obedience of the Law, to the Father, Son, and Holy Ghost; Hear Oh Lord, holy Father, Almighty eternal God; and send thy Holy Angel *Michael*, who may protect, keep, preserve and visit me, dwelling in this Tabernacle, by him who liveth, &c.

When you would operate, have respect to the Lunations: they are to be chosen in those moneths, when the ☉ Rules in ♊ and ♍ ♈ ♌ ♎ ♉, in these moneths you may begin.

In the Name of the Lord beginneth this most Holy Art, which the most high God Administered to *Solomon* by his Angel upon the Altar, that thereby suddenly in a short space of time, he was established in the knowledge of all Sciences; and know, that in these Orations are contained all Sciences, Lawful and unlawful; First, if you pronounce the Orations of Memory, Eloquence, and understanding, and the stability thereof; they will be mightily increased, insomuch that you will hardly keep silence; for by a word all things were Created, and by the virtue of that word all created beings stand, and every Sacrament, and that Word is God. Therefore let the Operator be constant in his faith, and confidently believe, that he shall obtain such knowledge and wisdome, in the pronouncing these Orations, for with God nothing is impossible: therefore let the Operator proceed in his work, with faith, hope, and a constant desire: firmly believing; because we can obtain nothing but by faith; Therfore have no doubt in this Operation, whereof there are three species whereby the Art may be obtained.

The first species is Oration, and reason of a Godly mind, not by attempting a voyce of deprecation, but by reading and repeating the same in the inward parts. The second species is fasting and praying, for the praying man God heareth. The third species is chastity; he that would operate in this Art, let him be clean and chast by the space of nine dayes at least; and before you begin, it is necessary that you know the time of the ☽. for in the prime of the ☽. it is proper to operate in this Art: and when you begin so sacred an Art, have a care to abstain from all mortal sins, at least while you are proceeding in this work until it be finished and compleated: and when you begin to operate, say this verse kneeling: Lift up the light of thy Countenance upon me, Oh Lord my God, and forsake not me thy servant N. that trusts in thee: Then say three times *Pater Noster*, &c. And assert that thou wilt never commit wilfull perjury, but alwayes persevere in faith and hope. This being done, with bended knees in the place wherein thou wilt operate, say,

> Our help is in the Name of the Lord, who hath made Heaven and earth: And I will enter into the Invocation of the most high, unto him who enlightneth and purifieth my Soul and Conscience, which dwelleth under the help of the most high, and continueth under the protection of the God of Heaven: O Lord open and unfold the doubts of my Heart, and change me into a new man by thy love: be thou Oh Lord unto me true faith, the hope of my life, and perfect charity, to declare thy wonders. Let us pray:

Then say the Oration following:

> Oh God my God, who from the beginning hast Created all things out of nothing, and reformest all things by thy Spirit; restore my Conscience, and heal my understanding, that I may glorify thee in all my thoughts, words and deeds; through him who liveth and reigneth with thee forever, *Amen.*

Now in the Name of *Christ*, on the first day of the Month, in which thou wouldst acquire Memory, Eloquence and Understanding, and stability thereof, with a perfect, good and contrite heart, and sorrow for thy sins committed; thou maist begin to pronounce these Orations following, which appertain to the obtaining of Memory and all Sciences, and which were composed and delivered by the Angel to *Solomon*, from the hand of God.

The first and last Oration of this art, is Alpha and Omega: Oh God omnipotent, &c.

This following is an Oration of four Languages, which is this:

Hely, Schemat, Azatan, honiel sichut, tam, imel, Iatatandema, Jetromiam, Theos: Oh Holy and strong God, *Hamacha, mal, Gottneman, Alazaman, Actuaar, Secheahal, Salmazan, zay, zojeracim, Lam hay, Masaraman, grensi zamach, heliamat, seman, selmar, yetrosaman muchaer, vesar, hasarian Azaniz, Azamet, Amathemach, hersomini.* And thou most Holy and just God, incomprehensible in all thy works, which are Holy just and good; *Magol, Achelmetor, samalsace, yana, Eman,* and *cogige, maimegas, zemmail, Azanietan, illebatha sacraman, reonas, grome, zebaman, zeyhoman, zeonoma, melas, heman, hathoterma, yatarmam, semen, semetary, Amen.*

This Oration ought to follow the first of the ten above written.

To perform any work.

This is to follow the third Oration above:

I confesse, O *Theos hazamagielgezuzan, sazaman, Sathaman, getormantas, salathiel, nesomel, megal vuieghama, yazamir, zeyhaman, hamamal amna, nisza, deleth, hazamaloth, moy pamazathoran hanasuelnea, sacromomem, gegonoman, zaramacham Cades bachet girtassoman, gyseton palaphatos halathel Osachynan machay, Amen.*

This is a true and approved experiment, to understand all Arts and secrets of the World, to find out and dig up minerals and treasure; this was revealed by the Heavenly Angel in this Notory Art. For this Art doth also declare things to come, and rendereth the sense capable of all arts in a short time, by the Divine use thereof.

We are to speak also of the time and place. First therefore, all these precepts are to be observed and kept; and the Operator ought to be clean, chaste, to repent of his sins, and earnestly desire to cease from sinning as much as may be; and so let him proceed, and every work shall be investigated into him, by the divine ministery.

When thou wilt operate in the new Moon, kneeling say this verse: Lift up the light of thy Countenance upon us, Oh God, and forsake us not, Oh Lord our God. Then say three times the *Pater Noster:* And afterwards let him vow unto God, that he will never commit wilfull perjury, but alwayes persist in faith. This being done, at night say with bended knees before thy bed, Our help is in the Name of the Lord, &c. and this Psalm; Whoso dwelleth under the shadow of the wings of the most high, to the end; and the Lords Prayer, and the Prayer following.

Theos Pater vehemens; God of Angels, I Pray and invocate thee by thy most Holy Angels *Eliphamasay, Gelomiros, Gedo bonay, Saranana, Elomnia,* and by all thy Holy Names, by us not to be pronounced, which are these: *de. el. x p n k h t li g y y.* not to be spoken, or comprehended by humane sense; I beseech thee cleanse my Conscience with the Splendor of thy Name; illustrate and confirm my understanding with the sweet savour of thy Holy Spirit: O Lord Adorne my Soul, that I may understand and perfectly remember what I hear; reform my Heart, and restore my Heart, and restore my sense Oh Lord God, and heal my bowels: open my mouth most merciful God, and frame and temper my Tongue to the praise and glory of thy Name, by thy glorious and unspeakeable Name. O Lord, who art the Fountain of all goodness, and original of all piety, have patience with me, and give unto me a true understanding, to know whatsoever is fitting for me, and retain the same in Memory: thou who dost not presently Judge a sinner, but mercifully expectest repentance; I beseech thee, though unworthy, to wash away the filth of my sins and wickedness, and grant me my petitions, to the praise and glory of thy Holy Name; who livest and reignest one God in perfect Trinity, World without end, *Amen.*

Some other precepts to be observed in this work.

Fast the day following with bread and water, and give Almes; if it be the Lord's day, then give double Almes; be clean in body and mind; both thy self, and put on clean Cloaths.

The processe follows.

When thou wilt operate concerning any difficult Probleme or Question, with bended knees, before thy bed, make Confession unto God the Father; and having made thy Confession, say this Oration.

Send Oh Lord thy wisdome to assist me, that it may be with me, and labour with me, and that I may alwayes know what is acceptable before thee; and that unto me *N.* may be manifested the truth of this question or Art.

This being done, Thrice in the day following, when thou risest, give thanks to God Almighty, saying, Glory and honour, and benediction be unto him that sitteth on the Trone, and that liveth for ever and ever, *Amen*, with bended knees and stretched out hands.

But if thou desirest to understand any book, ask of some that hath knowledge therein, what that book treateth of: This being done, open the book, and read in it; and operate as at first three times, and alwayes when thou goest to sleep, write Alpha and Omega, and afterwards sleep on thy right side, putting the palme of thy hand under thy Ear, and thou shalt see in a dream all things thou desirest; and thou shalt hear the voyce of one informing and instructing thee in that book, or in any other faculty wherein thou wilt operate: And in the morning, open the book, and read therein; and thou shalt presently understand the same, as if thou hadst studied in it a long time: And alwayes remember to give thanks to God, as aforesaid.

Afterwards on the first day say this Oration:

Oh Father, Maker of all Creatures; by thy unspeakeable power wherewith thou hast made all things, stir up the same power, and come and save me, and protect me from all adversity of Soul and Body, *Amen.*

Of the Son say,

O Christ, Son of the living God, who art the splendor and figure of light, with whom there is no alteration nor shaddow of change; Thou Word of God most high, thou wisdome of the Father; open unto me, thy unworthy servant *N.* the veins of thy saving Spirit, that I may wisely understand, retain in Memory, and declare all thy wonders: Oh wisdome, who proceedest out of the mouth of the most high, powerfully reaching from end to end, sweetly disposing of all things in the World, come and teach me the way of prudence and wisdome. Oh Lord which didst give thy Holy Spirit to thy Disciples, to teach and illuminate their Hearts, grant unto me thy unworthy servant *N.* the same Spirit, and that I may always rejoyce in his consolation.

Other precepts.

Having finished these Orations, and given Almes, when thou entrest into thy Chamber, devoutly kneel down before thy bed, saying this Psalm: Have mercy upon me, O God, according to the multitude of thy great mercies, &c. and, In thee Oh Lord have I trusted, &c. Then rise up, and go to the wall, and stretch forth thy hands, having two nayles fixed, upon which thou maist stay up thy hands, and say this Prayer following with great devotion:

O God, who for us miserable sinners didst undergo the painful death upon the Crosse; to whom also *Abraham* offer'd up his son *Isaac*, I thy unworthy servant, a sinner perplexed with many evils, do this day offer up and Sacrifice unto thee my Soul and Body, that thou maist infuse into me thy Divine wisdome, and inspire me with the Spirit of Prophesy, wherewith thou didst inspire the Holy Prophets.

Afterwards say this Psalm; Oh Lord incline thine ears unto my words, &c. and add,

The Lord is my shepherd, and nothing shall I want: he shall set me down in green pastures, his servant *N.* he shall lead me upon the waters of refreshment, he converteth my Soul, and leadeth me *N.* upon the paths of his righteousness for his Holy Name: Let my evening Prayer ascend up unto thee Oh Lord, and let thy mercy descend upon me thy unworthy servant *N.* protect, save, blesse, and sanctify me, that I may have a shield against all the wicked darts of my enemies: defend me Oh Lord by the price of the blood of the just One, wherewith thou hast redeemed me; who livest and reignest God, whose wisdom hath laid the foundation of the Heaven, and formed the Earth, and placed the Sea in her bounds: and by the going forth of thy Word hast made all Creatures, and hath formed man out of the dust of the Earth, according to his own image and likeness; who gave to *Solomon* the son of King *David* inestimable wisdome: hath given to his Prophets the Spirit of Prophesy, and infused into Philosophers wonderfull Philosophical knowledge, confirmed the Apostles with fortitude, comforted and strengthened the Martyrs, who exalteth his elect from eternity, and provideth for them; Multiply Oh Lord God, thy mercy upon me thy unworthy servant *N.* by giving me a teachable wit, and an understanding adorned with virture and knowledge, a firm and sound Memory, that I may accomplish and retain whatsoever I endeavour, through the greatness of thy wonderful Name; lift up, Oh Lord my God, the light of thy countenance upon me, that hope in thee: Come and teach me, Oh Lord God of virtues, and shew me thy face, and I shall be safe.

Then add this Psalm: Unto thee Oh Lord do I lift up my Soul: Oh my God in thee do I trust; excepting that verse, *Confundantur*, &c.
Having fulfilled these things upon the wall, descend unto thy Bed, writing in thy right hand Alpha and Omega: then go to bed, and sleep on thy right side, holding thy hand under thy right Ear, and thou shalt see the greatness of God as thou hast desired. And in the morning, on thy knees,

before thy bed, give thanks unto God for those things he hath revealed to thee:

> I give thanks unto thee, Oh great and wonderful God, who hast given Salvation and knowledge of Arts unto me thy unworthy servant *N.* and confirm this Oh God, which thou hast wrought in me, in preserving me. I give thanks unto thee, O powerful Lord God, who createdst me miserable sinner out of nothing, when I was not, and when I was utterly lost; not redeemed, but by the precious blood of thy Son our Lord *Jesus Christ;* and when I was ignorant thou hast given unto me learning and knowledge: grant unto me thy servant *N.* O Lord *Jesus Christ,* that through this knowledge, I may be alwayes constant in thy Holy service, *Amen.*

These operations being devoutly compleated, give thanks daily with these last Orations. But when thou wouldst read, study, or dispute, say, Remember thy word unto thy Servant, O Lord, in which thou hast given me hope; this is my comforter in humility. Then add these Orations:

> Remember me O Lord of Lords, put good words and speech into my mouth, that I may be heard efficaciously and powerfully, to the praise, glory, and honour of thy glorious Name, which is Alpha and Omega, blessed for ever, World without end, *Amen.*

Then silently say these Orations.

> O Lord God, that daily workest new signs and unchangeable wonders, fill me with the spirit of wisedome, understanding and Eloquence; make my mouth as a sharp Sword, and my Tongue as an arrow elected, & confirm the words of my mouth to all wisdome: mollify the Hearts of the hearers to understand what they desire, *Elysenach, Tzacham,* &c.

The manner of Consecrating the Figure of Memory.

It ought to be consecrated with great faith, hope and charity; and being consecrated, to be kept and used in operation as followeth.

On the first day of the new Moon, having beheld the new Moon, put the Figure under your right Ear, and so consequently every other night, and seven times a day; the first hour of the morning saying this Psalm, *Qui habitat,* &c. throughout; and the Lords Prayer once, and this Oration *Theos Patyr* once in the first hour of the day: then say this

Psalm, *Confitebor tibi Domine*, &c. and the Lords Prayer twice, and the Oration *Theos Patyr* twice.

In the third hour of the day the Psalm *Benedicat anima mea Dominum* &c. the Lords Prayer thrice, and the Oration *Theos Patyr*.

In the sixth hour say this Psalm: *Appropinquet deprecato mea in conspectu tuo Domine, secundum eloquium tuum*. Grant unto me Memory, and hear my voyce according to thy great mercy, and according unto thy word grant Eloquence, and my lips shall shew forth thy majesty, when thou shalt teach me thy Glory: *Gloria patria*, &c, say the Lords Prayer nine times, and *Theos Patyr*.

In the nineth hour, say the Psalm *Beati immaculati in via*; the Lords Prayer 12 times, and *Theos Patyr*.

In the Evening say this Psalm, *Deus misereatur nostri*: the Lords Prayer 15 times, and *Theos Patyr* as often.

The last hour say this Psalm, *Deus Deus meus respice in me*, &c. & *Deus in adjutorium meum intende*, and *te Deum Laudamus*; the Lords Prayer once, and *Theos Patyr*: then say the Oration following twice.

O God, who hast divided all things in number, weight, and measure, in hours, nights, and dayes; who countest the number of the Stars, give unto me constancy and virtue, that in the true knowledge of this Art *N*. I may love thee, who knows the gifts of thy goodness, who livest and reignest, &c.

Four dayes the Figure of Memory ought to be consecrated with these Orations.

O Father of all Creatures, of the Sun and Moon.

Then on the last day let him bath himself, and put on clean garments, and clean[8] *Ornaments*, and in a clean place, suffumigate himself with Frankincense, and come in a convenient hour in the night with a light Kindled, but so that no man may see thee; and before the bed upon your knees say this Oration with great devotion.

O most great and most Holy Father, seven or nine times: then put the Figure with great reverence about your Head; and sleep in the Bed with

---

8   Lectisternium, a robe in which the Priests used to sleep in the temples, to receive the divine Oracles.

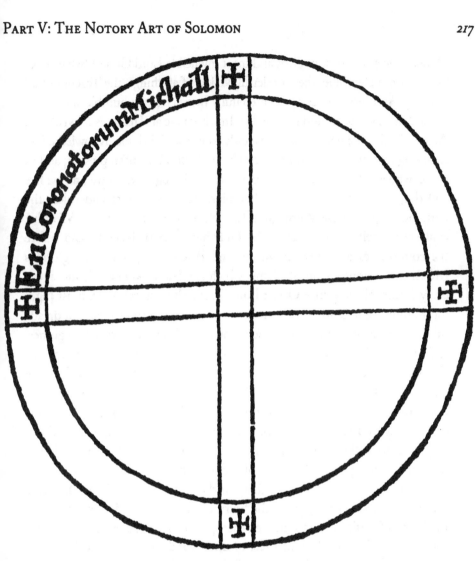

Figure 11. The Figure of Memory.

clean linnen vestiments, and doubt not but you shall obtain whatsoever you desire for this hath been proved by many, to whom such coelestial secrets of the Heavenly Kingdome are granted, *Amen.*

The Oration following ought to be said as you stand up.

O great God, Holy Father, most Holy Sanctifier of all Saints, three and one, most high King of Kings, most powerful God Almighty, most glorious and most wise Dispensor, Moderator, and Governour of all Creatures, visible and invisible: O mighty God, whose terrible and most mighty Majesty is to be feared, whose omnipotency the Heaven, the Earth, the Sea, Hell, and all things that are therein, do admire, reverence, tremble at, and obey.

O most powerful, most mighty, and most invincible Lord God of Sabaoth: O God incomprehensible; the wonderful Maker of all things, the Teacher of all learning, Arts and Sciences; who mercifully Instructest the humble and meek: O God of all wisdome and knowledge, In whom are all Treasures of wisdome, Arts and Sciences; who art able instantly to infuse Wisdome, Knowledg, and Learning into any man; whose Eye beholdeth all things past, present, and to come; who art the daily Searcher of all hearts; through whom we are, we live and dye; who sittest upon the Cherubins; who alone seest and rulest the bottomeless pit: whose Word gives Law throughout the universal World: I confesse my self this day before thy Holy and glorious Majesty, and before the company of all Heavenly virtues and Potentates, praying thy glorious Majesty, invocating thy great Name, which is a Name wonderful, and above every Name, blessing thee O Lord my God: I also beseech thee, most high, most omnipotent Lord, who alone art to be adored; O thou great and dreadful God Adonay, wonderful Dispensator of all beatitudes, of all Dignities, and of all goodness; Giver of all things, to whomsoever thou wilt, mercifully, aboundantly and permanently: send down upon me this day the gift of the grace of thy Holy Spirit. And now O most merciful God, who hast created *Adam* the first man, according to thy image and likeness; fortify the Temple of my body, and let thy Holy Spirit descend and dwell in my Heart, that I may shine forth the wonderful beams of thy Glory: as thou hast been pleased wonderfully to operate in thy faithful Saints; So O God, most wonderful King, and eternal glory, send forth from the seat of thy glorious Majesty, a seven-fold blessing of thy grace, the Spirit of Wisedome and Understanding, the Spirit of fortitude and Counsel, the Spirit of knowledge and Godliness, the Spirit of fear and love of thee, to understand thy wonderful Holy and occult mysteries, which thou art pleased to reveal, and which are fitting for thine to know, that I may comprehend the depth, goodness, and inestimable sweetness of thy most immense Mercy, Piety and Divinity. And now O most merciful Lord, who didst breath into the first Man the breath of life, be pleased this day to infuse into my Heart a true perfect perceiving, powerful and right understanding in all things; a quick, lasting, and indeficient Memory, and efficacious Eloquence; the sweet, quick and piercing Grace of thy Holy Spirit, and of the multitude of thy blessings, which thou bountifully bestowest: grant that I may despise all other things, and glorify, praise, adore, bless and magnify thee the King of Kings, and Lord of Lords; and always set forth thy praise, mercy, and omnipotency: that thy praise may always be in my mouth, and my Soul may be inflamed with thy Glory for ever before thee. O thou who art God omnipotent, King of all things, the greatest peace and perfectest wisdom, ineffable and inestimable sweetness and delight, the unexpressible joy of all good, the desire of all the blessed, their life, comfort, and glorious end; who was from eternity, and is and ever shall be virtue invincible, without parts or passions; Splendor and glory unquenchable; benediction, honour, praise, and venerable glory before all Worlds, since and everlastingly time without end, *Amen*.

The following Oration hath power to expell all lusts.

O Lord, Holy Father, omnipotent eternal God, of inestimable mercy and immense goodness; O most merciful *Jesus Christ*, repairer and restorer of mankind; O Holy Ghost, comforter and love of the faithful: who holdest all the Earth in thy fingers, and weighest all the Mountains and Hills in the World; who dost wonders past searching out, whose power there is nothing can resist, whose wayes are past finding out: defend my Soul, and deliver my Heart from the wicked cogitations of this World; extinguish and repress in me by thy power all the sparks of lust and fornication, that I may more intentively love thy works, and that the virtue of thy Holy Spirit may be increased in me, among the saving gifts of thy faithful, to the comfort and salvation of my Heart, Soul, and Body. O most great and most Holy God, Maker, Redeemer, and Restorer of mankind, I am thy servant, the Son of thy hand-maid, and the work of thy hands: O most merciful God and Redeemer, I cry and sigh before the sight of thy great Majesty, beseeching thee, with my whole Heart, to restore me a miserable sinner, and receive me to thy great mercy; give me Eloquence, Learning, and Knowledge, that those that shall hear my words, they may be mellif-luous in their Hearts; that seeing and hearing thy wisdome, the proud may be made humble, and hear and understand my words with great hu-mility, and consider the greatness and goodness of thy blessings, who livest and reignest now and for ever, *Amen*.

Note, that if you desire to know any thing that you are ignorant of, espe-cially of any Science, read this Oration: *I confess my self to thee this day, O God the Father of Heaven and Earth*, three times; and in the end express for what you desire to be heard; afterwards, in the Evening when you go to Bed, say the Oration *Theos* throughout, and the Psalm *Qui Habitat*, with this versicle, *Emitte Spiritum*; and go to sleep, and take the Figure for this purpose, and put it under the right Ear: and about the second or third hour of the night, thou shalt see thy desires, and know without doubt that which thou desirest to find out: and write in thy right hand Alpha and Omega, with the sign of the Cross, and put that hand under thy right Ear, and fast the day before; only once eating such meat as is used on fasting dayes.

[Finis.]

Appendix 1. Addenda
Found in Sloane 2731 and 3648

Sloane 2731 omits the 5th book, *Ars Notoria*, but instead inserts three folios (30–32), containing:

* A list of names, some with corrupt Hebrew lettering;
* An experiment relating to recovering stolen goods;
* Explanations of the circle and "triangles" of Solomon;
* Alternate versions of "The 5th Wandring prince Emoniel" and "the 7th spirit called Soleriel" from Book 2.

  These articles derive from Sloane 3648, which does include *Ars Notoria*, as well as extracts from Agrippa, Paracelsus, and de Abano. The first two articles are clearly unrelated to the *Lemegeton*. However, the "explanations" were included by Mathers in his edition of the *Goetia*. Since they are of exegetical nature, I have included them in this appendix.

The "explanations" refer to diagrams found in Book 1. They contain lists of sacred names with corresponding short phrases that are more of the character of prayers rather than etymologies. The lists contain corrupted versions of the names listed in the magic circle from the *Goetia*. They are based ultimately on Agrippa, *De Occulta Philosophia*, Book II, chapter 13 (Leiden: E.J. Brill, 1992), p. 289. Mathers supplied the title "Explanation of certain names used in this book Lemegeton," but given the content, it should read "The Explanation of the Circle of Solomon." Oddly, Mathers omitted the subheadings.

This is followed by two similar lists titled "The Explanation of the two triangles in the Parchment" and "The Explanation of Solomon's Triangle."

[The Explanation of the Circle of Solomon]

Eheie Kether[1]	Almighty God whose dwelling is in the highest heavens
Haioth [ha-Kados][2]	The great King of heaven and all the powers therein
Metatron[3]	And of all the holy hosts of Angels and Archangels
Reschith[4]	Hear the prayers of thy servant who put his whole trust in thee
Hagalgalim[5]	Lett thy holy Angells command assist me at this time and at all times
	P: M: sos[6]

Jehovah[7]	God Almighty God omnipotent hear my prayers
Hochmah[8]	Command thy holy Angels Above the fixed stars
Ophanim[9]	To be Assisting and Aiding of thy servants
Jophiel	That I may command all spirits of the Air fire water earth and hell
Masloth[10]	Soe that it may tend to thy glory and Mans good
	S. Z[11]

Jehovah	God Almighty God omnipotent hear my prayers
Elohim	God with us God be always present with us

---

1   S1 and S2 both read, "Eheid Rether."
2   S1 and S2 both read, "Haioth." Literally, "Holy living creatures."
3   S1, S2: "Metthraton."
4   S1, S2: "Reschith."
5   S1, S2: "Tagallalim." Reschith ha-Galgalim literally means "Primum Mobile."
6   P: M: Primum Mobile. This is actually the header for the previous five names.
7   In Agrippa, the name of God associated with the Sphere of the Zodiac is "Iod Jehovah." S1 and S2 simply read "Jehovah."
8   S1, S2: "Hadonath."
9   S1, S2: "Ophamim."
10   "Masloth" is the Hebrew word for Zodiac.
11   "Sphere of the Zodiac."

Binah	Strengthen us and support us both now and forever
Aralim	In these our undertakings which I doe as an Instrument in thy hands
Sabbathai[12]	Of thee the great God of Sabaoth

S. ♄

Hesed[13]	Thou great god governour and creator of all the Planets and host of heaven
Hasmalim[14]	Command them by the Almighty Power
Zedeck[15]	To be now present and assisting to us thy poor servants both now and forever

K: S. ♃

Elohim Gebor[16]	Most Almighty eternal and everliving Lord God
Seraphim	Command thy Seraphims
Camael. Madim[17]	To attend on us now at this time to assist us and defend us from all perils and dangers

S. ♂

Eloha	O Almighty God be present with us both now and forever
Tetragrammaton [18]	And let thy Almighty power and presence ever guard us and protect us at this present and forever
Raphael	Lett thy holy Angell Raphael wait upon us at at this present and forever

---

12 S1, S2: "Zabbathÿ." C adds, "(should read Shabbathii)." "Sabbathai" is Hebrew for Saturn.

13 S1, S2: "Hesel." C adds "(should be Chesed)."

14 C adds, "(should be Chashmalim)."

15 S1, S2: "Zedez." C adds "(should be Zedeq)." "Zedeck" is Hebrew for Jupiter.

16 S1, S2: "Elokim Geber." C adds "(should be Gibor)."

17 S1, S2: "Camael Modim." C silently corrects to "Madim." "Madim" is Hebrew for Mars.

18 Agrippa does not have "Tetragrammaton," but following the pattern of the others this should probably read "Tiphareth" or "Malachim."

Schemes[19]	To Assist us in this our undertakings
	S. ☉

Jehovah	God Almighty God omnipotent hear my prayers
Sabaoth	Thou great God of Sabaoths
Nezah[20]	All seeing God
Elohim	God be present with us and let thy presence be now and always present with us
Haniel	Let thy holy Angel Haniell come and minister unto us at this present
	S. ♀

Elohim	God be present with us and let thy presence be now and always present wth us
Sabaoth	O thou great god of Sabaoths be present with us at this time and forever
Hodben[21]	Let thy Almighty power defend us and protect us both now and forever
Michael	Let Michael who is under thee Generall of thy heavenly host
Cockab[22]	Come and expell all evil and danger from us both now and forever
	S. ☿

Sadai	Thou great God of all wisdom and knowledge
Jesod[23]	Instruct thy poor and most humble servant
Cherubin	By thy holy Cherubins
Gabriel	By thy holy Angel Gabriel who is the Author and messenger of good tidings

---

19 C adds, "(or Shemesh)." "Schemesh" is the Hebrew word for the Sun.

20 S1, S2: "Vesah." C silently corrects to "Netzah (or Netzach)."

21 This probably derives from Agrippa's "Hod" (name of God, plus "Beni Elohim, which is the "order of the blessed" associated with Mercury. C adds "(should be Hod simply)."

22 "Cochab" is the Hebrew word for Mercury.

23 S1, S2: "Jesal." C adds, "(should be Iesod)."

Levanah[24]   Direct us and support us at this present and forever

S. ☽

The Explanation of the
two triangles in the Parchment

Alpha and omega	Thou O great God who art the beginning and the end who was before all Eternity and ever shall be
Tetragrammaton	Thou God of mighty power be ever present with us to guard us and protect us and let thy holy presence be now and always with us
Tetragrammaton	Thou God of almighty power be ever present with us to guard us and protect us and let thy holy presence be now and always with us
Soluzen	I command thou spirit of what Region soever thou art to come into this circle
Halliza	and Appear in human shape
Bellatar[25]	and speak to us audably in our mother tongue
Bellonoy[26]	and shew and discover to us all treasures that thou knowest of or that is in thy keeping and deliver it to us quietly
Hallÿ Fra[27]	and answer us all such questions as we shall demand without any defect now at this time

The Explanation of Solomon's Triangle

Anephezaton	Thou great God of all the heavenly host
Tetragrammaton	Thou God of almighty power be ever present with us to guard us and protect us and let thy holy presence be now and always with us
Primeumaton	Thou who art the first and last let all spirits be subject to us and let the spirit be bound in this Triangle that disturbs this place

---

[24] S1, S2: "Zenanah." C silently corrects to "Levanah."

[25] C reads, "Bellator (or Ballaton)."

[26] C adds, "(or Bellony)."

[27] C reads, "Hallii. Hra."

Michael	By thy holy Angel Michael until I shall discharge him[28]
North Angel	Tetragrammaton. Thou God of almighty power be ever present with us to guard us and protect us and let thy holy presence be now and always with us
Candle	To be a light to our understandings and attend us now in our undertakings and defend us from all evil and danger both of soul and body

East Angel South and West are all on

The Middle Square 𝕹 Jehovah

Rash:

�7 Joh:

Thow Vniversall God of Heaven and all the hosts therein and of the Earth Sea and Air and all the Creatures therein

Thou, before thy presence all spirits both infernall Airy and all others do fear and tremble let them be now at this time and forever be in subjection to me at the word of thy most holy name Jehovah

---

28   C omits the rest of the text.

APPENDIX 2. JOHANN WEYER, PSEUDOMONARCHIA DAEMONUM

Pseudomonarchia Dæmonum.

O curas hominum, ô quantum est in rebus inane?

Johann Wier, *Pseudomonarchia daemonum.*
Salomons notes of conjuration

[Ah, human cares! Ah, how much futility in the world!. C. Lucilius, *Satires of Persius*]

<*An inventarie of the names, shapes, powers, governement, and effects of divels and spirits, of their severall segniories and degrees: a strange discourse woorth the reading.*>

Lectoris

Ne *Sathanicæ factionis monopolium usqueadeo porro delitescat, hanc Dæmonum Pseudomonarchiam, ex Acharonticorum Vasallorum archivo subtractam, in hujus Operis de Dæmonum præstigiis calce annectere volui, ut effascinatorum id genus hominum, qui se magos jactitare non erubescunt, curiositas, præstigiæ, vanitas, dolus, imposturæ, deliria, mens elusa, & manifesta mendacia, quinimo non ferendæ blasphemiæ, omnium mortalium, qui in mediæ lucis splendore hallucinari nolint,*

Reader.

oculis clarissimè appareant, hoc
potissimum seculo scelestissimo, quo
Christi regnum tam enormi
impunitaque tyrannide impetitur ab
iis qui Beliali palàm sacramentum
præstitêre, stipendium etiam justum
hauddubie recepturi: quibus &
perditas has horas libenter dedico, si
forte ex immensa Dei misericordia
convertantur & vivant: quod ex
animo iis precor, sitque felix &
faustum. Ne autem curiosulus aliquis,
fascino nimis detentus, hoc stultitiæ
argumentum temere imitari audeat,
voces hinc inde prætermisi studio, ut
universa delinquendi occasio
præcideretur. Inscribitur vero à
maleferiato hoc hominum genere
Officium spirituum, vel, Liber
officiorum spirituum, seu, Liber
dictus Empto. Salomonis, de
principibus & regibus dæmoniorum,
qui cogi possunt divina virtute &
humana. At mihi nuncupabitur
Pseudomonarchia Dæmonum.

Pseudomonarchia Dæmonum

Primus Rex, qui est de potestate Orientis, dicitur Baël, apparens tribus capitibus, quorum unum assimilatur bufoni alterum homini, tertium feli. Rauca loquitur voce, formator morum & insignis certator, reddit hominem invisibilem & sapientem. Huic obediunt sexagintasex legiones.

§ 2. Agares Dux primus sub potestate Orientis, apparet benevolus in senioris hominis

(1) <*Baell*>. Their first <and principall> king (which is of the power of the east) is called *Baëll* who when he is conjured up, appeareth with three heads; the first, like a tode; the second, like a man; the third, like a cat. He speaketh with a hoarse voice, he maketh a man go invisible [and wise], he hath under his obedience and rule sixtie and six legions of divels.

(2) *Agares*. The first duke under the power of the east, <is named *Agares*,> he commeth up mildile [i.e. he appears

forma, equitans in crocodilo, & in manu accipitrem portans. Cuncta linguarum genera docet optime: fugitantes reverti facit, & permanentes fugere: prælaturas & dignitates dimittit, & tripudiare facit spiritus terræ: & est de ordine Virtutum, sub sua potestate habens triginta & unam legiones.

willingly] in the likenes of a faire old man, riding upon a crocodile, and carrieng a hawke on his fist; hee teacheth presentlie all maner of toongs, he fetcheth backe all such as runne awaie, and maketh them runne that stand still; he overthroweth all dignities <supernaturall and temporall,> hee maketh earthquakes, [lit. "and makes spirits of the earth dance"] and is of the order of vertues, having under his regiment thirtie one legions.

§ 3. Marbas, alias Barbas, Præses magnus, se manifestans in fortissimi leonis specie, sed ab exorcista accitus humana induitur forma, & de occultis plene respondet, morbos invehit & tollit, promovet sapientiam artiumque mechanicarum cognitionem, homines adhæc in aliam mutat formā. Præest trigintasex legionibus.

(3) *Marbas, alias Barbas* is a great president, and appeareth in the forme of a mightie lion; but at the commandement of a conjuror commeth up in the likenes of a man, and answereth fullie as touching anie thing which is hidden or secret: he bringeth diseases, and cureth them, he promoteth wisedome, and the knowledge of mechanicall arts, or handicrafts; he changeth men into other shapes, and under his presidencie or gouvernement are thirtie six legions of divels conteined.

§ 4. Pruflas, alibi invenitur Bufas, magnus Princeps & Dux est, cujus mansio circa turrim Babylonis, & videtur in eo flamma foris, caput autem assimilatur magno nycticoraci. Autor est & promotor discordiarum, bellorum, rixarum & mendaciorum. Omnibus in locis non intromittatur. Ad quæsita respondet abunde. Sub sunt huic legiones vinginti sex, partim ex ordine Throni, partim Angelorum.

[(4) Pruflas, otherwise found as Bufas, is a great prince and duke, whose abode is around the Tower of Babylon, and there he is seen like a flame outside. His head however is like that of a great night hawk. He is the author and promoter of discord, war, quarrels, and falsehood. He may not be admitted into every place. He responds generously to your requests. Under him are twenty-six legions, partly of the order of Thrones, and partly of the order of Angels.][1]

---

1   Translation missing in Scot.

§ 5. Amon vel Aamon
Marchio magnus & potens, prodit
in lupi forma caudam habens
serpentinam, & flammam
evomens. Hominis autem indutus
speciem, caninos ostentat dentes,
& caput magno nycticoraci simile.
Princeps omnium fortissimus est,
intelligens præterita & futura, hinc
& gratiam concilians omnium
amicorum & inimicorum.
Quadraginta imperat legionibus.

(5) *Amon*, or *Aamon*, is a great and
mightie marques, and commeth abroad
in the likenes of a woolfe, having a
serpents taile, <spetting out and breath-
ing> [vomiting] flames of fier; when he
putteth on the shape of a man, he
sheweth out dogs teeth, and a great
head like to a mightie <raven> [night
hawk]; he is the strongest prince of all
other, and understandeth of all things
past and to come, he procureth favor,
and reconcileth both freends and foes,
and ruleth fourtie legions of divels.

§ 6. Barbatos magnus Comes
& Dux, apparet in signo Sagittarii
silvestris cum quatuor regibus
tubas ferentibus. Intelligit cantus
avium, canum latratus, mugitus
boum & cunctorum animalium:
thesauros item à magis &
incantatoribus reconditos, detegit:
Et est ex ordine Virtutum, partim
Dominationum. Triginta præsidet
legionibus. Novit præterita &
futura: tam amicorum quam
inimicorum animos conciliat.

(6) *Barbatos*, a great countie or earle,
and also a duke, he appeareth in *Signo
sagittarii sylvestris*, with foure kings,
which bring companies and great troopes.
He understandeth the singing of birds,
the barking of dogs, the lowings of
bullocks, and the voice of all living
creatures. He detecteth treasures hidden
by magicians and inchanters, and is of the
order of vertues, which in part beare rule:
he knoweth all things past, and to come,
and reconcileth freends and powers; and
governeth thirtie legions of divels by his
authoritie.

§ 7. Buer Præses magnus
conspicitur in signo *. Absolute
docet philosophiam, practicam,
ethica item & logica, & herbarum
vires: Dat optimos familiares:
Ægros sanitati restituere novit,
maxime & homines. Quinquaginta
legionum habet imperium.

(7) *Buer* is a great president, and is
seene in this signe [*]; he absolutelie
teacheth philosophie morall and naturall,
and also logicke, and the vertue of herbes:
he giveth the best familiars, he can heale
all diseases, speciallie of men, and
reigneth over fiftie legions.

§ 8. Gusoyn Dux magnus &
fortis, apparet in forma zenophali.
Explicate respondet & vere de
præsentibus, præteritis, futuris &

(8) *Gusoin* [Gusoyn] is a great duke,
and a strong, appearing in the forme of a
Xenophilus, he answereth all things,
present, past, and to come, expounding all

occultis. Amicoram & inimicorum gratiam reddit: Dignitates confert & honores conformat. Præest quadragintaquinque legionibus.

§ 9. Botis, alibi Otis, magnus Præses & Comes, Prodit in viperæ specie deterrima: Et siquando formam induit humanam dentes ostendit magnos & cornua duo, manu gladium acutum portans. Dat perfecte responsa vera de præsentius, præteritis, futuris & abstrusis. Tam amicos quam hostes conciliat. Sexaginta imperat legionibus.

§ 10. Bathym, alibi Marthim Dux magnus & fortis: Visitur constitutione viri fortissimi cum cauda serpentina, equo pallido insidens. Virtutes herbarum & lapidum pretiosorum intelligit. Cursu velocissimo hominem de regione in regionem transfert. Huic triginta subsunt legiones.

§ 11. Pursan, alias Curson, magnus Rex, prodit ut homo facie leonina, viperam portans ferocissimam, ursoque insidens, quem semper præcedunt tubæ. Callet præsentia, præterita & futura: Aperit occulta, thesauros detegit: Corpus humanum suscipit & aëreum. Vere respondet de rebus terrenis & occultis, de divinitate & mundi creatione: Familiares parit optimos: Cui parent vigintiduo legiones, partim de ordine Virtutum, partim ex ordine Throni.

questions. He reconcileth freendship, and distributeth honours and dignities, and ruleth over fourtie [and five] legions of divels.

(9) *Botis*, otherwise *Otis*, a great president and an earle he commeth foorth in the shape of an ouglie [lit. "worst"] viper, and if he put on humane shape, he sheweth great teeth, and two hornes, carrieng a sharpe sword in his hand: he giveth answers of things present, past, and to come, and reconcileth friends, and foes, ruling sixtie legions.

(10) *Bathin* [Bathym], sometimes called *Mathim* [Marthim], a great duke and a strong, he is seene in the shape of a verie strong man, with a serpents taile, sitting on a pale horsse, understanding the vertues of hearbs and pretious stones, transferring men suddenlie from countrie to countrie, and ruleth thirtie legions of divels.

(11) *Purson* [Pursan], *alias Curson*, a great king, he commeth foorth like a man with a lions face, carrieng a most cruell viper, and riding on a beare; and before him go alwaies trumpets, he knoweth <things hidden, and can tell> all things present, past, and to come: [he discloses hidden things,] he bewraieth treasure, he can take a bodie either humane or aierie; he answereth truelie of all things earthlie and secret, of the divinitie and creation of the world, and bringeth foorth the best familiars; and there obeie him two and twentie legions of divels, partlie of the order of vertues, & partlie of the order of thrones.

§ 12. Eligor, alias Abigor, Dux magnus, apparet ut miles pulcherrimus, lanceam, vexillum & sceptrum portans. Plene de occultis respondet atque bellis, & quomodo milites occurrere debeant: Futura scit, & gratiam apud omnes dominos & milites conciliat. Præsidet sexaginta legionibus.

(12) *Eligor, alias Abigor*, is a great duke, and appeereth as a goodlie [handsome] knight, carrieng a lance, an ensigne, and a scepter: he answereth fullie of things hidden, and of warres, and how souldiers should meete: he knoweth things to come, and procureth the favour of lords and knights, governing sixtie legions of divels.

§ 13. Loray, alias Oray, magnus Marchio, se ostendens in forma sagittarii pulcherrimi, pharetram & arcum gestantis: author existit omnium præliorum, & vulnera putrefacit quæ à sagittariis infliguntur, quos objicit optimos tribus diebus. Triginta dominatur legionibus.

(13) *Leraie* [Loray], *alias Oray*, a great marquesse, shewing himselfe in the likenesse of a galant [handsome] archer, carrieng a bowe and a quiver, he is author of all battels, he dooth putrifie all such wounds as are made with arrowes by archers, *Quos optimos objicit tribus diebus*, [who best drives away mobs from the days (?)] and he hath regiment over thirtie legions.

§ 14. Valefar, alias Malaphar, Dux est fortis, forma leonis prodiens & capite latronis. Familiaritatem parit suis, donec laqueo suspendantur. Decem præsidet legionibus.

(14) *Valefar, alias Malephar* [Malaphar], is a strong duke, comming foorth in the shape of a lion, and the head of a theefe [or "barking"], he is verie familiar with them to whom he maketh himself acquainted, till he hath brought them to the gallowes, and ruleth ten legions.

§ 15. Morax, alias Foraii, magnus Comes & Præses: Similis tauro visitur: Et si quando humanam faciem assumit, admirabilem in Astronomia & in omnibus artibus liberalibus reddit hominem: parit etiam famulos non malos & sapientes: novit & herbarum & pretiosorum lapidum potentiam. Imperat triginta sex legionibus.

(15) *Morax, alias Foraii*, a great earle and a president, he is seene like a bull, and if he take unto him a mans face, he maketh men wonderfull cunning in astronomie, & in all the liberall sciences: he giveth good familiars and wise, knowing the power & vertue of hearbs and stones which are pretious, and ruleth thirtie six legions.

§ 16. Ipes, alias Ayperos est magnus Comes & Princeps, apparens quidem specie angelica, interim leone obscurior & turpis, capite leonis, pedibus anserinis, cauda leporina. Præterita & futura novit: Redditque hominem ingeniosum & audacem. Legiones huic obediunt trigintasex.

(16) *Ipos* [Ipes], *alias Ayporos* [Ayperos], is a great earle and a prince, appeering in the shape of an angell, and yet indeed more obscure and filthie than a lion, with a lions head, a gooses feet, and a hares taile: he knoweth things to come and past, he maketh a man wittie, and bold, and hath under his jurisdiction thirtie six legions.

§ 17. Naberus, alias Cerberus, Marchio est fortis, forma corvi se ostentans: Si quando loquitur, raucam edit vocem. Reddit & hominem amabilem & artium intelligentem, cum primis in Rhetoricis eximium. Prælaturarum & dignitatum jacturam parit. Novendecim legiones hunc audiunt.

(17) *Naberius* [Naberus], *alias Cerberus*, is a valiant marquesse, shewing himselfe in the forme of a crowe, when he speaketh with a hoarse voice: he maketh a man amiable and cunning in all arts, and speciallie in rhetorike, he procureth the losse of prelacies and dignities: nineteene legions heare <and obeie> him.

§. 18. Glasya labolas, alias Caacrinolaas vel Caassimolar magnus Præses: Qui progreditur ut canis habens alas gryphi. Artium cognitionem dat, interim dux omnium homicidarum. Præsentia & futura intelligit. Tam amicorum quam inimicorum animos demeretur: Et hominem reddit invisibilem. Imperium habet triginta sex legionum.

(18) *Glasya Labolas, alias Caacrinolaas,* or *Caassimolar*, is a great president, who commeth foorth like a dog, and hath wings like a griffen, he giveth the knowledge of arts, and is the captaine of all mansleiers: he understandeth things present and to come, he gaineth the minds and love of freends and foes, he maketh a man go invisible, and hath the rule of six and thirtie legions.

§ 19. Zepar Dux magnus, apparens uti miles, inflammansque virorum amore mulieres, & quando ipsi jussum fuerit, earum formam in aliam transmutat, donec dilectis suis fruantur. Steriles quoque eas facit. Vigintisex huic parent legiones.

(19) *Zepar* is a great duke, appearing as a souldier, inflaming women with the loove of men, and when he is bidden he changeth their shape, untill they maie enjoie their beloved, he also maketh them barren, and six and twentie legions are at his obeie and commandement.

§ 20. Byleth Rex magnus & terribilis, in equo pallido equitans, quem præcedunt tubæ, symphoniæ, & cuncta Musicæ genera. Quum autem coram exorcista se ostentat, turgidus ira & furore videtur, ut decipiat. Exorcista vero tum sibi prudenter caveat: Atque ut fastum ei adimat, in manu suscipiat baculum corili, cum quo orientem & meridiem versus, foris juxta circulum manum extendet, facietque triangulum. Cæterum si manum non extendit, & intrare jubet, atque spirituum Vinculum ille renuerit, ad lectionem progrediatur exorcista: mox ingredietur item submissus, ibi stando & faciendo quodcunque jufferit exorcista ipsi Byleth regi, eritque securus. Si vero contumacior fuerit, nec primo jussu circulum ingredi voluerit, reddetur forte timidior exorcista: Vel si Vinculum spirituum minus habuerit, sciet haud dubie exorcista, malignos spiritus postea eum non verituros, at semper viliorem habituros. Item si ineptior sit locus triangulo deducendo juxta circulum, tunc vas vino plenum ponatur: Et intelliget exorcista certissimè, quum è domo sua egressus fuerit cum sociis suis, prædictum Byleth sibi fautorem fore, benevolum, & coram ipso submissum quando progredietur. Venientem vero exorcista benigne suscipiat, & de ipsius fastu glorietur: Propterea quoque eundem adorabit, quemadmodum alii reges, quia nihil dicit absque aliis principibus. Item si hic Byleth

(20) *Bileth* [Byleth] is a great king and a terrible, riding on a pale horsse, before whome go trumpets, and all kind of melodious musicke. When he is called up by an exorcist, he appeareth rough [turgid] and furious, to deceive him. Then let the exorcist or conjuror take heed to himself; and to allaje his courage, let him hold a *hazell bat* [rod, staff, or stick] in his hand, wherewithall he must reach out toward the east and south, and make a *triangle* without besides the *circle*; but if he hold not out his hand unto him, and he bid him come in, and he still refuse the bond or chain of spirits; let the conjuror proceed to reading, and by and by he will submit himselfe, and come in, and doo whatsoever the exorcist commandeth him, and he shalbe safe. If *Bileth* the king be more stubborne, and refuse to enter into the circle at the first call, and the conjuror shew himselfe fearfull, or if he have not the chaine of spirits, certeinelie he will never feare nor regard him after. Also, if the place be unapt for a triangle to be made without the circle, then set there a boll of wine, and the exorcist shall certeinlie knowe when he commeth out of his house, with his fellowes, and that the foresaid *Bileth* will be his helper, his friend, and obedient unto him when he commeth foorth. And when he commeth, let the exorcist receive him courteouslie, and glorifie him in his pride, and therfore he shall adore him as other kings doo, bicause he saith nothing without other princes. Also, if he be cited by an exorcist, alwaies a *silver ring* of the middle finger of the left hand must be held against the exorcists face, as they doo for *Amaimon*. And the dominion and power of so great a prince is not to be pretermitted [i.e. overlooked]; for there is

accitus fuerit ab aliquo exorcista, semper tenendus ad exorcistæ faciem annulus argenteus medii digiti manus sinistræ, quemadmodum pro Amaymone. Nec est prætermittenda dominatio & potestas tanti principis, quoniam nullus est sub potestate & dominatione exorcistæ alius, qui viros & mulieres in delirio detinet, donec exorcistæ voluntatem explerint: Et fuit ex ordine Potestatum, sperans se ad septimum Thronum rediturum, quod minus credibile. Imperat octogintaquinque legionibus.

none under the power & dominion of the conjuror, but he that deteineth both men and women in doting [better: "foolish" or "silly"] love, till the exorcist hath had his pleasure. He is of the orders of powers, hoping to returne to the seaventh throne, which is not altogether credible, and he ruleth eightie five legions.

§ 21. Sytry, alias Bitru, magnus Princeps, leopardi facie apparens, habensque alas velut gryphi. Quando autem humanam assumit formam, mire pulcher videtur. Incendit virum mulieris amore, mulierem vicissim alterius desiderio incitat. Jussus secreta libenter detegit feminarum, eas ridens ludificansque, ut se luxuriose nudent. Huic sexaginta legiones obsequuntur.

(21) *Sitri* [Sytry], *alias Bitru*, is a great prince, appeering with the face of a leopard, and having wings as a griffen: when he taketh humane shape, he is verie beautiful, he inflameth a man with a womans love, and also stirreth up women to love men, being commanded he willinglie deteineth [discloses] secrets of women, laughing at them and mocking them, to make them luxuriouslie naked, and there obeie him sixtie legions.

§ 22. Paymon obedit magis Lucifero quam alii reges. Lucifer hic intelligendus, qui in profunditate scientiæ suæ demersus, Deo assimilari voluit, & ob hanc arrogantiam in exitium projectus est. De quo dictum est: Omnis lapis pretiosus operimentum tuum [*Ezech.* 28]. Paymon autem cogitur virtute divina, ut se sistat coram exorcista: ubi hominis induit simulachrum, insidens dromedario, coronaque

(22) *Paimon* is more obedient in *Lucifer* than other kings are. *Lucifer* is heere to be understood he that was drowned in the depth of his knowledge: he would needs be like God, and for his arrogancie was throwne out into destruction, of whome it is said; Everie pretious stone is thy covering (*Ezech.* 88 [28.13].). *Paimon* is constrained by divine vertue to stand before the exorcist; where he putteth on the likenesse of a man: he sitteth on a beast called a dromedarie, which is a swift runner, and weareth a

insignitus lucidissima, & vultu fœmineo. Hunc præcedit exercitus cum tubis & cimbalis bene sonantibus, atque omnibus instrumentis Musicis, primo cum ingenti clamore & rugitu apparens, sicut in Empto. Salomonis, & arte declaratur. Et si Paymon hic quandoque loquitur, ut minus ab exorcista intelligatur, propterea is non tepescat: sed ubi porrexerit illi primam chartam ut voto suo obsequatur, jubebit quoque ut distincte & aperte respondeat ad quæsita, & de universa philosophia & prudentia vel scientia, & de cæteris arcanis. Et si voles cognoscere dispositionem mundi, & qualis sit terra, aut quid eam fustineat in aqua, aut aliquid aliud, & quid sit abyssus, & ubi est ventus & unde veniat, abunde te docebit. Accedant & consecrationes tam de libationibus quam aliis. Confert hic dignitates & confirmationes. Resistentes sibi suo vinculo deprimit, & exorcistæ subjicit. Bonos comparat famulos, & artium omnium intellectum. Notandum, quod in advocando hunc Paymonem, Aquilonem versus exorcistam conspicere oporteat, quæ ibi hujus sit hospi-tium. Accitum vero intrepide constanterque suscipiat, interroget, & ab eo petat quicquid voluerit, nec dubie impetrabit. At ne creatorem oblivioni tradat, cavendum exorcistæ, propter ea quæ præmissa fuerunt de Paymone. Sunt qui dicunt, eum ex ordine Dominationum fuisse: sed aliis placet, ex ordine Cherubin.

glorious crowne, and hath an effeminate countenance. There goeth before him an host of men with trumpets and well sounding cymbals, and all musicall instruments. At the first he appeereth with a great crie and roring, as in *Circulo* [Empto.] *Salomonis*, and in the art is declared. And if this *Paimon* speake sometime that the conjuror understand him not, let him not therefore be dismaied. But when he hath delivered him the first obligation to observe his desire, he must bid him also answer him distinctlie and plainelie to the questions he shall aske you, of all philosophie, wisedome, and science, and of all other secret things. And if you will knowe the disposition of the world, and what the earth is, or what holdeth it up in the water, or any other thing, or what is *Abyssus*, or where the wind is, or from whence it commeth, he will teach you aboundantlie. Consecrations also as well of sacrifices [offerings, libations] as otherwise may be reckoned. He giveth dignities and confirmations; he bindeth them that resist him in his owne chaines, and subjecteth them to the conjuror; he prepareth good familiars, and hath the understanding of all arts. Note, that at the calling up of him, the exorcist must looke towards the northwest, bicause there is his house. When he is called up, let the exorcist receive him constantlie without feare, let him aske what questions or demands he list, and no doubt he shall obteine the same of him. And the exorcist must beware he forget not the creator, for those things, which have beene rehearsed before of *Paimon*, some saie he is of the order of dominations; others saie, of the order of cherubim. There follow him two hundred legions, partlie of the order of

Hunc sequuntur legiones ducentæ, partim ex ordine Angelorum, partim Potestatum. Notandum adhæc, si Paymon solus fuerit citatus per aliquam libationem aut sacrificium, duo reges magni comitantur, scilicet Bebal & Abalam, & alii potentes. In hujus exercitu sunt vigintiquinque legiones: Quia spiritus his subjecti, non semper ipsis adsunt, nisi ut appareant, divina virtute compellantur.

angels, and partlie of potestates. Note that if *Paimon* be cited alone by an offering or sacrifice, two kings followe him; to wit, *Beball & Abalam*, & other potentates: in his host are twentie five legions, bicause the spirits subject to them are not alwaies with them, except they be compelled to appeere by divine vertue.

§ 23. Regem Belial aliqui dicunt statim post Luciferum fuisse creatum, ideoque sentiunt ipsum esse patrem & seductorem eorum qui ex Ordine ceciderunt. Cecidit enim prius inter alios digniores & sapientiores, qui præcedebant Michaëlem & alios cœlestes angelos, qui decrant. Quamvis autem Belial ipsos qui in terram dejecti fuerint, præcesserit: alios tamen qui in cœlo mansere, non antecessit. Cogitur hic divina virtute, cum accipit sacrificia, munera & holocausta, ut vicissim det immolantibus responsa vera: At per horam in veritate non perdurat, nisi potentia divina compellatur, ut dictum est. Angelicam assumit imagine in impense pulchram, in igneo curru sedens. Blande loquitur. Tribuit dignitates & prælaturas senatorias, gratiam item amicorum, & optimos famulos. Imperium habet octoginta legionum, ex ordine partim Virtutum, partim Angelorum. Forma exorcistæ invenitur in Vinculo Spirituum.

(23) Some saie that the king *Beliall* was created immediatlie after *Lucifer*, and therefore they thinke that he was father and seducer of them which fell being of the orders. For he fell first among the worthier and wiser sort, which went before *Michael* and other heavenlie angels, which were lacking. Although *Beliall* went before all them that were throwne downe to the earth, yet he went not before them that tarried in heaven. This *Beliall* is constrained by divine venue, when he taketh sacrifices, gifts, and [burnt] offer-ings, that he againe may give unto the offerers true answers. But he tarrieth not one houre in the truth, except he be constrained by the divine power, as is said. He taketh the forme of a beautifull angell, sitting in a firie chariot; he speaketh faire, he distributeth preferments of senatorship, and the favour of friends, and excellent familiars: he hath rule over eightie legions, partlie of the order of vertues, partlie of angels; he is found in the forme of an exorcist in the bonds of spirits. The exorcist must consider, that this *Beliall* doth in everie thing assist his subjects. If he will not submit himselfe, let the bond of spirits be read: the spirits

Observandum exorcistæ, hunc
Belial in omnibus succurrere suis
subditis: Si autem se submittere
noluerit, Vinculum Spirituum
legatur, quo sapientissimus
Salomon eos cum suis legionibus
in vase vitreo relegavit: Et relegati
cum omnibus legionibus fuere
septuagintaduo reges, quorum
primus erat Bileth, secundus
Belial, deinde Asmoday, & circirer
mille millia legionum. Illud
proculdubio à magistro Salomone
didiciste me fateor: Sed causam
relegationis me non docuit,
crediderim tamen propter
arrogantiam ipsius Belial. Sunt
quidam necromantici, qui asserunt,
ipsum Salomonem quodam die
astutia cujusdam mulieris
seductum, orando se inclinasse
versus simulacrum Belial nomine.
Quod tamen fidem non meretur:
Sed potius sentiendum, ut dictum
est, propter superbiam &
arrogantiam, relegatos esse in
magno vase, projectos in Babylone
in puteum grandem valde.
Enimvero prudentissimus Salomon
divina potentia suas exequebatur
operationes, quæ etiam nunquam
eum destituit: propterea
simulachrum non adorasse ipsum
sentiendum est, alioqui divina
virtute spiritus cogere nequivisset.
Hic autem Belial cum tribus
regibus in puteo fuit. At
Babylonienses ad hæc
exhorrescentes, rati se thesaurum
amplum in puteo inventuros,
unanimi consilio in puteum
descenderunt, detegeruntque &
confregere vas, unde mox egressi

chaine is sent for him, wherewith wise
Salomon gathered them togither with their
legions in a brasen vessell, where were
inclosed among all the legions seventie
two kings, of whome the cheefe was
Bileth, the second was *Beliall*, the third
Asmoday, and above a thousand thousand
legions. Without doubt (I must confesse)
I learned this of my maister *Salomon*; but
he told me not why he gathered them
together, and shut them up so: but I
beleeve it was for the pride of this *Beliall*.
Certeine nigromancers doo saie, that
Salomon, being on a certeine daie seduced
by the craft of a certeine woman, inclined
himselfe to praie before the same idoll,
Beliall by name: which is not credible.
And therefore we must rather thinke (as
it is said) that they were gathered together in that great brasen vessell for
pride and arrogancie, and throwne into a
deepe lake or hole in *Babylon*. For wise
Salomon did accomplish his workes by the
divine power, which never forsooke him.
And therefore we must thinke he wor-
shipped not the image *Beliall*; for then he
could not have constrained the spirits by
divine vertue: for this *Beliall*, with three
kings were in the lake. But the
Babylonians woondering at the matter,
supposed that they should find therein a
great quantitie of treasure, and therefore
with one consent went downe into the
lake, and uncovered and brake the vessell,
out of the which immediatlie flew the
capteine divels, and were delivered to
their former and proper places. But this
Beliall entred into a certeine image, and
there gave answer to them that offered
and sacrificed unto him: as *Tocz.* in his
sentences reporteth, and the Babylonians
did worship and sacrifice thereunto.

captivi, in proprium locum porto sunt rejecti. Belial vero ingressus quoddam simulachrum, dabat responsa sibi immolantibus & sacrificantibus, ut testatur Tocz in dictis suis: Et Babylonienses adorantes sacrificaverunt eidem.

§ 24. Bune Dux magnus & fortis, apparet ut draco, tribus capitibus, tertium vero assimilatur homini. Muta loquitur voce: Mortuos locum mutare facit, & dæmones supra defunctorum sepulchra congregari: omnimodo hominem locupletat, redditque loquacem & sapientem: ad quæsita vere respondet. Huic legiones parent triginta.

(24) *Bune* is a great and a strong Duke, he appeareth as a dragon with three heads, the third whereof is like to a man; he speaketh with a divine voice, he maketh the dead to change their place, and divels to assemble upon the sepulchers of the dead: he greatlie inricheth a man, and maketh him eloquent and wise, answering trulie to all demands, and thirtie legions obeie him.

§ 25. Forneus magnus Marchio, similis monstro marino, reddit hominem in Rhetoricis admirabilem, optima fama & linguarum peritia ornat, tam amicis quam inimicis gratum facit. Subsunt huic vigintinovem legiones, ex ordine partim Thronorum, partim Angelorum.

(25) *Forneus* is a great marquesse, like unto a monster of the sea, he maketh men woondeffull in rhetorike, he adorneth a man with a good name, and the knowledge of toongs, and maketh one beloved as well of foes as freends: there are under him nine and twentie legions, of the order partlie of thrones, and partlie of angels.

§ 26. Roneve Marchio & Comes, assimilatur monstro. Singularem in Rhetoricis intelligcntiam confert, famulos item fidos, linguarum cognitionem, amicorum & inimicorum favorem. Huic obediunt legiones novendecim.

(26) *Ronove* [Roneve] a marquesse and an earle, he is resembled to a monster, he bringeth singular understanding in rhetorike, faithfull servants, knowledge of toongs, favour of freends and foes; and nineteene legions obeie him.

(27) *Berith* is a great and a terrible duke, and hath three names. Of some he is called *Beall*; of the Jewes *Berithi* [Berith]; of Nigromancers *Bolfry* [Bolfri]: he commeth foorth as a red souldier, with red clothing, and upon a horsse of that

§ 27. Berith Dux magnus & terribilis: tribus nuncupatur nominibus, à quibusdam Beal, à Judæis Berith, à necromanticis

Bolfri. Prodit ut miles ruber cum vestitu rubro, & equo ejusdem coloris coronaque ornatus. Vere de præsentibus, præterius & futuris respondet. Virtute divina per annulum magicæ artis ad horam scilicet cogitur. Mendax etiam est. In aurum cuncta metallorum genera mutat. Dignitatibus ornat easdemque confirmat: Claram subtilemque edit vocem. Viginti sex legiones huic subsunt.

colour, and a crowne on his head. He answereth trulie of things present, past, and to come. He is compelled at a certeine houre, through divine vertue, by a ring of art magicke. He is also a lier, he turneth all mettals into gold, he adorneth a man with dignities, and confirmeth them, he speaketh with a cleare and a subtill voice, and six and twentie legions are under him.

§ 28. Astaroth Dux magnus & fortis, prodiens angelica specie turpissima, insidensque in dracone infernali, & viperam portans manu dextra. Vere respondet de præteritis, præsentibus, futuris & occultis. Libenter de spirituum creatore, & eorundem lapsu loquitur, quomodo peccaverint & ceciderint. Se spontè non prolapsum esse dicit. Reddit hominem mire eruditum in artibus liberalibus. Quadraginta legionibus imperat. Ab hoc quilibet exocista caveat, ne prope nimis cum admittat, ob fœtorem intolerabilem quem expirat. Itaque annulum argenteum magicum in manu sua juxta faciem teneat, quo se ab injuria facile tuebitur.

(28) *Astaroth* is a great and a strong duke, comming foorth in the shape of a fowle angell, sitting upon an infernall dragon, and carrieng on his right hand a viper: he answereth trulie to matters present, past, and to come, and also of all secrets. He talketh willinglie of the creator of spirits, and of their fall, and how they sinned and fell: he saith he fell not of his owne accord. He maketh a man woonderfull learned in the liberall sciences, he ruleth fourtie legions. Let everie exorcist take heed, that he admit him not too neere him, bicause of his stinking breath [lit. "because of the intolerable stench that he exhales"]. And therefore let the conjuror hold neere to his face a magicall [silver] ring, and that shall defend him.

§ 29. Forras vel Forcas magnus Præses est: visitur forma viri fortissimi, & in humana specie vires herbarum & lapidum preciosorum intelligit. Plene docet Logica, Ethica & corundem partes. Reddit hominem invisibilem, ingeniosum, loquacem & vivacem: Amissa recuperat,

(29) *Foras* [Forras], *alias Forcas* is a great president, and is seene in the forme of a strong man, and in humane shape, he understandeth the vertue of hearbs and pretious stones: he teacheth fullie logicke, ethicke, and their parts: he maketh a man invisible, wittie, eloquent, and to live long; he recovereth things lost, and discovereth [discloses]

thesauros detegit. Dominium viginti novem legionum habet.

treasures, and is lord over nine and twentie legions.

§ 30. Furfur Comes est magnus, apparens ut cervus cauda flammea. In omnibus mentitur, nisi in triangulum intro ducatur. Jussus angelicam assumit imaginem. Rauca loquitur voce: amorem inter virum & mulierem libenter conciliat: novit & concitare fulgura, coruscationes & tonitrua in iis partibus ubi jussum fuerit. De occultis & divinis rebus bene respondet. Imperat legionibus vigintisex.

(30) *Furfur* is a great earle, appearing as an hart, with a firie taile, he lieth in everie thing, except he be brought up within a triangle; being bidden, he taketh angelicall forme, he speaketh with a hoarse voice, and willinglie maketh love betweene man and wife [or simply "woman"]; he raiseth thunders and lightnings, and blasts. Where he is commanded, he answereth well, both of secret and also of divine things, and hath rule and dominion over six and twentie legions.

§ 31. Marchocias magnus Marchio est. Se ostentat specie lupæ ferocissimæ cum alis gryphi, cauda serpentina, & ex ore nescio quid evomens. Quum hominis imaginem induit, pugnator est optimus. Ad quæsita vere respondet: fidelis in cunctis exorcistæ mandatis. Fuit ordinis Dominationum. Huic subjacent legiones triginta. Sperat se post mille ducentos annos ad septimum Thronum reversurum: sed ea spe falsus est.

(31) *Marchosias* [Marchocias] is a great marquesse, he sheweth himselfe in the shape of a cruell shee woolfe, with a griphens wings, with a serpents taile, and spetting I cannot tell what out of his mouth. When he is in a mans shape, he is an excellent fighter, he answereth all questions trulie, he is faithfull in all the conjurors businesse [commands], he was of the order of dominations, under him are thirtie legions: he hopeth after 1200 yeares to returne to the seventh throne, but he is deceived in that hope.

§ 32. Malphas magnus Præses, conspicitur corvo similis: sed hominis idolum indutus rauca fatur voce. Domos & turres ingentes mire extruit, & obvios cito facit artifices maximos: Hostium vero ædes & turres dejicit. Famulos suppeditat non malos. Sacrificia libenter suscipit, at sacrificatores omnes fallit. Quadraginta huic parent legiones.

(32) *Malphas* is a great president, he is seene like a crowe, but being cloathed with humane image, speaketh with a hoarse voice, he buildeth houses and high towres wonderfullie, and quicklie bringeth artificers togither, he throweth downe also the enimies edifications, he helpeth to good familiars, he receiveth sacrifices willinglie, but he deceiveth all the sacrificers, there obeie him fourtie legions.

§ 33. Vepar, alias Separ, Dux magnus & fortis: Similis syreni: Ductor est aquarum & navium armis onustarum. Ut mare jussu magistri turgidum navibusque plenum appareat, efficit: contra inimicos exorcistæ per dies tres vulneribus putrescentibus vermesque producentibus homines inficit, à quibus tamen negotio absoluto sanantur omnes. Imperat legionibus vigintinovem.

§34. Sabnac, alias Salmac, Marchio magnus & fortis: prodit ut miles armatus, capite leonis, in pallido equo infidens. Hominis formam transmutat mire: Turres magnas armis plenas ædificat, item castra & civitates. Triginta dies ex mandato exorcistæ homini vulnera putrida & verminantia infligit. Familiares conciliat bonos: dominium exercens quinquaginta legionum.

§ 35. Sydonay, alias Asmoday, Rex magnus, fortis & potens: Visitur tribus capitibus, quorum primum assimilatur capiti tauri, alterum hominis, tertium arietis. Cauda ejus serpentina, ex ore flammam eructat, pedes anserini. Super dracone infernali sedet, in manu lanceam & vexillum portans. Præcedit alios qui sub potestate Amaymonis sunt. Cum hujus officia exercet exorcista, fit fortis, cautus & in pedibus stans: si vero coopertus fuerit, ut in omnibus detegatur, efficiet: Quod si non fecerit exorcista, ab Amaymone in cunctis decipietur: Sed mox cum

(33) *Vepar, alias Separ*, a great duke and a strong, he is like a mermaid, he is the guide of the waters, and of ships laden with armour; he bringeth to passe (at the commandement of his master) that the sea shalbe rough and stormie, and shall appeare full of shippes; he killeth men in three daies, with putrifieng their wounds, and producing maggots into them; howbeit, they maie be all healed with diligence, he ruleth nine and twentie legions.

(34) *Sabnacke* [Sabnac], *alias Salmac*, is a great marquesse and a strong, he commeth foorth as an armed soldier with a lions head, sitting on a pale horsse, he dooth marvelouslie change mans forme and favor, he buildeth high towres full of weapons, and also castels and cities; he inflicteth men thirtie daies with wounds both rotten and full of maggots, at the exorcists commandement, he provideth good familiars, and hath dominion over fiftie legions.

(35) *Sidonay* [Sydonay], *alias Asmoday,* a great king, strong and mightie, he is seene with three heads, whereof the first is like a bull, the second like a man, the third like a ram, he hath a serpents taile, he belcheth flames out of his mouth, he hath feete like a goose, he sitteth on an infernall dragon, he carrieth a lance and a flag in his hand, he goeth before others, which are under the power of *Amaymon*. When the conjuror exerciseth this office, let him be abroad [brave], let him be warie [courageous] and standing on his feete; <if his cap be on his head> [if he is afraid he will be overwhelmed], he will cause all his dooings to be bewraied [divulged], which if he doo not, the

ipsum in prædicta forma conspicit, appellabit illum nomine suo, inquiens: Tu vero es Asmoday. Ipse non negabit: Et mox ad terram. Dat annulum virtutum: Docet absolute Geometriam, Arithmeticam, Astronomiam, Mechanicam: Ad interrogata plene & vere respondet: Hominem reddit invisibilem: Loca thesaurorum ostendit & custodit, si fuerit de legionibus Amaymonis. In sua potestate legiones septuaginta duas habet.

§ 36. Gaap, alias Tap, Præses magnus & Princeps: in signo Meridiei apparet: sed quum humanam assumit faciem, ductor est præcipuorum quatuor regum, tam potens ut Byleth. Extiterunt autem quidam necromantici, qui huic libamina & holocausta obtulere, & ut eundem evocarent, artem exercuere, dicentes sapientissimum Salomonem eam composuisse, quod falsum est: imo fuit Cham filius Noë, qui primus post diluvium cœpit malignos invocare spiritus, invocavit autem Byleth, & composuit artem in suo nomine, & librum, qui multis mathematicis est cognitus. Fiebant autem holocausta, libamina, munera, & multa nefaria, quæ operabantur exorcistæ admistis sanctissimis Dei nominibus, quæ

exorcist shalbe deceived by *Amaymon* in everie thing. But so soone as he seeth him in the forme aforesaid, he shall call him by his name, saieng; Thou art *Asmoday*; he will not denie it, and by and by he boweth downe to the ground; he giveth the ring of venues, he absolutelie teacheth geometrie, arythmetike, astronomie, and handicrafts [mechanics]. To all demands he answereth fullie and trulie, he maketh a man invisible, he sheweth the places where treasure lieth, and gardeth it, if it be among the legions of *Amaymon*, he hath under his power seventie two legions.

(36) *Gaap, alias Tap*, a great president and a prince, he appeareth in a meridionall signe, and when he taketh humane shape he is the guide of the foure principall kings, as mightie as *Bileth*. There were certeine necromancers that offered sacrifices and burnt offerings unto him; and to call him up, they exercised an art, saieng that *Salomon* the wise made it. Which is false: for it was rather *Cham*, the sonne of *Noah*, who after the floud began first to invocate wicked spirits. He invocated *Bileth*, and made an art in his name, and a booke which is knowne to manie mathematicians.[2] There were burnt offerings and sacrifices made, and gifts given, and much wickednes wrought by the exorcists, who mingled therewithall the holie names of God, the which in that art are everie where expressed. Marie [Certainly] there is an epistle of those names written by *Salomon*, as also write

2 The reference is probably to the *Book of Bilt* (or Bilath), see Hermann Gollancz, *Sepher Maphteah Shelomoh* (London: Oxford University Press, 1914), fol. 42a–46a. It also occurs in British Library Oriental MS 14759.

in eadem arte sparsim exprimuntur. Epistola vero de iis nominibus est conscripta à Salomone, uti & scribunt Helias Hierosolymitanus & Heliseus. Notandum, si aliquis exorcista habuerit artem Beleth, nec ipsum coram se sistere possit aut videre, nisi per artem: Quomodo autem eundem continere oporteat, non est explicandum, quum sit nefandum, & nihil à Salomone de ejus dignitate & officio didicerim, hoc tamen non silebo, ipsum reddere hominem admirabilem in philosophia & artibus omnibus liberalibus. Facit ad amorem, odium, invisibilitatem & consecrationem eorum quæ sunt de dominatione Amaymonis: Et de potestate alterius exorcistæ tradit familiares, & vera perfecte responsa de præsentibus, præteritis & futuris. Velocissimo transcursu in varias regiones traducit hom-inem. Sexagintasex præest legionibus, & fuit de Potestatum ordine.

§ 37. Chax, alias Scox, Dux est & Marchio magnus: Similis ciconiæ rauca voce & subtili. Mirabiliter aufert visum, auditum & intellectum jussu exorcistæ: aufert pecuniam ex qualibet domo regia, & reportat post mille ducentos annos, si jussus fuerit: abripit & equos. Fidelis esse in omnibus mandatis putatur: ac licet se obsecuturum exorcistæ promittat, non tamen in omnibus facit. Mendax est, nisi in triangulum introducatur:

Helias Hierosolymitanus and *Helisæus*. It is to be noted, that if anie exorcist have the art of *Bileth*, and cannot make him stand before him, nor see him, I may not bewraie how and declare the meanes to conteine him, bicause it is abhomination, and for that I have learned nothing from *Salomon* of his dignitie and office. But yet I will not hide this; to wit, that he maketh a man woonderfull in philosophie and all the liberall sciences: he maketh love, hatred, insensibilitie, invisibilitie, consecration, and consecration of those things that are belonging unto the domi-nation of *Amaymon*, and delivereth familiars out of the possession of other conjurors, answering truly and perfectly of things present, past, & to come, & transferreth men most speedilie into other nations, he ruleth sixtie six legions, & was of the order of potestats.

(37) *Shax* [Chax], *alias Scox*, is a darke and a great marquesse, like unto a storke, with a hoarse and subtill voice: he dooth marvellouslie take awaie the sight, hearing and understanding of anie man, at the commandement of the conjuror: he taketh awaie monie out of everie kings house, and carrieth it backe after 1200 yeares, if he be commanded, he is a horssestealer, he is thought to be faithfull in all commandements: and although he prom-ise to be obedient to the conjuror in all things; yet is he not so, he is a lier, except he be brought into a triangle, and there

introductus autem loquitur de rebus divinis & reconditis thesauris, qui à malignis spiritibus non custodiuntur. Promittit insuper se collaturum optimos famulos, qui accepti sunt, si non fuerint deceptores. Huic subjacent legiones triginta.

he speaketh divinelie, and telleth of things which are hidden, and not kept of wicked spirits, he promiseth good familiars, which are accepted if they be not deceivers, he hath thirtie legions.

§ 38. Pucel Dux magnus & fortis, apparet in specie angelica, sed obscura valde: loquitur de occultis: docet Geometriam & omnes artes liberales: sonitus facit ingentes, & sonare aquas ubi non sunt, easdem & calefacit & harum balnea recuperandæ sanitati servientia certis temporibus, distemperat jussu exorcistæ. Fuit de ordine Potestatum, habetque in sua potestate legiones quadragintaocto.

(38) *Procell* is a great and a strong duke, appearing in the shape of an angell, but speaketh verie darklie of things hidden, he teacheth geometrie and all the liberall arts, he maketh great noises, and causeth the waters to rore, where are none, he warmeth waters, and distempereth bathes at certeine times, as the exorcist appointeth him, he was of the order of potestats, and hath fourtie eight legions under his power.

§ 38 [sic]. Furcas miles est: prodit similitudine sævi hominis cum longa barba, & capillitio cano. In equo pallido insidet, portans in manu telum acutum. Docet perfecte practicam, philosophiam, rhetoricam, logicam, chiromantiam, astronomiam, piromantiam, & earum partes. Huic parent viginti legiones.

(38) *Furcas* is a knight and commeth foorth in the similitude of a cruell man, with a long beard and a hoarie head, he sitteth on a pale horsse, carrieng in his hand a sharpe weapon [dart or spear], he perfectlie teacheth practike philosophie, rhetorike, logike, astronomie, chiromancie, pyromancie, and their parts: there obeie him twentie legions.

§ 39. Murmur magnus Dux & Comes: Apparet militis forma, equitans in vulture, & ducali corona comptus. Hunc præcedunt duo ministri tubis magnis: Philosophiam absolute docet. Cogit animas coram exorcista apparere, ut interrogatæ respondeant ad ipsius quæsita. Fuit

(39) *Murmur* is a great duke and an earle, appearing in the shape of a souldier, riding on a griphen [vulture], with a dukes crowne on his head; there go before him two of his ministers, with great trumpets, he teacheth philosophie absolutelie, he constraineth soules to come before the exorcist, to answer what he shall aske them, he was of the order

de ordine partim Thronorum, partim Angelorum.

partlie of thrones, and partlie of angels, <and ruleth thirtie legions.>

§ 40. Caym magnus Præses, formam assumens merulæ: at quum hominem induit, respondet in favilla ardente, ferens in manu glagium [sic gladium] acutissimum. Præ cæteris sapienter argumentari facit: Tribuit intellectum omnium volatilium, mugitus boum, latratus canum, & sonitus aquarum: de futuris optime respondet. Fuit ex ordine Angelorum. Præsidet legionibus triginta.

(40) *Caim* [Caym] is a great president, taking the forme of a thrush [blackbird], but when he putteth on man's shape, he answereth in burning ashes, carrieng in his hand a most sharpe swoord, he maketh the best disputers, he giveth men the understanding of all birds, of the lowing of bullocks, and barking of dogs, and also of the sound and noise of waters, he answereth best of things to come, he was of the order of angels, and ruleth thirtie legions of divels.

§ 41. Raum vel Raym Comes est magnus: Ut corvus visitur: Sed cum assumit humanam faciem, si ab exorcista jussus fuerit, mirè ex regis domo vel alia suffuratur, & ad locum sibi designatum transfert. Civitates destruit: Dignitatum despectum ingerit. Novit præsentia, præterita & futura. Favorem tam hostium quam amicorum conciliat. Fuit ex ordine Thronorum. Præest legionibus triginta.

(41) *Raum*, or *Raim* is a great earle, he is seene as a crowe, but when he putteth on humane shape, at the commandement of the exorcist, he stealeth woonderfullie out of the kings house, and carrieth it whether he is assigned, he destroieth cities, and hath great despite unto dignities, he knoweth things present, past, and to come, and reconcileth freends and foes, he was of the order of thrones, and governeth thirtie legions.

§ 42. Halphas Comes magnus, prodit similis ciconiæ rauca voce. Insigniter ædificat oppida ampla armis plena: Bellum movet, & jussus, homines bellicosos ad designatum locum mittit obviam. Subsunt huic viginti sex legiones.

(42) *Halphas* is a great earle, and commeth abroad like a storke, with a hoarse voice, he notablie buildeth up townes full of munition and weapons, he sendeth men of warre to places appointed, and hath under him six and twentie legions.

§ 43. Focalor Dux magnus, prodit velut homo, habens alas gryphi forma. Accepta humana figura, interficit homines & in

(43) *Focalor* is a great duke comming foorth as a man, with wings like a griphen, he killeth men, and drowneth them in the waters, and overturneth ships

aquis submergit. Imperat mari &
vento, navesque bellicas subvertit.
Notandum omni exorcistæ, si huic
mandetur, ne homines lædat,
libenter obsequitur. Sperat se post
mille annos reversurum ad
septimum Thronum, sed fallitur.
Triginta legionibus imperat.

§ 44. Vine magnus Rex &
Comes: se ostentat ut leo in equo
nigro insidens, portansque viperam
in manu. Amplas turres libenter
ædificat: Lapideas domus extruit,
rivos reddit turgidos: Ad exorcistæ
mandatum respondet de occultis,
maleficis, præsentibus, præteritis &
futuris.

§ 45. Bifrons, monstri
similitudine conspicitur. Ubi
humanam assumit imaginem, reddit
hominem in Astrologia mirabilem,
planetarum mansiones absolute
docens, idem præstat in Geometria,
& mensuris aliis. Vires herbarum,
lapidum pretiosorum & lignorum
intelligit. Corpora mortuorum de
loco ad locum transmutat: Candelas
super defunctorum sepulchra
inflammare videtur. Huic subjacent
vinginti sex legiones.

§ 46. Gamygyn magnus
Marchio: in forma equi parvi
visitur: at ubi hominis
simulachrum assumit, raucam edit
vocem, de omnibus artibus
liberalibus differens: efficit quoque,
ut coram exorcista conveniant
animæ in mari exeuntes, & quæ
degunt in purgatorio (quod dicitur
Cartagra, id est, afflictio

of warre, commanding and ruling both
winds and seas. And let the conjuror note,
that if he bid him hurt no man, he
willinglie consenteth thereto: he hopeth
after 1000 yeares to returne to the seventh
throne, but he is deceived, he hath three
legions.

(44) *Vine* is a great king and an earle,
he showeth himselfe as a lion, riding on a
blacke horsse, and carrieth a viper in his
hand, he gladlie buildeth large towres, he
throweth downe stone walles, and maketh
waters rough. At the commandement of
the exorcist he answereth of things
hidden, of witches, and of things present,
past, and to come.

(45) *Bifrons* is seene in the similitude
of a monster, when he taketh the image
of a man, he maketh one woonderfull
cunning in astrologie, absolutelie declaring the mansions of the planets, he dooth
the like in geometrie, and other
admesurements, he perfectlie
understandeth the strength and vertue of
hearbs, pretious stones, and woods, he
changeth dead bodies from place to place,
he seemeth to light candles upon the
sepulchres of the dead, and hath under
him six and twentie legions.

(46) *Gamigin* [Gamygyn] is a great
marquesse, and is seene in the forme of a
little horsse, when he taketh humane
shape he speaketh with a hoarse voice,
disputing of all liberall sciences; he
bringeth also to passe, that the soules,
which are drowned in the sea, or which
dwell in purgatorie (which is called
Cartagra, that is, affliction of soules) shall
take aierie bodies, and evidentlie appeare

animarum) & corpora aërea suscipiunt, apparentque evidenter, & ad interrogata respondent. Permanet apud exorcistam, donec ipsius votum expleverit. Triginta legiones in sua habet potestate.

and answer to interrogatories at the conjurors commandement; he tarrieth with the exorcist, untill he have accomplished his desire, and hath thirtie legions under him.

§ 47. Zagam magnus Rex & Præses: ut taurus prodit cum alis ad modum gryphi: sed assumpta hominis forma, reddit hominem ingeniosum: transmutat cuncta metallorum genera in monetas illius ditionis, & aquam in vinum, & è diverso: sanguinem quoque in oleum, & contra: & stultum in sapientem. Præest triginta tribus legionibus.

(47) *Zagan* [Zagam] is a great king and a president, he commeth abroad like a bull, with griphens wings, but when he taketh humane shape, he maketh men wittie, he turneth all mettals into the coine of that dominion, and turneth water into wine, and wine into water, he also turneth bloud into <wine> [oil], & <wine> [oil] into bloud, & a foole into a wise man, he is head of thirtie and three legions.

§ 48. Orias Marchio magnus, visitur ut leo, in equo fortissimo equitans, cauda serpentina: in dextera portat duos grandes serpentes etiam exibilantes. Callet planetarum mansiones, & vires sidereas perfecte docet. Transmutat homines: confert dignitates, prælaturas & confirmationes: Item amicorum & hostium favorem. Præsidet legionibus triginta.

(48) *Orias* is a great marquesse, and is seene as a lion riding on a strong horsse, with a serpents taile, and carrieth in his right hand two great serpents hissing, he knoweth the mansion of planets and perfectlie teacheth the vertues of the starres, he transformeth men, he giveth dignities, prelacies, and confirmations, and also the favour of freends and foes, and hath under him thirtie legions.

§ 49. Volac magnus Præses: progreditur uti puer alis angeli, super dracone equitans duobus capitibus. De occultis thesauris perfecte respondet, & ubi serpentes videantur, quos & viribus dedestitutos tradit in exorcistæ manus. Dominium habet legionum triginta.

(49) *Valac* [Volac] is a great president, and commeth abroad with angels wings like a boie, riding on a twoheaded dragon, he perfectlie answereth of treasure hidden, and where serpents may be seene, which he delivereth into the conjurors hands, void of anie force or strength, and hath dominion over thirtie legions of divels.

§ 50. Gomory Dux fortis & potens: apparet ut mulier

(50) *Gomory* a strong and a mightie duke, he appeareth like a faire woman,

pulcherrima: ac ducali cingitur corona, in camelo equitans. Bene & vere respondet de præteritis, præsentibus, futuris, & occultis thesauris ubi lateant. Conciliat amorem mulierum, & maxime puellarum. Imperat legionibus vigintisex.

§ 51. Decarabia vel Carabia, magnus Rex & Comes: venit similis *. Vires herbarum & lapidum pretiosorum novit: efficit ut aves coram exorcista volent, & velut familiares ac domesticæ morentur, bibant & cantillent suo more. Parent huic triginta legiones.

§ 52. Amduscias Dux magnus & fortis: procedit ut unicornu: in humana similiter forma, quando coram magistro suo se fistit: Et si præcipiatur, efficit facile ut tubæ & symphoniæ omniaque musicorum instrumentorum genera audiantur, nec tamen conspectui appareant: ut item arbores ad exorcistæ genu se inclinent. Optimus est una cum famulis. Imperium habet vigintinovem legionum.

§ 53. Andras magnus Marchio: visitur forma angelica, capite nycticoraci nigro simili, in lupo nigro & fortissimo equitans, bajulansque manu gladium acutissimum. Novit interficere dominum, servum & coadjutores: author est discordiarum. Dominatur legionibus triginta.

with a duchesse crownet about hir midle, riding on a camell, he answereth well and truelie of things present, past, and to come, and of treasure hid, and where it lieth: he procureth the love of women, especiallie of maids, and hath six and twentie legions.

(51) *Decarabia* or *Carabia*, he commeth like a *3 and knoweth the force of herbes and pretious stones, and maketh all birds flie before the exorcist, and to tarrie with him, as though they were tame, and that they shall drinke and sing, as their maner is, and hath thirtie legions.

(52) *Amduscias* a great and a strong duke, he commeth foorth as an unicorne, when he standeth before his maister in humane shape, being commanded, he easilie bringeth to passe, that trumpets and all musicall instruments may be heard and not seene, and also that trees shall bend and incline, according to the conjurors will, he is excellent among familiars, and hath nine and twentie legions.

(53) *Andras* is a great marquesse, and is seene in an angels shape with a head like a blacke night raven, riding upon a blacke and a verie strong woolfe, flourishing with a sharpe sword in his hand, he can kill the maister, the servant, and all assistants, he is author of discords, and ruleth thirtie legions.

---

3   The asterisk in Weyer's text seems to mark the omission of a word noticed in the manuscript (ellipses) See paragraph 56 where this is more clearly the case.

§ 54. Androalphus Marchio magnus, apparens ut pavo: graves edit sonitus: Et in humana forma docet perfecte geometriam & mensuram spectantia: reddit hominem in argumentando argutum, & in astronomia prudentem, eundemque in avis speciem transmutat. Triginta huic subsunt legiones.

(54) *Andrealphus* [Androalphus] is a great marquesse, appearing as a pecocke, he raiseth great noises, and in humane shape perfectlie teacheth geometrie, and all things belonging to admeasurements, he maketh a man to be a subtill disputer, and cunning in astronomie, and transformeth a man into the likenes of a bird, and there are under him thirtie legions.

§ 55. Oze Præses magnus, procedit similis leopardo: sed hominem mentitus, reddit prudentem in artibus liberalibus: vere resondet de divinis & occultis: transmutat hominis formam: & ad eam insaniam eum redigit, ut sibi persuadeat esse quod non est, quemadmodum se esse regem vel papam, & coronam in capite gestare: duratque id regnum horam.

(55) *Ose* [Oze] is a great president, and commeth foorth like a leopard, and counterfeting to be a man, he maketh one cunning in the liberall sciences, he answereth truelie of divine and secret things, he transformeth a mans shape, and bringeth a man to that madnes that he thinketh himselfe to be that which he is not; as that he is a king or a pope, or that he weareth a crowne on his head, *Durátque id regnum ad horam* [and makes the kingdom of time endure (?).]

§ 56. Aym vel Haborym Dux magnus & fortis: progreditur tribus capitibus, primo serpenti, simili, altero homini duos * habenti, tertio felino. In vipera equitat, ingentem facem ardentem portans, cujus flamma succenditur castrum vel civitas. Omnibus modis ingeniosum reddit hom-inem: de abstrusis rebus vere respondet. Imperat legionibus vigintisex.

(56) *Aym* or *Haborim* [Haborym] is a great duke and a strong, he commeth foorth with three heads, the first like a serpent, the second like a man having two *4 the third like a cat, he rideth on a viper, carrieng in his hand a light fier brand, with the flame whereof castels and cities are fiered, he maketh one wittie everie kind of waie, he answereth truelie of privie matters, and reigneth over twentie six legions.

§ 57. Orobas magnus Prin-ceps: procedit equo conformis: hominis autem indutus idoltum,

(57) *Orobas* is a great prince, he commeth foorth like a horsse, but when he putteth on him a mans idol [image],

---

de virtute divina loquitur: vera dat responsa de præteritis, præsentibus, futuris, de divinitate & creatione: neminem decipit, nec tentari sinit: confert prælaturas & dignitates, amicorum item & hostium favorem. Præsidet legionibus viginti.

§ 58. Vapula Dux magnus & fortis: conspicitur ut leo alis ad modum gryphi. Reddit hominem subtilem & mirabilem in artibus mechanicis, philosophia, & scientiis quæ in libris continentur. Præfectus est trigintasex legionum.

§ 59. Cimeries magnus Marchio & fortis: imperans in partibus Africanis: docet perfecte Grammaticam, Logicam & Rhetoricam. Thesauros detegit, & occulta aperit. Facit ut homo cursu celerrimo videatur transmutari in militem. Equitat in equo nigro & grandi. Legionibus viginti præest.

§ 60. Amy Præses magnus: apparet in flamma ignea: sed humana assumpta forma, reddit hominem admirabilem in astrologia & omnibus artibus liberalibus. Famulos suppetit optimos: thesauros à spiritibus custoditos ostendit. Præfecturam habet legionem triginta sex, ex ordine partim angelorum, partim potestatum. Sperat se post mille ducentos annos ad Thronum septimum reversurum, quod credibile non est.

§ 61. Flauros dux fortis: conspicitur forma leopardi &

he talketh of divine vertue, he giveth true answers of things present, past, and to come, and of the divinitie, and of the creation, he deceiveth none, nor suffereth anie to be tempted, he giveth dignities and prelacies, and the favour of freends and foes, and hath rule over twentie legions.

(58) *Vapula* is a great duke and a strong, he is seene like a lion with griphens wings, he maketh a man subtill and wonderfull in handicrafts [mechanics], philosophie, and in sciences conteined in bookes, and is ruler over thirtie six legions.

(59) *Cimeries* is a great marquesse and a strong, ruling in the parts of *Aphrica* [Africa]; he teacheth perfectlie grammar, logicke, and rhetorike, he discovereth treasures and things hidden, he bringeth to passe, that a man shall seeme with expedition to be turned into a soldier, he rideth upon a great blacke horsse, and ruleth twentie legions.

(60) *Amy* is a great president, and appeareth in a flame of fier, but having taken mans shape, he maketh one marvelous in astrologie, and in all the liberall sciences, he procureth excellent familiars, he bewraieth treasures preserved by spirits, he hath the governement of thirtie six legions, he is partlie of the order of angels, partlie of potestats, he hopeth after a thousand two hundreth yeares to returne to the seventh throne: which is not credible.

(61) *Flauros* a strong duke, is seene in the forme of a terrible strong leopard, in

terribili. In humana specie vultum ostentat horrendum, & oculos flammeos. De præteritis, præsentibus & futuris plene & vere respondet. Si fuerit in triangulo, mentitut in cunctis, & fallit in aliis negotiis. Libenter loquitur de divinitate, mundi creatione & lapsu. Divina virtute cogitur, & omnes alii dæmones sive spiritus, ut omnes adversarios exorcistæ succendant & destruant. Et si virtute numinis ipsi imperatum fuerit, exorcistæ tentationem non permittit. Legiones viginti sub sua habet potestate.

humane shape, he sheweth a terrible countenance, and fierie eies, he answereth trulie and fullie of things present, past, and to come; if he be in a triangle, he lieth in all things and deceiveth in other things, and beguileth in other busines, he gladlie talketh of the divinitie, and of the creation of the world, and of the fall; he is constrained by divine vertue, and so are all divels or spirits, to burne and destroie all the conjurors adversaries. And if he be commanded, he suffereth the conjuror not to be tempted, and he hath twentie legions under him.

§ 62. Balam Rex magnus & terribilis: prodit tribus capitibus, primo tauri, altero hominis, tertio arietis: cauda adhæc serpentina, oculis flammeis, equitans in urso fortissimo, & accipitrem in manu portans. Raucam edit vocem: perfectè responet de præteritis, præsentibus & futuris: reddit hominem & invisibilem & prudentem. Quadraginta legionibus præsidet, & fuit ex ordine dominationum.

(62) *Balam* is a great and a terrible king, he commeth foorth with three heads, the first of a bull, the second of a man, the third of a ram, he hath a ser-pents taile, and flaming eies, riding upon a furious [very powerful] beare, and carrieng a hawke on his fist, he speaketh with a hoarse voice, answering perfectlie of things present, past, and to come, hee maketh a man invisible and wise, hee governeth fourtie legions, and was of the order of dominations.

§ 63. Alocer Dux magnus & fortis: procedit ut miles in equo vasto insidens: facies ejus leonina, rubicunda valde cum oculis flammeis: graviter loquitur: hom-inem reddit admirabilem in astronomia & in omnibus artibus liberalibus: confert bonam familiam. Dominatur triginta sex legionibus.

(63) *Allocer* [Alocer] is a strong duke and a great, he commeth foorth like a soldier, riding on a great horsse, he hath a lions face, verie red, and with flaming eies, he speaketh with a big voice, he maketh a man woonderfull in astronomie, and in all the liberall sciences, he bringeth good familiars, and ruleth thirtie six legions.

§ 64. Zaleos magnus Comes: apparet ut miles pulcherrimus in crocodilo equitans, & ducali ornatus corona, pacificus, &c.

§ 65. Wal Dux magnus & fortis: conspicitur ut dromedarius magnus ac terribilis: at in humana forma linguam sonat Ægyptiacam graviter. Hic præ cæteris amorem maxime mulierum conciliat: inde novit præsentia, præterita & futura: confert & gratiam amicorum atque inimicorum. De ordine fuit potestatum. Trigintaseptem legiones gubernat.

§ 66. Haagenti magnus Præses: ut taurus videtur, habens alas gryphi: sed assumpta facie humana, reddit hominem ingeniosum in quibuslibet: cuncta metalla in aurum transmutat, aquam in vinum, & ediverso. Tot legionibus imperat, quot Zagan.

§ 67. Phœnix magnus Marchio: apparet uti avis phœnix puerili voce: sed antequam se sistit coram exorcista, cantus emittit dulcissimos: tunc autem cavendum exorcistæ cum suis sociis, ne suavitati cantus aures accommodent, sed ille mox huic jubeat humanam assumere speciem, tunc mire loquetur de cunctis scientiis admirandis. Poëta est optimus & obediens. Sperat se post mille ducentos annos ad septimum thronum rediturum. Viginti præest legionibus.

(64) *Saleos* [Zaleos] is a great earle, he appeareth as a gallant [handsome] soldier, riding on a crocodile, and weareth a dukes crowne, peaceable, &c.

(65) *Vuall* [Wal] is a great duke and a strong, he is seene as a great and terrible dromedarie, but in humane forme, he soundeth out in a base [deep] voice the *Ægyptian* toong. This man above all other procureth the especiall love of women, and knoweth things present, past, and to come, procuring the love of freends and foes, he was of the order of potestats, and governeth thirtie seven legions.

(66) *Haagenti* is a great president, appearing like a great bull, having the wings of a griphen, but when he taketh humane shape, he maketh a man wise in everie thing, he changeth all mettals into gold, and changeth wine and water the one into the other, and commandeth as manie legions as *Zagan*.

(67) *Phœnix* is a great marquesse, appearing like the bird *Phoenix*, having a childs voice: but before he standeth still before the conjuror, he singeth manie sweet notes. Then the exorcist with his companions must beware he give no eare to the melodie, but must by and by bid him put on humane shape; then will he speake marvellouslie of all woonderfull sciences. He is an excellent poet, and obedient, he hopeth to returne to the seventh throne after a thousand two hundreth yeares, and governeth twentie legions.

§ 68. Stolas magnus Princeps: prodit forma nycticoracis: coram exorcista hominis simulachrum suscipit, docetque absolutè astronomiam. Herbarum & lapidum pretiosorum vires intelligit. Vigintisex legiones huic subjacent.

(68) *Stolas* is a great prince, appearing in the forme of a nightraven, before the exorcist, he taketh the image and shape of a man, and teacheth astronomie, absolutelie understanding the vertues of herbes and pretious stones; there are under him twentie six legions.

Legio 6666.

¶ *Note that a legion is 6 6 6 6, and now by multiplication count how manie legions doo arise out of everie particular.*

This was the work of one T. R. written in faire letters of red & blacke upon parchment, and made by him, Ann. 1570. to the maintenance of his living, the edifieng of the poore, and the glorie of gods holie name: as he himselfe saith.

Secretum secretorum tu operans sis secretus horum.

The secret of secrets; Thou that workst them, be secret in them

[Hours to Observe]

§ 69. Observa horas in quibus quatuor reges, scilicet Amoymon rex Orientalis, Gorson rex Meridionalis, Zymymar rex Septentrionalis, Goap rex & princeps Occidentalis possunt constringi, à tertia hora usque ad meridiem, à nona hora usque ad vesperas.

(69) The houres wherin principall divels may be bound, to wit, raised and restrained from dooing of hurt. *AMAYMON* king of the east, *Gorson* king of the south, *Zimimar* king of the north, *Goap* king and prince of the west, may be bound from the third houre, till noone, and from the ninth houre till evening.

Item Marchiones à nona usque ad completorium, vel à completorio usque ad finem diei.

Marquesses may be bound from the ninth houre till compline, and from compline till the end of the daie.

Item Duces à prima usque ad meridiem: & observatur cœlum clarum.

Dukes may be bound from the first houre till noone; and cleare wether is to be observed.

Item Prælati in aliqua hora diei.

Prelates may be bound in anie houre of the daie.

Item Milites ab aurora usque ad ortum solis, vel à vesperis usque ad finem solis.

Knights from daie dawning, till sunne rising; or from evensong, till the sunne set.

Item Præses in aliqua hora diei non potest constringi, nisi rex cui paret, invocaretur, & nec in crepusculo noctis.

A President may not be bound in anie houre of the daie, except the king, whome he obeieth, be invocated; nor in the shutting of the evening.

Item Comites omni hora diei, dum sunt in locis campestribus vel sylvestribus, quo homines non solent accedere, &c.

Counties or erles may be bound at anie houre of the daie, so it be in the woods or feelds, where men resort not.

Citatio Prædictorum spirituum

The forme of adjuring or citing of the spirits aforesaid to arise and appeare.

§ 1 Ubi quem volueris spiritum, hujus nomen & officium supra cognosces: inprimis autem ab omni pollutione, minimum tres vel quatuor dies mundus esto in prima citatione, sic & spiritus postea obsequentiores erunt: fac & circulum, & voca spiritum cum multa intentione: primum vero annulum in manu contineto: inde hanc recitato benedictionem tuo nomine & socii, si præsto fuerit, & effectum tui instituti sortieris, nec detrimentum à spiritibus senties: imo tuæ animæ perditionem.

(1) WHEN you will have anie spirit,you must know his name and office; you must also fast, and be cleane from all pollusion, three or foure daies before; so will the spirit be the more obedient unto you. Then make a circle, and call up the spirit with great intention,and holding a ring in your hand, rehearse in your owne name, and your companions (for one must alwaies be with you) this praier following, and so no spirit shall annoie you, and your purpose shall take effect.5

§ 2. In nomine Domini nostri Jesu Christi + patris & + filii & + spiritus sancti: sancta trinitas & inseparabilis unitas te invoco, ut sis mihi salus & defensio & protectio corporis & animæ meæ, & om-

(2) In the name of our Lord Jesus Christ the + father + and the sonne + and the Hollie-ghost + holie trinitie and unseparable unitie, I call upon thee, that thou maiest be my salvation and defense, and the protection of my bodie and soule,

---

3   Scot adds, "(And note how this agreeth with popish charmes and conjurations.)."

nium rerum mearum. Per virtutem
sanctæ crucis + & per virtutem
passionis tuæ deprecor te domine
Jesu Christe, per merita beatissimæ
Mariæ virginis & matris tuæ atque
omnium sanctorum tuorum, ut
mihi concedas gratiam & potestatem divinam super omnes
malignos spiritus, ut quoscunque
nominibus invocavero, statim ex
omni parte conveniant, &
voluntatem meam perfecte
adimpleant, quod mihi nihil
nocentes, neque timorem
inferentes, sed potius obedientes &
ministrantes, tua districte virtute
præcipiente, mandata mea
perficiant, Amen. Sanctus sanctus
sanctus dominus Deus Sabaoth,
qui venturus es judicare vivos &
mortuos: tu qui es A & Ω primus
& novissimus, Rex regum &
dominus dominantium Joth
Aglanabrath El abiel anathi
Enathiel Amazin sedomel gayes
tolima Elias ischiros athanatos
ymas heli Messias, per hæc tua
sancta nomina & per omnia alia
invoco te & obsecro te domine
Jesu Christe, per tuam nativitatem,
per baptismum tuum, per
passionem & crucem tuam, per
ascensionem tuam, per adventum
spiritus sancti paracliti, per
amaritudinem animæ tuæ; quando
exivit de corpore tuo, per quinque
vulnera tua, per sanguinem &
aquam, quæ exierant de corpore
tuo, per virtutem tuam, per sacramentum quod dedisti discipulis
tuis pridie quam passus fuisti: per
sanctam trinitatem, per individuam
vnitatem, per beatam Mariam

and of all my goods through the vertue of
thy holie crosse, and through the vertue
of thy passion, I beseech thee O Lord
Jesus Christ, by the merits of thy blessed
mother S. *Marie*, and of all thy saints,
that thou give me grace and divine power
over all the wicked spirits, so as which of
them soever I doo call by name, they may
come by and by from everie coast, and
accomplish my will, that they neither be
hurtfull or fearefull unto me, but rather
obedient and diligent about me. And
through thy vertue streightlie commanding them, let them fulfill my
commandements, Amen. Holie, holie,
Lord God of sabboth, which wilt come to
judge the quicke and the dead, thou
which art *A* and *Omega*, first and last,
King of kings and Lord of lords, *Ioth,
Aglanabrath, El, Abiel,* <Anathiel> [anathi
Enathiel], *Amazim, Sedomel, Gayes,*
[Tolima, Elias, Ischiros, Athanatos, Ymas
Heli, Messias, <Tolimi, Elias, Ischiros,
Athanatos, Imas>. By these thy holie
names, and by all other I doo call upon
thee, and beseech thee O Lord Jesus
Christ, by thy nativitie and baptisme, by
thy crosse and passion, by thine ascension
and by the comming of the Holie-ghost,
by the bitternesse of thy soule when it
departed from thy bodie, by thy five
wounds, by the bloud and water which
went out of thy bodie, by thy vertue, by
the sacrament which thou gavest thy
disciples the daie before thou sufferedst,
by the holie trinitie, and by the insepa-
rable unitie, by blessed Marie thy mother,
by thine angels, archangels, prophets,
patriarchs, and by all thy saints, and by all
the sacraments which are made in thine
honour, I doo worship and beseech thee,
blesse and desire thee, to accept these
prayers, conjurations, and words of my

matrem tuam, per angelos &
archangelos, per prophetas &
patriarchas, & per omnes sanctos
tuos, & per omnia sacramenta quæ
fiunt in honore tuo: adoro te &
obsecro te, benedico tibi & rogo,
ut acceptes orationes has &
conjurationes & verba oris mei,
quibus uti voluero. Peto Domine
Iesu Christe: da mihi virtutem &
potestatem tuam super omnes
angelos tuos, qui de cœlo ejecti
sunt ad decipiendum genus
humanum, ad attrahendum eos, ad
constringendum, ad ligandum eos
pariter & solvendum: Et ad
congregandum eos coram me, &
ad præcipiendum eis ut omnia,
quæ possunt, faciant, & verba mea
vocemque meam nullo modo
contemnant: sed mihi & dictis
meis obediant, & me timeant, per
humanitatem & misericordiam &
gratiam tuam deprecor & peto te
adonay amay hortan vigedora
mytay hel suranat ysion ysyesy &
per omnia nomina tua sancta, per
omnes sanctos & sanctas tuas per
angelos & archangelos, potestates,
dominationes & virtutes, & per
illud nomen per quod Salomon
contringebat dæmones, &
conclusit ipsos Elhroch eban her
agle goth joth othie venoch nabrat,
& per omnia sacra nomina quæ
scripta sunt in hoc libro & per
virtutem eorundem, quatenus me
potentem facias congregare &
constringere omnes tuos spiritus
de cœlo depulsos, ut mihi veraciter
de omnibus meis interrogatis, de
quibus quæram, responsionem
veracem tribuant, & omnibus meis

mouth, which I will use. I require thee O
Lord Jesus Christ, that thou give me thy
vertue & power over all thine angels
(which were throwne downe from heaven
to deceive mankind) to drawe them to
me, to tie and bind them, & also to loose
them, to gather them togither before me,
& to command them to doo all that they
can, and that by no meanes they
contemne my voice, or the words of my
mouth; but that they obeie me and my
saiengs, and feare me. I beseech thee by
thine humanitie, mercie and grace, and I
require thee *Adonay, Amay, Horta, Vege
dora, Mitai, Hel, Suranat, Ysion, Ysesy*, and
by all thy holie names, and by all thine
holie he saints and she saints, by all thine
angels and archangels, powers, dominations, and vertues, and by that name that
Salomon did bind the divels, and shut
them up, *Elhrach, Ebanher, Agle, Goth,
Ioth, Othie, Venoch, Nabrat*, and by all
thine holie names which are written in
this booke, and by the vertue of them all,
that thou enable me to congregate all thy
spirits throwne downe from heaven, that
they may give me a true answer of all my
demands, and that they satisfie all my
requests, without the hurt of my bodie or
soule, or any thing else that is mine,
through our Lord Jesus Christ thy sonne,
which liveth and reigneth with thee in the
unitie of the Holie-ghost, one God world
without end.

mandatis illi satisfaciant sine
læsione corporis & animæ meæ &
omnium ad me pertinentium, per
Dominum nostrum Jesum
Christum filium tuum, qui tecum
vivit & regnat in unitate spiritus
sancti Deus per omnia secula.

§ 3. O pater omnipotens, ô fili
sapiens, ô spiritus sancte corda
hominum illustrans, ô vos tres in
personis, una vero deitas in sub-
stantia: qui Adam & Evæ in
peccatis eorum pepercistis, &
propter eorum peccata mortem
subiisti tu fili turpissimam, in
lignoque sanctæ crucis sustinuisti:
ô misericordissime, quando ad
tuam confugio misericordiam, &
supplico modis omnibus quibus
possum, per hæc nomina sancta tui
filii, scilicet A & Ω, & per omnia
alia sua nomina, quatenus
concedas mihi virtutem & potestatem tuam, ut valeam tuos
spiritus qui de cœlo ejecti sunt,
ante me citare, & ut ipsi mecum
loquantur, & mandata mea
perficiant statim & sine mora, cum
eorum voluntate, sine omni
læsione corporis, animæ &
bonorum meorum, &c. Continua
ut in libro *6 Annuli Salomonis
continetur.

§ 4. O summa & æterna virtus
Altissimi, qui te disponente his

(3) Oh father omnipotent, oh wise
sonne, oh Holie-ghost, the searcher of
harts, oh you three in persons, one true
godhead in substance, which didst spare
Adam and *Eve* in their sins; and oh thou
sonne, which diedst for their sinnes a
most filthie [disgraceful] death, susteining
it upon the holie crosse; oh thou most
mercifull, when I flie unto thy mercie, and
beseech thee by all the means I can, by
these the holie names of thy sonne; to
wit, *A* and *Omega*, and all other his
names, grant me thy vertue and power,
that I may be able to cite before me, thy
spirits which were throwne downe from
heaven, & that they may speake with me,
& dispatch by & by without delaie, &
with a good will, & without the hurt of
my bodie, soule, or goods, &c: as is
conteined in the booke called *Annulus
Salomonis*.

(4) Oh great and eternall vertue of
the highest, which through disposition,
these being called to judgement, *Vaicheon,*

---

6   Note ellipsis. The missing word is probably "Quatuor;" the book *Quatuor Annuli
     Salomonis* ("The Four Rings of Solomon") exists in several manuscripts, including
     Sloane 3847.
7   Note ellipsis.

judicio vocatis *7 vaycheon
stimulamaton ezphares
tetragrammaton olyoram irion
esytion existion eryona onela
brasym noym messias sother
emanuël sabaoth adonay, te adoro,
te invoco, totius mentis viribus
meis imploro, quatenus per te
præsentes orationes &
consecrationes & conjurationes
consecrentur videlicet, &
ubicunque maligni spiritus in
virtute tuorum nominum sunt
vocati, & omni parte conveniant,
& voluntatem mei exorcisatoris
diligenter adimpleant, fiat fiat fiat,
Amen.

§ 5. Hæc blasphema &
execranda hujus mundi fæx &
sentina pœnam in magos
prophanos bene constitutam, pro
scelerato mentis ausu jure meretur.

*Stimulamaton, Esphares, Tetragrammaton,
Olioram, Cryon* [irion], *Esytion, Existion,
Eriona, Onela, Brasim, Noym, Messias,
Soter, Emanuel, Sabboth* [Sabaoth], *Adonay,*
I worship thee, I invocate thee, I imploie
thee with all the strength of my mind,
that by thee, my present praiers, consecrations, and conjurations be hallowed: and
whersoever wicked spirits are called, in
the vertue of thy names, they may come
togither from everie coast, and diligentlie
fulfill the will of me the exorcist. *Fiat,
fiat, fiat, Amen.*

[(5). This kind of blasphemy and
cursing constitutes the worst kind of
refuse and dregs of the earth, and punish-
ment of these profane magi is well
deserved.]

Finis

Appendix 3. Comparison of Goetia with Weyer

Table 3 compares the names of the spirits and order in which they are found in both Weyer and the *Goetia*. The numbers correspond to the order of the spirits, equal sign indicates that the name of the spirit in Weyer is the same as in the *Goetia*. Note that the third spirit in the *Goetia*, Vassago, is not found in Weyer. The last three spirits in the *Goetia*, Seere, Dantalion, and Andromalis, are also not found in Weyer.

Table 3. Comparison of Goetia *with Weyer.*

GOETIA		WEYER		*GOETIA*		WEYER	
1.	Bael	1.	Baël [Baell]	37.	Phoenix	67.	=
2.	Agares	2.	=	38.	Halphas	42.	=
3.	**Vassago**			39.	Malphas	31.	=
4.	Gamigin	46.	Gamygyn	40.	Raum	41.	=, Raym
5.	Marbas	3.	=, Barbas	41.	Focalor	43.	=
6.	Valefar	14.	=, Malaphar	42.	Vepar	32.	=, Separ
7.	Amon	5.	=, Aamon	43.	Sabnach	33.	Sabnac, Salmac
8.	Barbatos	6.	=	44.	Shax	36.	Chax, Scox
9.	Paimon	22	=	45.	Vine	44.	=
10.	Buer	7.	=	46.	Bifrons	45.	=
11.	Gusoin	8.	Gusoyn [Gusoin]	47.	Vual	65.	Wal [Vuall]
12.	Sitri	21	Sytry / Bitru	48.	Haagenti	66.	=
13.	Beleth	20.	Byleth [Bileth]	49.	Procel	37.	Pucel [Prucel]

Table 3.   Comparison of Goetia *with Weyer (cont.).*

GOETIA	WEYER	GOETIA	WEYER
14. Leraye	13. Loray [Leraie], Oray	50. Furcas	38. =
15. Eligor	12. =, Abigor	51. Balam	62. =
16. Zepar	19. =	52. Alloces	63. Alocer [Allocer]
17. Botis	9. =, Otis	53. Caim	40. Caym
18. Bathin	10. Bathym [Bathin], Marthim [Mathim]	54. Murmur	39. =
19. Saleos	64. Zaleos [Saleos]	55. Orobas	57. =
20. Purson	11. Pursan [Purson], Curson	56. Gemory	50. Gomory
21. Morax	15. =, Foraii	57. Ose	55. Oze [Ose]
22. Ipos	16. Ipes [Ipos], Ayperos [Ayporos]	58. Amy	60. =
23. Aim	56. Aym, Haborym	59. Orias	48. =
24. Naberius	17. Naberus [Naberius], Cerberus	60. Vapula	58. =
25. Glasya Labolas	18. =, Caacrinolaas [*Gaacrinolaas*, or *Caassimolar*]	61. Zagan	47. Zagam [Zagan]
26. Bune	23 =	62. Valac	49. Volac [Valac]
27. Ronove	25 =	63. Andras	53. =
28. Berith	26 =	64. Flauros	61. =
29. Astaroth	27 =	65. Andrealphus	54. Androalphus [Andrealphus]
30. Forneus	24 =	66. Cimeies	59. Cimeries
31. Foras	28 = / Forcas	67. Amduscias	52. =
32. Asmoday	34. Sidonay, Asmoday	68. Belial	
33. Gaap	35. =, Tap	69. Decarabia	51. =, Carabia
34. Furtur	29. Furfur	70. **Seere**	
35. Marchosias	30. Marchocias	71. **Dantalion**	
36. Stolas	68. =	72. **Andromalius**	

Appendix 4. Other Examples of Some of the Drawings

Figure 12.   Sigil for Baal, from Harley 6483.

Figure 13.   Sigil for Agares, from Harley 6483.

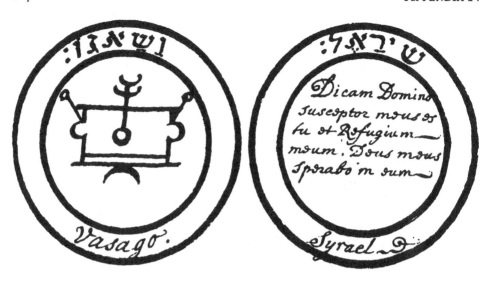

Figure 14.   Sigil for Vasago, from Harley 6483.

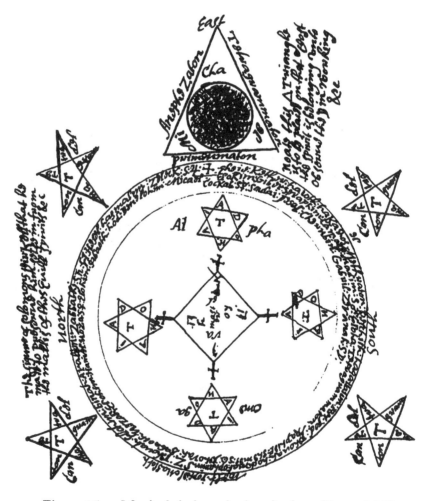

Figure 15.   Magical circle and triangle, from Sloane 3648.

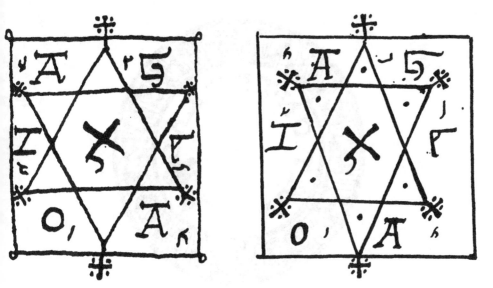

*Figure 16.   Hexagram to be worn as a Lamin, from the Hebrew
manuscript of the* Clavicula Salomonis (Sepher Mafteah Shelomoh),
*Hermann Gollancz (London: Oxford University Press, 1914),
fol. 38a (left); Or. 14759 (right).*

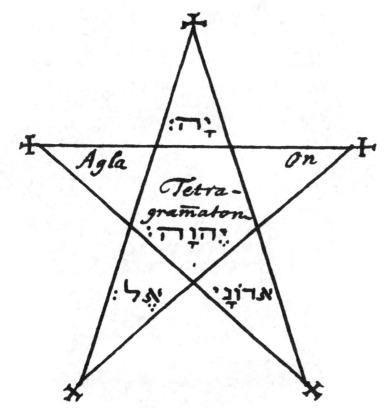

Figure 17.   Pentagram, from Harley 6483.

Figure 18.   The Magic Ring, from Sloane 2731.

Figure 19.   Brass vessel, from Sloane 2731.

Figure 20.   Sigil for Carmasiel, from Harley 6483.

Figure 21.   Sigils for some of Carmasiel's dukes, from Harley 6483.

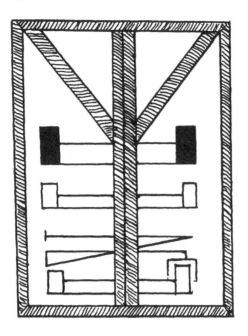
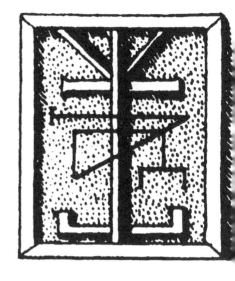

Figure 22.   The Seal of Solomon, from Harley 6483 (left) and Magical Calendar *(right) (Edinburgh: Magnum Opus Hermetic Sourceworks, 1979).*

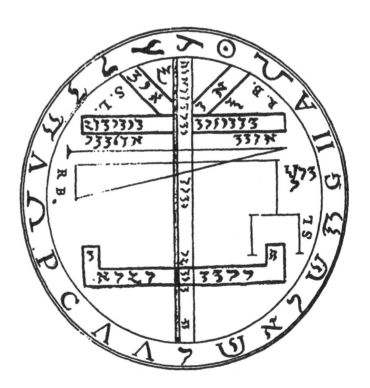

Figure 23.   Seal of Solomon, frontispiece from British Library manuscript Lans. 1203, Les Véritables Clavicules de Salomon, *Traduites de l'Hebreux en langue Latine, Par le Rabin ABOGNAZAR.*

Saturn	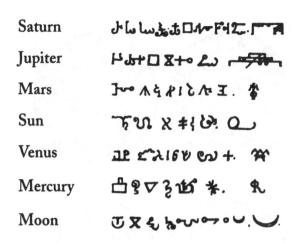
Jupiter	
Mars	
Sun	
Venus	
Mercury	
Moon	

Figure 24. Characters of the seven planets, from The Magical Calendar.

Aries

Taurus

Gemini

Cancer

Leo

Virgo

Libra

Scorpio

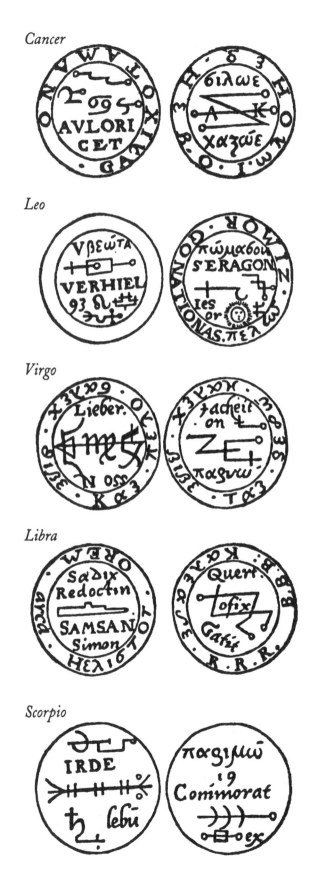

Figure 25.   Sigilla, nempe XII signorum zodiaci, from Paracelsus,
                    Archidoxis magicae, Liber II. [1]

Edition used is Paracelsus, *Sämtlich Werke*, ed. Karl Sudhoff (Berlin, 1933), Band 14,
pp. 475–77.

Figure 26.   The Almadel, from Gollancz, Sepher Maphteah Shelomoh, *fol 20b. Note, too, the drawing at the bottom showing how the candles are to be constructed with feet to support the Almadel.*

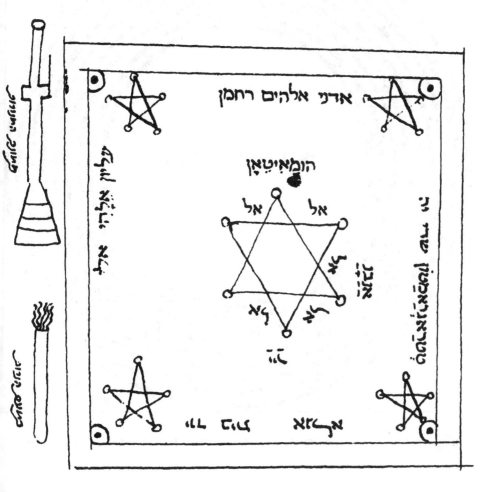

Figure 27. "*Picture of the Almadel,*" *from Or. MS 6360.*

Figure 28. First note of the art of grammar, from Sloane 1712, fol. 14v.

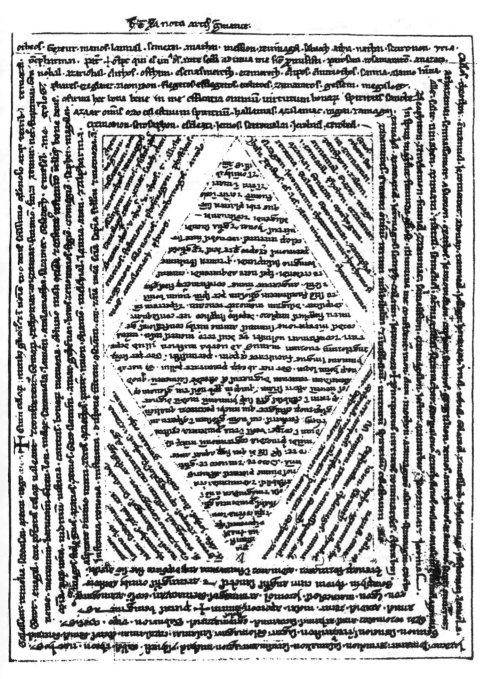

Figure 29.   Second note of the art of grammar, from Sloane 1712, fol. 15r.

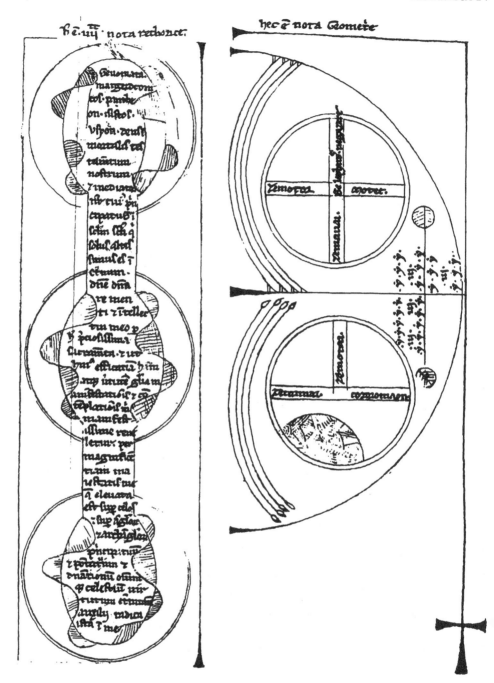

Figure 30.   Fourth note of rhetoric and the note of geometry,
from Sloane 1712, fol. 19r.

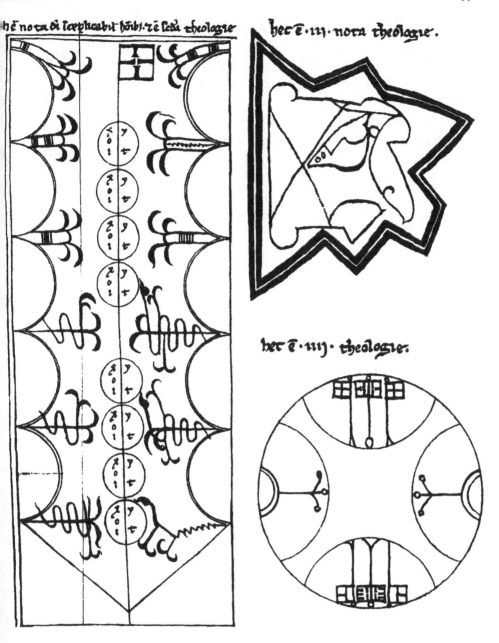

*Figure 31. Second, third, and fourth notes of theology,
from Sloane 1712, fol 21v.*

Index
